NORTON ANTHOLOGY OF
WESTERN MUSIC

Volume 3: The Twentieth Century and After

SEVENTH EDITION

NORTON ANTHOLOGY OF
WESTERN MUSIC

Volume 3: The Twentieth Century and After

SEVENTH EDITION

Edited by

J. PETER BURKHOLDER

and

CLAUDE V. PALISCA

W. W. NORTON & COMPANY

NEW YORK · LONDON

W. W. Norton & Company has been independent since its founding in 1923, when William Warder Norton and Mary D. Herter Norton first published lectures delivered at the People's Institute, the adult education division of New York City's Cooper Union. The firm soon expanded its program beyond the Institute, publishing books by celebrated academics from America and abroad. By mid-century, the two major pillars of Norton's publishing program—trade books and college texts— were firmly established. In the 1950s, the Norton family transferred control of the company to its employees, and today—with a staff of four hundred and a comparable number of trade, college, and professional titles published each year—W. W. Norton & Company stands as the largest and oldest publishing house owned wholly by its employees.

Director of Production, College: Jane Searle

Composition: David Botwinik

Manufacturing: Quad Graphics, Taunton, Massachussetts

ISBN 978-0-393-92163-2 (pbk.)

W. W. Norton & Company, Inc., 500 Fifth Avenue, New York, N.Y. 10110
wwnorton.com

W. W. Norton & Company Ltd., Castle House, 75/76 Wells Street, London W1T 3QT

3 4 5 6 7 8 9 0

CONTENTS

MAKING CONNECTIONS:
How to Use This Anthology

The *Norton Anthology of Western Music* (NAWM) is a companion to *A History of Western Music*, Ninth Edition (HWM), and *Concise History of Western Music*, Fifth Edition (CHWM). It is also designed to stand by itself as a collection representing the most significant traditions, trends, genres, national schools, innovations, and historical developments in the history of music in Europe and the Americas.

The editions of the scores are the best available for which permission could be secured, including several editions especially prepared for NAWM. Where no publication or editor is cited, Claude V. Palisca or I have edited the music from the original source. All foreign-language texts are accompanied by English translations either in the score or immediately following it. Texts that follow the score are arranged to show their poetic form and feature translations by one or both coeditors, except where another translator is credited. Most translations are literal to a fault, corresponding to the original line by line, often word for word, to facilitate understanding of the ways the composer has set the text.

Each selection is followed by a detailed commentary, separate from the discussion of the piece in HWM or CHWM, that describes the piece's origins, points out its important features and stylistic traits, and addresses issues of performance practice, including any unusual aspects of notation.

Recordings

An anthology of musical scores is greatly enhanced by recordings. Excellent, authoritative recorded performances of all the items in NAWM are included on the *Norton Recorded Anthology of Western Music*. These recordings are available in a variety of formats, including a three-volume set of mp3 discs, corresponding to the three volumes of NAWM, and a Concise mp3 disc including 109 works that are featured in CHWM (indicated in NAWM by the icon `concise ⌐⟩`). All of these recordings are also available online as part of Total Access, a suite of media resources that comes with every new copy of HWM and CHWM. In addition to recordings, Total Access includes listening quizzes for every item in NAWM and stunning Metropolitan Opera videos of a dozen of the operatic scenes in this anthology, from Gluck's *Orfeo ed Euridice* (NAWM 110) to John Adams's *Doctor Atomic* (219). The availability of a Metropolitan Opera video is indicated by a ▶ symbol at the end of a commentary.

Many of the recordings that accompany this anthology are new to this edition. The recordings feature some of the best performers and ensembles working today, alongside classic recordings from earlier generations. For music composed prior to 1780, the performers on the recordings use period instruments and seek to reflect the performance practice of the time, to the extent that we understand it today.

The recordings also include performances with period instruments for several works composed during the late eighteenth and nineteenth centuries, including symphonies by Haydn, Mozart, Beethoven, Berlioz, and Schumann and vocal works by Mendelssohn and Stephen Foster. The ragtime and jazz recordings all feature the original artists, and several of the twentieth- and twenty-first-century pieces appear in performances by the composer or by the performers for whom they were written. In many periods and genres, musicians were expected to improvise, embellish, or otherwise alter the written music, as evident in many of the performances on the accompanying recordings. When these or other discrepancies occur between score and recording, we have provided an explanation in the commentary.

To make it easier to coordinate listening with the study of the scores, timings have been added to the scores at major sections, themes, and other events in the music, especially those pointed out in the commentaries. Timings have also been added to texts and translations for many of the vocal works with multiple stanzas, repetitive forms, or long texts, to make it easier to listen while following the words rather than the score.

Why These Pieces?

We have aimed to include outstanding works that represent their makers, genres, and times. Only a small fraction of the music worthy of attention could be included, making it important for us to choose pieces that could accomplish several purposes at once. Knowing the thinking behind our choices will help students and teachers make the best use of this collection. The rest of this preface explains several of the themes that determined our selections.

Placing Music in Historical Context

The title *Norton Anthology of Western Music* needs one important qualifier: this is a historical anthology of the Western musical tradition. Rather than serve up great works to be studied in splendid isolation, this anthology seeks to place each piece in a historical context, relating it to the society from which it came and to other music that the composer used as model or inspiration. Studying music in its contexts can illuminate the choices composers made, the values of the society they lived in, and the meanings of the pieces themselves. Just as composers did not create in a musical void, standing aloof from their predecessors and contemporaries, so the historically oriented listener must have access to the primary material in order to establish connections. This anthology invites students and teachers to make such connections.

Breadth and Depth of Repertoire

Making connections depends on having a wide range of examples. The repertoire in this edition of NAWM is broader and more diverse than ever before.

Among the thirty-nine new additions, excerpts from J. S. Bach's *Well-Tempered Clavier* and *St. Matthew Passion* (NAWM 102 and 104), a complete string quartet and symphony by Haydn (118 and 119), the first movement of Mendelssohn's Violin Concerto (139), and choral works by Schubert (141) and Bruckner (157) enhance the already extensive coverage of major composers from the eighteenth and nineteenth centuries. The twentieth century is represented by over fifty selections, including new works by Strauss, Ravel, Weill, Villa-Lobos, Revueltas, Varèse, and Bernstein. For the first time, music from the twenty-first century is featured, with pieces by Saariaho, Golijov, Carter, Adams, and Higdon (216–220), each of which simultaneously extends a trend of the late twentieth century and harks back to music of an earlier era. Coverage of early music is expanded with motets by Petrus de Cruce (23), Vitry (25), and Gombert (50); secular songs by Machaut (27), Landini (31), Josquin (42), and Cara (55); an anthem by Tallis (48); a divertissement by Lully (85b); and instrumental pieces by Holborne (67), Byrd (69), Couperin (97c), and Telemann (99).

Women composers are represented across the centuries—in the twelfth century by Hildegard of Bingen (7) and Comtessa de Dia (9); in the seventeenth by Barbara Strozzi (77) and Elisabeth-Claude Jacquet de la Guerre (88); in the nineteenth by Fanny Mendelssohn Hensel (133), Clara Schumann (142), and Amy Beach (162); in the twentieth by Bessie Smith (182), Ruth Crawford Seeger (194), and Sofia Gubaidulina (213); and in the twenty-first by Kaija Saariaho (216) and Jennifer Higdon (220).

Music of Spain and Latin America is well represented, with a medieval cantiga (12), a Renaissance motet and mass (52a and b), a secular villancico (54), works for vihuela (68a and b), a South American Christmas villancico (91), the first opera composed and staged in the New World (90), a chamber aria by Brazil's Heitor Villa-Lobos (190), a symphonic homage by Mexico's Silvestre Revueltas (191), and a Passion by Argentine composer Osvaldo Golijov (217). The African American traditions of ragtime, blues, and jazz are included, with a Joplin rag (164), Bessie Smith's *Back Water Blues* (182), Louis Armstrong's rendition of *West End Blues* (183), Duke Ellington's *Cotton Tail* (184), and Charlie Parker and Dizzy Gillespie's *Anthropology* (197). Also here are classics of band literature, from Sousa (163) to Persichetti (199). The coverage of American and East European music is extensive, including works by sixteen composers from Eastern Europe and twenty-nine working in the United States.

Breadth of repertoire is matched by depth. Several composers are represented by more than one work to permit comparison of early and later styles (for example, Du Fay, Monteverdi, Beethoven, Schubert, Schoenberg, Stravinsky, Varèse, Cage, and Adams) and to show distinct approaches by a single composer to diverse genres (for example, Adam de la Halle, Machaut, Du Fay, Josquin, Byrd, Lassus, Bach, Handel, Pergolesi, Haydn, Mozart, Beethoven, Schubert, Schumann, Mendelssohn, and Brahms). Instead of relying solely on excerpts to give a taste of multimovement genres, NAWM includes complete examples of a Gregorian chant Mass, Baroque keyboard suite, Corelli trio sonata, Vivaldi concerto, Bach cantata, and Haydn string quartet and symphony to show how such works are constructed and what types of movements they contain. In the same spirit, complete scenes from operas by Monteverdi, Rameau, Handel, Mozart, Rossini, Meyerbeer, Weber, Verdi, Berg, Saariaho, and Adams demonstrate how differently these composers construct a scene.

Styles and Genres

Perhaps the primary role of a historical anthology is to present examples of the most important styles and genres in music history and to trace their development through time. The generally chronological organization of NAWM follows the order in which these selections are discussed in HWM. Volume 1 highlights changes in both style and genre from ancient Greece (1–2), medieval monophony (3–13), and early polyphony (14–24) through the fourteenth century (25–32); the first, middle, and later generations of Renaissance composers (33–38, 39–45, and 46–70); and the early, middle, and late Baroque period (71–84, 85–95, and 96–106). Volume 2 includes the Classic era (107–124) and the first and second halves of the nineteenth century (125–148 and 149–163). Volume 3 focuses on the twentieth century, divided by World War II (164–196 and 197–215), and the twenty-first century (216–220).

Genres, styles, conventions, and forms develop only because composers pick up ideas from each other and replicate or build on them in their own music, a process that can be observed again and again through the pieces in this anthology. The monophonic songs of the troubadours in southern France (8–9) inspired those of the trouvères in the north (10), Minnesinger in Germany (11), and cantiga composers in Spain (12). Later generations of poet-musicians, active in the fourteenth century, wrote polyphonic secular songs and codified standard forms for them, notably the French virelai (27 and 39), rondeau (28 and 35), and ballade (29 and 36) and the Italian madrigal, caccia, and ballata (30–32). In the Renaissance, new forms and styles of secular song emerged with the Spanish villancico (54), German Lied (41), Italian frottola and madrigal (55–59 and 71–72), and new types of song in French (42–43 and 60–62) and in English (63–65). In the nineteenth century, the song for voice and piano became the mainstay of home music-making, exemplified by the Lieder of Schubert and Schumann (128–130) and the parlor songs of Stephen Foster (131), but then splintered into two different traditions: art songs, like those of Fauré (159) and Ives (180), and popular songs, like those by Gershwin, Smith, and Oliver (181–183). Outgrowths of the art song include the orchestral song, such as Mahler's *Kindertotenlieder* (165), and the song for voice and chamber ensemble, as in Boulez's *Le marteau sans maître* (202).

Similar paths can be traced in religious music from Gregorian chant (3–5) to the modern style of Pärt (215); in Passions from J. S. Bach (104) to Golijov (217); and in opera from its creation in Italy (73–75) through its diffusion to other lands (76, 85, 89, and 90) and the many changes in style throughout the eighteenth (93, 98, 105, 107–110, and 124), nineteenth (145–154), twentieth (166, 174, 186, and 200), and twenty-first centuries (216 and 219). Exploring and explaining changes in these and other genres is a central theme of this anthology and of HWM and CHWM.

Musicians frequently use an old word to mean new things, so that the very nature of a genre may change. Through this anthology, the listener can follow the motet as it changes from a work that adds text to existing music (21a) to a new work based on chant (21c). It then acquires greater rhythmic diversity among the voices (22 and 23) and rich rhythmic patterning in the lowest voice (22), leading to the isorhythmic motets of Vitry (25). Next, the motet is redefined as a newly composed Latin sacred work with equal voices in works by Dunstable (34), Josquin (44), Gombert (50), Victoria (52a), and Lassus (53). Finally, the meaning of *motet* is broadened in the seventeenth century to embrace sacred works with instrumental accompaniment for any number of voices from one (79) to many (78 and 86). Even more surprising is the change in meaning of *concerto*, which in the early seventeenth century designated a work for voices and instruments, such as Schütz's sacred concertos (81), but came to mean a piece for one or more solo instruments with orchestra. The latter type is represented here by a Vivaldi violin concerto (96), illustrating the genre's first maturity in the late Baroque; piano concerto movements from the Classic era by J. C. Bach (117) and Mozart (122), showing the latter's debt to the former; Mendelssohn's Violin Concerto (139), representing the Romantic concerto; and Schnittke's Concerto Grosso No. 1 (214), a postmodern reinterpretation of a Baroque genre.

Similar chains of development can be seen in instrumental music. Dance music in the Middle Ages (13) and Renaissance (66–67) led to stylized dances of many types: songs in the form of dances, such as Dowland's *Flow, my tears* (65); independent pieces for keyboard or lute, including those by Gaultier (87), Chopin (134), and Dvořák (161); keyboard dance suites in the Baroque period, such as those by Jacquet de la Guerre (88) and François Couperin (97), a genre revived in the modern era by Ravel (168), Schoenberg (173), and others; and dance movements in other works, including Corelli's trio sonatas (94d) and symphonies from Haydn (119c) to Shostakovich (189). Ballets or dance episodes appear in operas, as in the scenes included here from Lully's *Armide* (85b), Gluck's *Orfeo ed Euridice* (110), and Berg's *Wozzeck* (174b). Stravinsky's *Rite of Spring* (176) and Copland's *Appalachian Spring* (195), known today primarily as orchestral works, were originally composed as dance music for ballets, as was Milhaud's *La création du monde* (185). More generally, dance rhythms infect many vocal and instrumental works, including the air in minuet rhythm from Lully's opera *Armide* (85c); Araujo's *Los coflades de la estleya* (91) and Torrejón y Velasco's *La púrpura de la rosa* (90), both full of Spanish dance rhythms; the aria in gigue rhythm in Scarlatti's cantata *Clori vezzosa, e bella* (92b); the sarabande-influenced aria from Handel's opera *Giulio Cesare* (105b); the waltzes in Schumann's *Carnaval* (132); Gottschalk's *Souvenir de Porto Rico* (137), suffused with rhythms from Latin American dances; and the seguidilla from Bizet's *Carmen* (152).

The canzonas of Gabrieli (70) and others established a tradition of extended instrumental works in several sections with contrasting meters, tempos, and moods, leading to the sonatas of Marini (84) and the multimovement sonatas of Corelli (94) and later composers. Out of this tradition grew the chamber music of Telemann (99); the string quartet, represented here by Haydn (118), Beethoven (127), Ruth Crawford Seeger (194), and George Crumb (205); string quintets, including Schubert's (141); and chamber works with piano, such as Clara Schumann's Piano Trio (142) and piano quintets by Brahms (156) and Amy Beach (162). The symphony grew from its Italian beginnings, represented by Sammartini (115), to become the major instrumental genre of the late eighteenth and nineteenth centuries, dominated by Austrian and German composers such as Stamitz (116), Haydn (119), Mozart (123), and Beethoven (126). Symphonists after Beethoven reinterpreted the tradition in varying ways, including Berlioz's programmatic *Symphonie fantastique* (138), reconceptions of form in Schumann's Fourth Symphony (140) and Tchaikovsky's *Pathétique* Symphony (160), and Brahms's embrace of the past in his Fourth Symphony (155).

The symphony was a continuing presence in the twentieth century, represented here by Webern (175), Stravinsky (177), Hindemith (187), Shostakovich (189), Still (196), and Persichetti (199).

Descriptive instrumental passages in opera, like Rameau's picture of a stormy sea in *Hippolyte et Aricie* (98), inspired composers to write instrumental music intended to convey a mood, character, scene, or story, as in the character pieces of Couperin (97), Schumann (132), Liszt (136), Gottschalk (137), Scriabin (170), Satie (171), and Cowell (193) and the orchestral tone poems and descriptive pieces by Strauss (158), Debussy (167), Penderecki (208), Adams (211), and Higdon (220).

As suggested by these descriptions, almost every genre has roots in an earlier one. Here is where the evolutionary metaphor so often applied to music history seems most applicable, tracing lines of development both within and among genres. This anthology provides ample material for making these connections.

Techniques

In addition to genres, composers often learn techniques from their contemporaries or predecessors and extend them in new ways. Compositional practices that start in one genre or tradition often cross boundaries over time. To give just one example, imitative counterpoint, developed in the medieval canon (24) and caccia (31), became a structural principle in Renaissance vocal music from the late fifteenth century through the early seventeenth century, illustrated by Busnoys's chanson *Je ne puis vivre* (39), Josquin's motet *Ave Maria . . . virgo serena* (44), and Weelkes's madrigal *As Vesta was* (64). The technique was brought into instrumental music through the canzona (70) and ricercare (83), and the latter developed into the fugue (95, 100, and 102). Fugal passages occur in many genres, from oratorios (106c and 143) to symphonies (123, 126, and 138), and imitation remains a device learned by every student of Western music.

Forms morph into new forms or combine with others. Binary form, invented for dance music (66a, 87, and 88), was used for abstract sonata movements by Corelli (94d), Domenico Scarlatti (113), and others and developed into sonata form as used in piano sonatas (114, 121, and 125), chamber works (118a, 141, 156, and 162), and symphonies (115, 116, 119a, 123, 126, and 140). A small binary form could also be expanded by serving as the theme for a movement in rondo form, as in the finales of Haydn's *Joke* String Quartet (118d) and Symphony No. 88 in G Major (119d). The elements of sonata form could in turn be combined with ritornello form in a concerto first movement (117 and 122) or with rondo form in a sonata-rondo, used often for finales (127b).

Styles also cross genres and traditions. Vocal music served as the basis for early instrumental works, like the intabulations and variations of Narváez (68). Moreover, the styles and gestures of vocal music have been imitated by instrumental composers again and again, including recitative and vocal monody in Marini's violin sonata (84), singing styles in piano sonatas by C. P. E. Bach (114) and Mozart (121), and bel canto operatic style in Chopin's nocturnes (135). Musicians cannot afford to know only the literature for their own instrument, because composers are constantly borrowing ideas from other repertoires, and performers need to know how to reflect these allusions to other styles in their performances.

Several selections document the influence of vernacular and traditional music on art music. Medieval English singers improvised polyphony with parallel thirds and sixths, which entered notated music in the thirteenth-century *Sumer is icumen in* (24), fifteenth-century carols (33), and the works of English composer John Dunstable (34) and exercised a profound influence on Continental composers such as Binchois (35) and Du Fay (37 and 38). Debussy adapted the texture and melodic idiom of Asian music to his own orchestral conception in *Nuages* (167). Satie borrowed from Parisian café music in *Embryons desséchés* (171). Stravinsky simulated Russian folk polyphony in *The Rite of Spring* (176). Bartók borrowed elements of Hungarian peasant song in *Staccato and Legato* (178) and Serbo-Croatian song and Bulgarian dance styles in his *Music for Strings, Percussion and Celesta* (179). Milhaud's *La création du monde* (185) and Weill's *Die Dreigroschenoper* (186) draw on jazz and blues, and Still's *Afro-American Symphony* (196) incorporates the twelve-bar blues, the African American spiritual, and instrumental sounds from jazz. Sheng makes the cellist imitate the sounds and playing styles of Chinese instruments in his *Seven Tunes Heard in China* (209), and Villa-Lobos, Revueltas, and Golijov combine styles and rhythms from Latin America with European genres and techniques. Influences also go the other way; Foster's *Jeanie with the Light Brown Hair* (131) includes a brief cadenza, an idea borrowed from opera, and "Cool" from Bernstein's Broadway musical *West Side Story* (198) mixes fugue and twelve-tone technique with elements of pop, bebop, and cool jazz styles.

Twentieth-century composers have introduced a constant stream of innovations, and this anthology includes a number of pioneering works. Notable are Schoenberg's *Pierrot lunaire* (172), his most famous atonal piece and the first to use Sprechstimme; his Piano Suite (173), the first complete twelve-tone work; Webern's Symphony (175), a model of *Klangfarbenmelodie* and pointillism; Stravinsky's *Rite of Spring* (176), whose propulsive rhythm and block construction influenced so many later composers; Varèse's *Hyperprism* (192) and *Poème électronique* (206), which reconceive music as sound masses moving through space; Cowell's *The Banshee* (193), based on new sounds produced by playing directly on the strings of a piano; Ruth Crawford Seeger's *String Quartet 1931* (194), whose novel approach to counterpoint made it a classic of the American experimentalist tradition; Cage's *Sonatas and Interludes* (203) for prepared piano and *Music of Changes* (204), one of the first pieces composed using chance operations; Boulez's *Le marteau sans maître* (202), which extends serialism to duration and dynamics; Crumb's *Black Angels* (205), full of new sounds from an electrified string quartet; Babbitt's *Philomel* (207), an early example of combining a live singer with electronic music on tape; Penderecki's *Threnody* (208), which produces novel clusters of sound from a string orchestra; Adams's *Short Ride in a Fast Machine* (211), which applies minimalist techniques to create a gradually changing canvas of sound; and Ligeti's *Vertige* (212), an exercise in micropolyphony.

Learning from History

Besides learning from their contemporaries and immediate predecessors, many composers have reached back across the centuries to revive old methods or genres, often producing something remarkably new in the process. Inspired by the ancient Greek idea of suiting music to the rhythm and mood of the words, illustrated here by the *Epitaph of Seikilos* (1), Renaissance composers sought to capture the accents and feelings of the text, evident in motets by Josquin (44) and Lassus (53), in the new genre of the madrigal (56–59, 64, and 71–72), and in the *musique mesurée* of Le Jeune (62). Among the tools Renaissance composers borrowed from ancient Greek music and music theory was chromaticism, found in Euripides' *Orestes* (2); after madrigal composers like Rore (57), Marenzio (58), and Gesualdo (59) used it as an expressive device, it became a common feature in instrumental music as well, such as in Frescobaldi's chromatic ricercare (83), and later composers from Bach (100–101) to Wagner (149) made it an increasingly central part of the musical language. In a classic example of creating something really new by reaching into the distant past, the attempt to revive the principles of ancient Greek tragedy led to the invention of opera and recitative in Peri's *Euridice* (73).

Romantic and modern composers have often sought to revive the spirit of earlier music. Recollections of Baroque music include Beethoven's fugue in his String Quartet in C♯ Minor (127a), Brahms's chaconne in the finale of his Fourth Symphony (155), Schoenberg's passacaglia in *Nacht* from *Pierrot lunaire* (172a), and evocations of J. S. Bach's music by Villa-Lobos (190), Sheng (209), and Golijov (217). Bruckner's *Virga Jesse* (157) combines elements of Renaissance motet style with Romantic harmony. Webern's twelve-tone Symphony (175) contains elaborate canons modeled on those of the Renaissance, and Reich's *Tehillim* (210) reconciles canons with minimalist procedures. Messiaen borrowed the isorhythmic techniques of Vitry (25) and Machaut (26a) in his *Quartet for the End of Time* (201), and Saariaho's *L'amour de loin* (216) evokes the lament of a medieval troubadour in the modernist style of spectral music.

Reworkings

In addition to drawing on general styles, genres, and techniques, composers have often reworked particular compositions, a process that can be traced through numerous examples in this anthology. In one notable case, a single chant gave rise to a chain of polyphonic accretions. *Viderunt omnes* (3d) was elaborated by Leoninus and colleagues in an organum for two voices (17), which in turn was refreshed by his successors with new clausulae (18) that substituted for certain passages in the original setting. His younger colleague Perotinus composed a four-voice organum on the same chant (19). Meanwhile, anonymous musicians fitted words to the upper parts of some of the clausulae, creating the new genre of the motet (21a). Later composers borrowed the tenor line of a clausula (21b) or a passage from the original *Viderunt omnes* chant (21c and 22) and added new voices to create ever more elaborate motets.

NAWM contains many other instances in which composers reworked existing music into new pieces, a recurring thread in music history. Anonymous medieval church musicians added monophonic tropes (6) to the chant *Puer natus* (3a) and developed early types of polyphony that add other voices to a chant (14–15). Machaut based the Kyrie of his *La Messe de Nostre Dame* (26a) on the chant *Kyrie Cunctipotens Genitor* (3b) and the Gloria (26b) on a chant Gloria (a variant of 3c). Many Renaissance composers wrote masses that rework existing models using a fascinating variety of methods, including Du Fay's cantus-firmus mass based on his own polyphonic ballade *Se la face ay pale* (38a and b), Josquin's paraphrase mass on the chant hymn *Pange lingua* (45), and Victoria's imitation mass on his own motet *O magnum mysterium* (52a and b). Du Fay elaborated a Gregorian hymn in fauxbourdon style (37), and Luther recast another chant hymn (46a) as a Reformation chorale (46b), later used by J. S. Bach as the basis for a cantata (103). Luther's chorale *Ein feste Burg* (46c) was set in four parts by Johann Walter (46d), one of over a hundred reworkings of that famous tune. J. S. Bach's setting of *Durch Adams Fall* (101) exemplifies an entire genre of chorale preludes for organ, and his *St. Matthew Passion* includes a chorale (104e) whose tune was taken from a secular Renaissance song set by Isaac (41).

Such elaborations of existing material are not confined to religious music. Narváez's *Cancion Milles regres* (68a) is a reworking for vihuela of Josquin's chanson *Mille regretz* (43), and Byrd's *John come kiss me now* (69) offers sixteen variations for keyboard of a popular song of his day. Gottschalk's *Souvenir de Porto Rico* (137) uses a melody of Puerto Rican street musicians. Berlioz's *Symphonie fantastique* (138) and Crumb's *Black Angels* (205) both borrow phrases from the Gregorian chant *Dies irae*. Luther's *Ein feste Burg* (46c) makes a dramatic appearance in Meyerbeer's opera *Les Huguenots* (147) as a symbol of the Reformation. Puccini borrowed two Japanese songs to depict his title character in *Madama Butterfly* (151), and identified her American husband with *The Star-Spangled Banner*. The Coronation scene from Musorgsky's *Boris Godunov* (153) incorporates a Russian folk song, and Stravinsky's *Rite of Spring* (176) uses several. The repeating bass figure in the chaconne finale of Brahms's Fourth Symphony (155) is adapted from a chaconne movement of a Bach cantata. The theme of the finale of Beach's Piano Quintet (162) is modeled on a theme from Brahms's Piano Quintet (156). Ives's *General William Booth Enters into Heaven* (180) is based on a hymn tune and quotes a drum pattern and a minstrel show song. Both Ellington's *Cotton Tail* (184) and Parker and Gillespie's *Anthropology* (197) borrow the harmonic progression from the chorus of Gershwin's song *I Got Rhythm* (181). Copland's *Appalachian Spring* (195) includes variations on a Shaker hymn, and the first movement of Sheng's *Seven Tunes Heard in China* (209) varies the melody of a Chinese song.

Improvisation

Improvisation has been part of the Western tradition since ancient times. Every type of medieval organum (14–19) was an improvisatory practice before it was a written one. Singers and instrumentalists from the Renaissance to the early nineteenth century often improvised ornaments and embellishments to decorate the written music, as represented on many of the recordings that accompany this anthology. Lutenists and keyboard players demonstrated their skill through elaborate improvisations, exploring a mode or introducing another work; from these developed the written tradition of the toccata and prelude, represented by examples from Frescobaldi (82), Jacquet de la Guerre (88a), Buxtehude (95), and J. S. Bach (100a and 102a). Part of the individuality of the keyboard music of C. P. E. Bach (114), Schumann (132), Hensel (133), Chopin (135), Liszt (136), Rachmaninoff (169), and Scriabin (170) derives from textures or passages that sound improvisatory, however carefully calculated they may be. The invention of

sound recording has made possible the preservation of improvisations themselves, which are a fundamental part of the blues and jazz tradition, represented
here in the recordings of Scott Joplin and Jelly Roll Morton playing Joplin's
Maple Leaf Rag (164a and b), Bessie Smith's blues (182), Louis Armstrong's
performance on King Oliver's *West End Blues* (183b), Ben Webster's solo in
Ellington's *Cotton Tail* (184), and Charlie Parker's solo in *Anthropology* (197).

Reception

Certain pieces won a place in this anthology because contemporary critics or the
composers themselves singled them out. A legend developed that when some
Catholic leaders sought to ban polyphonic music from church services, Palestrina
saved it by composing his *Pope Marcellus Mass* (51). Giovanni Maria Artusi attacked
Monteverdi's *Cruda Amarilli* (71) in his 1600 treatise, provoking a spirited and
now famous defense from Monteverdi. Caccini wrote that *Vedrò 'l mio sol* (72) was
one of his pioneering attempts to write a new type of solo song. Cesti's *Intorno
all'idol mio* (76b) was one of the most frequently cited arias of the mid-seventeenth
century. Athanasius Kircher praised the final scene of Carissimi's *Jephte* (80) as a
triumph of the powers of musical expression. Jean-Jacques Rousseau roundly
criticized and Jean le Rond d'Alembert carefully analyzed Lully's monologue in
Armide, Enfin il est en ma puissance (85c). Pergolesi's *La serva padrona* (107) was a
hit with the public in Italy and provoked a battle between critics in France, and
his *Stabat mater* (111) was one of the most widely praised and performed works of
religious music from its time. The opening chorus of Haydn's *The Creation* (120)
was hailed as the height of the sublime in music. The first movement of Beethoven's
Eroica Symphony (126) and Stravinsky's *The Rite of Spring* (176) were both objects
of critical uproars after their premieres. Britten's *Peter Grimes* (200) was the first
English opera to win international acclaim in over two centuries, and Higdon's
blue cathedral (220) has been one of the most frequently performed new pieces of
orchestral music in the past twenty-five years. The reactions to these compositions
are exemplars of "reception history," a field that has attracted considerable
attention among teachers and historians.

Relation to Politics

Finally, musical influences are not the only connections that can be made among
these pieces. For example, many grew out of a specific political context, and
studying the ways those links are reflected in the music can be illuminating.
Walther von der Vogelweide's *Palästinalied* (11) is a crusade song, celebrating the
Christian warriors from Western Europe who sought to wrest the Holy Land from
the Muslims. *Fole acostumance/Dominus* (21b) attacks hypocrisy and deception in
the church and in French politics. Du Fay's *Resvellies vous* (36) and Peri's *Euridice*
(73) were both written for aristocratic weddings, and many other works in NAWM
were composed for royal or aristocratic patrons. Indeed, Lully's operas and
church music (85–86) were part of a political program to glorify King Louis XIV
of France and centralize his power through the arts. Gay's *The Beggar's Opera* (109)
spoofed social norms by taking a criminal as its hero. Beethoven originally
dedicated his *Eroica* Symphony (126) to Napoleon, whom he saw as the embodiment
of republican ideals, then tore up the dedication when Napoleon named himself

emperor. Political commentary is a recurrent theme in twentieth-century music, including Berg's appeal for better treatment of the poor in *Wozzeck* (174), Weill's satire of social class structure in *Die Dreigroschenoper* (186), Britten's condemnation of social ostracism in *Peter Grimes* (200), Crumb's reflections on the Vietnam War in *Black Angels* (205), and Penderecki's memorial for the first victims of nuclear war (208). Sometimes the role of politics is unclear, even if inescapable; musicians and critics are still trying to puzzle out the intended meanings of Hindemith's *Symphony Mathis der Maler* (187), written in Germany during the Nazi era, and Shostakovich's Fifth Symphony (189), composed in the Soviet Union during the height of Stalin's repression.

Your Turn

All of these and many other potential connections can be made through the works in this anthology. But they remain unrealized until you, the reader, make them real for yourself. We invite you to study each piece for what it shares with others as well as for its own distinctive qualities. You will encounter much that is unfamiliar, perhaps including pieces you will grow to love and others that may never suit your tastes. At the end, the goal is to understand as much as possible about why those who created this music made the choices they did, and how each piece represents a genre, style, trend, and time that played an important role in our long and ever-changing tradition of Western music.

—J. Peter Burkholder
February 2014

ACKNOWLEDGMENTS

The creative efforts of many people are represented in these pages. W. W. Norton and I appreciate the individuals and publishers cited in the source notes who granted permission to reprint or adapt material under copyright. I am especially grateful to John Hajdu Heyer for his edition of Lully's *Te Deum*, to Edward H. Roesner for his edition of *Viderunt omnes* by Leoninus and colleagues, and to Rebecca A. Baltzer for her editions of *Factum est salutare/Dominus* and *Fole acostumance/Dominus* and her editorial revisions of Adam de la Halle's *De ma dame vient/Dieus, comment porroie/Omnes*, which were prepared specifically for NAWM. Thomas J. Mathiesen kindly provided phonetic transliterations of the Greek poetry and new engravings of the music for NAWM 1 and 2. David Botwinik contributed the beautiful layout and elegantly typeset several items that were not reproduced from existing editions. Laura Dallman typeset the first movement of Persichetti's *Symphony for Band* (NAWM 199), and Nathan Landes scanned several new selections. Daniel T. Rogers researched the background to each of the works added to this edition. I had assistance in writing several of the commentaries on new items, from Laura Dallman (NAWM 67, 69, 168, 186, 190, 191, 199, and 220), Harry Haskell (157, 159, and 216–218), Nathan Landes (206), and Amanda Sewell (219). Katherine Baber offered ideas for the commentary on *West Side Story* (198). Lewis Lockwood and Alan Gosman generously provided portions of their edition of Beethoven's *Eroica* sketchbook prior to publication (126). Daniel R. Melamed provided helpful editorial comments on commentaries for the new Telemann and Bach items (99, 102, and 104) and drafted some of the text for the last, on *Erbarme dich*. Giuliano Di Bacco and Michael Long helped with Italian and Latin translations for new medieval items (25 and 31). I am deeply indebted to all of them for their assistance.

Members of the Editorial Advisory Board for HWM—Michael Alan Anderson, Arved Ashby, Gregory Barnett, James A. Borders, Mauro Calcagno, Drew Edward Davies, Andrew Dell'Antonio, Charles Dill, Don Fader, Andrew Flory, Rebecca L. Gerber, Jonathan Gibson, Robert O. Gjerdingen, David Grayson, Helen M. Greenwald, James Grier, Karen Henson, D. Kern Holoman, Steven Johnson, Lewis Lockwood, Michael P. Long, Melanie Lowe, Rebecca Maloy, Michael Marissen, Mary Sue Morrow, Margaret Notley, Gretchen Peters, Heather Platt, Hilary Poriss, John Rice, Margaret Rorke, Jesse Rosenberg, Stephanie P. Schlagel, Carl B. Schmidt, W. Anthony Sheppard, Christopher J. Smith, Larry Starr, Pamela F. Starr, Russell Stinson, Susan Youens, Charles Youmans, and Laurel Zeiss—made very helpful suggestions, from choice of repertoire to details in the commentaries. Bryan Christian, Barbara Russano Hanning, Ralph Locke,

Massimo Ossi, William F. Prizer, Kristen Strandberg, Michael Strasser, Charles Whitman, Natalie Williams, and many other colleagues, students, and friends offered ideas and useful corrections. Over three hundred instructors provided extensive feedback about the previous edition and suggestions for changes. Their help has made this a much better anthology, and I am very grateful.

Assembling the recordings was an especially complex task. I began with an initial list, matching editions to recordings wherever possible. Roger Hickman found other high-quality recordings. He also worked with Ronnie Thomas from Naxos to ensure that the mastering of each recording was precise. Randall Foster, licensing director of Naxos, oversaw the production of the recordings and, with the assistance of his staff, negotiated a license for each track—a laborious and complicated effort. Their enthusiastic work brought the recordings to fruition, and I greatly appreciate their contributions.

In addition, I remain indebted to the many people who assisted in preparing the previous editions, especially John Anderies, Rika Asai, Katherine Baber, David N. Baker, Nicole Baker, Jonathan Bellman, Jane A. Bernstein, Geoffrey Block, Ira L. Braus, Michael Broyles, Anna Maria Busse Berger, Catherine J. Cole, Vincent Corrigan, Felix O. Cox, Richard Crawford, Stephen A. Crist, Drew Edward Davies, Luis Dávila, Andrew Dell'Antonio, Charles Dill, Matthew Dirst, Cathy Ann Elias, Paul Elliott, Margot Fassler, Kristine Forney, James Franklin, Jonathan Gibson, Jonathan Glixon, Halina Goldberg, Robert A. Green, James Grier, Bruce Gustafson, Barbara Russano Hanning, Kunio Hara, Stephen E. Hefling, Jan Herlinger, Roger Hickman, Robert Hopkins, Steven Huebner, David R. Hurley, Steven Johnson, Jeffrey Kallberg, William Kinderman, Gesa Kordes, Dennis Leclaire, Luiz Fernando Lopes, Melanie Lowe, Kathryn Lowerre, Claudia Macdonald, Jeffrey Magee, Roberta Montemorra Marvin, Alan Matheson, Thomas J. Mathiesen, Daniel Melamed, Alison Mero, David Metzer, Felicia Miyakawa, Kevin N. Moll, Margaret Murata, Russell E. Murray, Jessie Ann Owens, Heather Platt, William F. Prizer, Brent C. Reidy, Samuel Rosenberg, Ann Shaffer, Alexander Silbiger, Jeremy L. Smith, Rex Sprouse, Pamela F. Starr, Derek Stauff, Scott Stewart, Kristen Strandberg, R. Larry Todd, Patrick Warfield, Stephen A. Willier, Travis Yeager, Christopher Young, and Neal Zaslow. Their contributions continue to enhance this new edition.

It has been a pleasure to work with the staff at W. W. Norton. Justin Hoffman oversaw and coordinated the entire NAWM project, facilitated communication between all of the project's contributors, offered encouragement, and made the schedule work when I fell behind. Courtney Hirschey copyedited the entire manuscript and suggested numerous improvements. Kathleen Karcher contacted rights holders and secured permissions for the works in the anthology. Barbara Curialle proofread, making further refinements to the text, and Pamela Lawson project edited, cheerfully tolerating my last minute revisions. Nicole Schilder scanned scores for new selections, and Jane Searle oversaw production of both NAWM and HWM. Maribeth Anderson Payne, music editor, has been a constant source of ideas and enthusiasm for NAWM as well as HWM, and her careful scrutiny of the commentaries helped make them clearer and more accurate. I cannot thank them all enough for their skill, dedication, care, and counsel.

Thanks finally but most of all to my family, especially my parents Donald and Jean Burkholder, who introduced me to the love of music; Bill, Joanne, and Sylvie Burkholder, whose enthusiasm renewed my own; and P. Douglas McKinney, whose patient support and encouragement have sustained me through three editions over more than a dozen years. My father passed away as I was preparing this edition. He never learned to play an instrument but loved to listen to music, especially the classics from Bach through Bartók. During my more than thirty years as a music historian, knowing he would read and share with others everything I wrote about music, I have always written with him in mind, trying to make my writing clear and accessible not only to scholars and students but to him and all lovers of music. It is a habit too ingrained to break. I miss him, but his spirit is still with me and on every page of this anthology.

—*J. Peter Burkholder*
February 2014

PITCH DESIGNATIONS

In this anthology, a note referred to without regard to its octave register is designated by a capital letter (A). A note in a particular octave is designated in italics, using the following system:

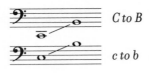 *C to B*

c to b

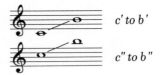 *c' to b'*

c" to b"

NORTON ANTHOLOGY OF
WESTERN MUSIC

Volume 3: The Twentieth Century and After

SEVENTH EDITION

Scott Joplin (1867/8–1917)

Maple Leaf Rag

Piano rag
1899

From Scott Joplin, *Maple Leaf Rag* (Sedalia, Mo: John Stark & Son, 1899). Reprinted in Scott Joplin, *Complete Piano Works*, ed. Vera Brodsky Lawrence (New York: The New York Public Library, 1971), 26–28.

Scott Joplin named his *Maple Leaf Rag* after the Maple Leaf Club in Sedalia, Missouri, where he performed regularly as a pianist in the late 1890s. Instead of selling the piece outright to a publisher, as was a frequent practice of composers at the time, he negotiated with his publisher, John Stark, for a royalty of one cent per copy. The first year only about four hundred copies were sold, but eventually buyers took home more than a million copies, making it the most famous piano rag in history and the first piece by an African American to sell so well. Although ragtime was a type of popular music, Joplin intended his rags as classical works, equivalent to other stylized dances, such as Chopin's mazurkas and waltzes (compare NAWM 134).

The form of a rag is like that of a march, with two repeated sixteen-measure strains followed by a trio, usually in a key a fourth higher, that features two more strains. *Maple Leaf Rag* is unusual in that it lacks the typical four-measure introduction, repeats the first strain once again after the second strain and before the trio, and returns to the original key in the last strain. Thus its form is AABBACCDD, in which the C strain is in the subdominant D♭ major and the others in the tonic A♭ major. The contrasts of melody and figuration between and within strains are strong, as in Sousa's march (NAWM 163), but the logical form and several recurring rhythmic figures lend the piece a satisfying unity.

In a rag, the left-hand accompaniment keeps a steady beat in eighth notes while the right hand plays syncopated figures above it. The most common accompanimental pattern for rags is the alternation of a bass octave on the beat with chords on the offbeats, as at measures 17 and 49, but *Maple Leaf Rag* also includes other patterns, like those at measures 1 and 9. Throughout the rag, the syncopations in the right hand vary tremendously, with well over a dozen different possible combinations of rhythms within a measure. Longer or accented notes often fall on the sixteenth note just before or just after the beat. At times the pattern of accents seems to set up a meter of $\frac{3}{16}$ in the right hand against $\frac{2}{4}$ in the left, as at measures 1–4 and 17–27. These constantly changing rhythms give the music much of its energy. But the harmony is also colorful, with chromatic passing tones, lowered sixth chords (measure 5), changes of mode (to minor in measure 7), diminished seventh chords (measure 9), ninth chords (measures 31 and 49), and other effects. All strains but the first begin away from the tonic chord, and all cadences involve some chromaticism, providing momentum toward resolution.

The accompanying recording includes two performances. The first is by Scott Joplin himself, recorded on a player piano roll in April 1916. Player pianos literally play themselves, with an internal mechanism that depresses the keys. As a paper roll passes over a metal cylinder that has a small hole for each key on the piano keyboard, a suction pump draws in air wherever a hole is cut in the paper, and a mechanism presses the corresponding key, sounding that note. Many famous pianists—including several composers, such as Joplin—recorded music this way. Piano rolls were one form in which music was sold in the late nineteenth and early twentieth centuries, and they helped to popularize Joplin's music. His roll gives us a good sense of his playing: steady, clear, and not too fast (he often admonished players not to play ragtime fast). He adds notes and flourishes here and there, especially to the bass line.

The second performance is by Jelly Roll Morton (1890–1941), recorded in June 1938 for the Library of Congress as part of a project by Alan Lomax to record, document, and preserve the work of artists who had contributed to the jazz and blues traditions. Morton was one of the pioneers of jazz, and his playing shows the characteristics of the early New Orleans style. While Joplin played the piece more or less as notated (as a classical piece would be played), Morton renders the sixteenth notes in the swinging style associated with jazz, in which the notes on the beat (here, on each eighth note) are elongated and those on the offbeats shortened, creating a rhythm like triplets alternating eighth and sixteenth notes. Moreover, he freely changes the material, adding an introduction (based on the second half of the first strain), adding new syncopations, changing the accompanimental patterns in the left hand, introducing a fair amount of chromaticism, and altering some passages almost beyond recognition. His performance imitates the sound of a New Orleans jazz band, the right hand suggesting the style of the trumpet and clarinet melody instruments, and the left the trombone and piano (see NAWM 183). He also omits the repetitions of the first two strains, to keep the piece under the three- to four-minute limit for 78-rpm records, resulting in the form Intro ABACCDD.

Gustav Mahler (1860–1911)

Kindertotenlieder: No. 1, *Nun will die Sonn' so hell aufgeh'n*

Orchestral song cycle

1901

concise 🔊

From Gustav Mahler, *Songs of a Wayfarer and Kindertotenlieder* in full score (New York: Dover), 59–73. Dover Publications, Inc.

Nun will die Sonn' so hell aufgeh'n,
Als sei kein Unglück die Nacht gescheh'n!
Das Unglück geschah nur mir allein!
Die Sonne, sie scheinet allgemein!

Du musst nicht die Nacht in dir verschränken,
Musst sie ins ew'ge Licht versenken!
Ein Lämplein verlosch in meinem Zelt!
Heil sei dem Freudenlicht der Welt!

Now would the sun so brightly rise
as if no misfortune had happened during the night!
The misfortune happened to me alone!
The sun, it shines on everyone!

You must not enfold the night within you,
You must immerse it in everlasting light!
A little lamp went out in my tent!
Hail to the joy-light of the world!

— FRIEDRICH RÜCKERT

Gustav Mahler's *Kindertotenlieder* (Songs on the Death of Children) is a cycle of five songs for solo voice and orchestra on poems by Friedrich Rückert about the deaths of children and the feelings of grieving parents. Rückert wrote the poems after his own two children died from scarlet fever, but when Mahler wrote the first three songs in the cycle during a two-week period in the summer of 1901, including the song shown here, he was unmarried and childless. He was attracted to the poems because of the intense emotions they conveyed, the painful irony of a parent mourning a child instead of the other way around, and perhaps the coincidence that Rückert's son was named Ernst, the name of Mahler's beloved younger brother, who died at age thirteen. By the time Mahler finished the cycle in 1904, he was married and a father, and his wife Alma later recalled that she thought he was tempting fate by continuing to work on these songs. The cycle was first performed in Vienna in January 1905.

In the first song, *Nun will die Sonn' so hell aufgeh'n*, Rückert's text is not comforting, but bitterly ironic. The speaker's child has died during the night, but the sun shines anyway as if nothing had happened; the sorrow is his alone, and neither the world nor the sun seems to care.

Mahler's setting heightens these ironies. Despite being scored for full orchestra, the music is mostly a thin texture of two or three contrapuntal lines, sometimes over drones or simple ostinatos, as if the few instruments that are playing at any one moment were alone in a vast world. The counterpoint does not follow traditional rules, but instead emphasizes plaintive dissonances. The opening duet of horn and oboe sounds stark, its bare harmonic fourths and octaves empty. The apparently joyful words "Now would the sun so brightly rise" are set to a mournful descending melody that emphasizes half-steps, an emblem of sadness since the Renaissance madrigal, and accompanied by half-step motives in horn and bassoon. Yet for the next line, which tells of the misfortune that occurred during the night, the music slowly shifts to major through a rising chromatic melody over a reassuring rocking figure, and the cadence is in a radiant D major. The misalignment of mood between text and music makes clear that the sun is not a source of joy for the poet today, but an uncaring and even mocking observer.

An orchestral interlude leads the music back to minor for the second couplet (at measure 22). Here the music varies what we have already heard, but the mismatch of mood is gone; the poet's sense of being alone with his misfortune is clearly etched by the mournful melody, and the bright D-major cadence is perfectly suited to the sentiment that the sun shines on everyone, although the poet is left to feel even more alone in his misery.

The music sounds as if it will repeat once more (measures 41–47), but instead the singer inverts the melody and heads in a new direction (at measure 47). This third couplet is the only one in the poem not to mention misfortune or the sun directly, so Mahler gives it new music, developing the half-step motive, chromatic motion, and other ideas already heard. The words suggest a path out of despair— you must not give in to darkness by holding it in yourself, but must bathe it in endless light—but the music reaches a new height of dissonance, chromaticism, and intensity, suggesting that such advice could not be followed easily, if at all.

The final couplet (measure 67) returns to the music of the first couplet, with intensified emphasis on melodic seconds through rhythmic diminution. Here, though, the major-mode cadence in the voice is followed by another cadential phrase, repeating the words "to the joy-light of the world!" to mournful music first heard in the orchestra (compare measures 79–82 with measures 17–20) and closing in a poignant D minor.

The very simplicity of this music makes it even more affecting. The form is a modified AABA song form, yet the changing relationship between music and text along with subtle variations in the music keep it fresh. The contrasts between D minor and D major and between diatonic and chromatic passages are again simple, but wonderfully effective and typical of Mahler. The sparse use of instruments creates a transparent sound, yet the delicate counterpoint is suffused with chromaticism and dissonance to convey the sense of loss and hurt so poignantly articulated in the text. Each of the elements here is familiar, but the combination is new and unique—a formula that is characteristic of Mahler's modernist style.

Richard Strauss (1864–1949)

Salome, Op. 54: Scene 4, conclusion, *Ah! Ich habe deinen Mund geküsst*

Opera

1903–5

166

From Richard Strauss, *Salome* (Berlin: Adolph Fürstner, 1905; repr. New York: Dover, 1981), 346–52.

(Der Vorhang fällt schnell.)

Berlin, 20. Juni 1905.

SALOME

Ah! Ich habe deinen Mund geküsst, Jochanaan.	Ah! I have kissed your mouth, Jochanaan.
Ah! Ich habe ihn geküsst, deinen Mund,	Ah! I have kissed it, your mouth,
es war ein bitterer Geschmack	there was a bitter taste
auf deinen Lippen.	on your lips.
Hat es nach Blut geschmeckt?	Did it taste of blood?

1:23   Nein! Doch es schmeckte vielleicht nach Liebe . . .   No! But it tasted perhaps of love . . .

Sie sagen, dass die Liebe bitter schmecke . . .   They say that love tastes bitter . . .

2:16   Allein was tut's? Was tut's?   But what does it matter? What does it matter?

Ich habe deinen Mund geküsst, Jochanaan.   I have kissed your mouth, Jochanaan.

Ich habe ihn geküsst, deinen Mund.   I have kissed it, your mouth.

(The moon breaks through the clouds again and illuminates Salome.)

HEROD
(turning around)

Man töte dieses Weib!   Kill that woman!

(The soldiers rush at Salome and bury her under their shields.)

— OSCAR WILDE, TRANS. HEDWIG LACHMANN

Salome was Richard Strauss's third opera and first operatic success, after he achieved early renown as a composer of tone poems (see NAWM 158). He based it on Oscar Wilde's play *Salomé*, which Strauss saw in Berlin in 1903. Rather than work with a libretto prepared especially for the opera, as was standard practice, Strauss took the play itself, in the German translation by Hedwig Lachmann, and adapted it as a libretto by making judicious cuts. He sketched the opera by the end of 1904 and then began on the full score, finishing in June 1905. As the premiere drew near, Strauss and conductor Ernst von Schuch had to deal with protests from singers and orchestra members about the work's extreme difficulty. Marie Wittlich, the soprano singing the title role, was unwilling to perform Salome's Dance of the Seven Veils, and in the end a ballerina danced it in her stead. The premiere in Dresden on December 9, 1905, was a great success, earning thirty-eight curtain calls. Soon the opera was being staged in opera houses across Europe, and the royalties enabled Strauss to pay for a villa in the Bavarian mountain resort town of Garmisch, which he called "the house that *Salome* built."

There is much that is traditional in *Salome*. The operatic ideas of music representing emotion, delineating characters, and dramatizing the situation are as evident here as in the operas of Mozart, Weber, and Wagner. Like Wagner, Strauss builds the musical fabric from leitmotives associated with characters and ideas, and like many of his predecessors, he associates particular keys with certain characters. But the story is shocking, especially in its treatment of sexuality, and Strauss wrote music to match.

The ultimate source for Wilde's play is the accounts of the death of John the Baptist in the gospels of Matthew and Mark, especially the latter:

[King] Herod had sent and seized John [the Baptist], and bound him in prison for the sake of Herodias, his brother Philip's wife; because he had married her. For John said to Herod, "It is not lawful for you to have your brother's wife." And Herodias had a grudge against him, and wanted to kill him. But she could not, for Herod feared John, knowing that he was a righteous and holy man, and kept him safe. When he heard him, he was much perplexed; and yet he heard him gladly. But an opportunity came when Herod on his birthday gave a banquet for his courtiers and officers and the leading men of Galilee. For when Herodias' daughter came in and danced, she pleased Herod and his guests; and the king said to the girl, "Ask me for whatever you wish, and I will grant it." And he vowed to her, "Whatever you ask me, I will give you, even half my kingdom." And she went out, and said to her mother, "What shall I ask?" And she said, "The head of John the baptizer." And she came in immediately with haste to the king, and asked, saying, "I want you to give me at once the head of John the Baptist on a platter." And the king was exceedingly sorry; but because of his oaths and his guests he did not want to break his word to her. And immediately the king sent a soldier of the guard and gave orders to bring his head. He went and beheaded him in the prison, and brought his head on a platter, and gave it to the girl; and the girl gave it to her mother. (Mark 6:17–28, Revised Standard Version)

The biblical accounts do not give the name of Herodias's daughter, but the Jewish historian Josephus (37–ca. 100) identifies her in his *Jewish Antiquities* as Salome (although he does not link her to the death of John the Baptist). Several nineteenth-century writers elaborated on the Bible stories, including German poet Heinrich Heine and American poet J. C. Heywood, both of whom included scenes of Herodias kissing John's severed head. Wilde's play made Salome the central character, rather than Herod or Herodias, and made the engine of the drama Salome's erotic attraction to John, called Jochanaan in the play. In Wilde's version, it was Salome's idea, not her mother's, to ask for the head of Jochanaan on a silver platter. When she is given the head, she rapturously speaks to Jochanaan, telling him his body was beautiful, and if he had only looked at her and truly seen her he would have loved her. Then she kisses his lips.

The concluding passage given here begins just after that kiss. The example on the next page shows the elements of this passage in reduced score. A soft continuous trill in flutes and clarinets between A and B♭ sustains tension. Against it we hear in oboe and piccolo a leitmotive associated with Salome's desire for Jochanaan, a quick triadic figure (E–G–E–B) in which every note is dissonant against one of the notes in the trill. In between statements of this motive sounds a dissonant five-note chord (C♯–E–F×–G♯–A♯) in low strings, brass, winds, and organ. The level of dissonance is extreme, and at first each of these three elements seems to be in its own key: perhaps D minor for the trill, E minor for the motive, and C♯ minor with neighbor tones for the chord. Amid these sonic elements, Salome sings a highly chromatic melody akin to a recitative, saying "Ah, I have kissed your mouth, Jochanaan." Her first two phrases each end with a minor triad, first C♯ minor and then B♭ minor.

What sense can we make of the notes in this passage? The low chord in the orchestra is the primary sonority, combining a C♯-minor triad (C♯–E–G♯) with a diminished seventh chord (C♯–E–F×–A♯). All the other elements in this passage emphasize notes in this chord. The three triads, E minor, C♯ minor, and B♭ minor, each highlight a minor third that is part of the diminished seventh chord, spelled

enharmonically (respectively, E–G or E–F𝄪; C♯–E; and B♭–D♭ or A♯–C♯). The trill between A and B♭ (enharmonically, A and A♯) combines A♯ with its lower chromatic neighbor. The beginning, high, and low notes in Salome's vocal line are all in that diminished seventh chord as well. So as dissonant as the passage sounds, it is all centered on a traditional dissonance, the diminished seventh chord, which had been used as a dramatic expressive device for over two centuries (see, for example, Scarlatti's cantata *Clori vezzosa, e bella*, NAWM 92, and Weber's *Der Freischütz*, NAWM 148). Such an intensification of a traditional device is quintessentially modernist, combining elements from the tradition in novel ways to create a passage that is unlike anything heard before.

    Salome notes a bitter taste on Jochanaan's lips, asks if it was blood, then sings, "No! But it tasted perhaps of love" (rehearsal 357). Here the dissonance seems to resolve to a beautiful F-major triad, embellished by a hopeful arching motive in the violins. But this proves to be a false promise: the trill continues, the F-major chord quickly fades, and the E-minor motive and low dissonant chord return unchanged, making clear that no resolution has taken place. Salome comments, "They say that love tastes bitter."

But now comes the real resolution. As she sings, "What does it matter? I have kissed your mouth, Jochanaan," the harmony moves to an F♯-major triad (rehearsal 358), decorated by the arching violin motive and colored by E and A natural, then on to a glorious I$_4^6$–V^7–I cadence in C♯ major (rehearsal 359). In retrospect, we understand the whole passage from the beginning of this excerpt as a single chord progression in C♯: starting with hints of the minor tonic; moving through forms of the subdominant (the diminished seventh chord F×–A♯–C♯–E is VII^{o7} of V, F♯ major is IV, and F♯–A–C♯–E is iv^7); moving on to the dominant G♯ decorated with a I$_4^6$ cadential chord; and resolving to a brilliant major tonic chord. All the ambiguity and dissonance lead to this culminating moment, which is highlighted by simultaneous statements in the orchestra of all the leitmotives associated with Salome. C♯ is Salome's key throughout the opera, and C♯ major is linked to her erotic power and her ecstasy, particularly in her long dialogue with Jochanaan at the center of the opera and her monologue to his head shortly before this concluding passage.

Yet all is not well. Her home key quickly unravels, beginning with the crunching dissonance just before rehearsal 361, a combination of two clashing forms of the subdominant: F♯ major (F♯–A♯–C♯) and an augmented sixth chord (A–C♯–E–F×, spelled A–C♯–E–G). This composite chord is both colorful and functional: it recalls earlier dissonant sonorities in this passage and leads right back to C♯ major. The contrast between sweet consonance and this bitter dissonance with six notes sounding at once reminds us that Salome's moment of bliss is the result of a horrific act. The music once again moves away from C♯ major, now irrevocably, as Herod, in revulsion, orders Salome killed. The opera ends with the brass and timpani shouting out her motive, truncated to its first three notes, in a deadly C minor.

The plot is shocking, and so is the music. On first hearing, it sounds radically new. Yet every new element in the music is an extension or intensification of a traditional device. In this way, Strauss's opera exemplifies his brand of musical modernism.

Claude Debussy (1862–1918)

Nocturnes: No. 1, *Nuages* (Clouds)

Symphonic poem

1897–99

167

From Claude Debussy, *Nocturnes*, ed. Clinton F. Nieweg (New York: E. F. Kalmus, 1990, 2004), 2–18. Used by permission. The discussion of rotational form in the commentary that follows draws on James Hepokoski, "Clouds and Circles: Rotational Form in Debussy's 'Nuages,'" *Tijdschrift voor Musiektheorie* 15, no. 1 (2010): 1–17.

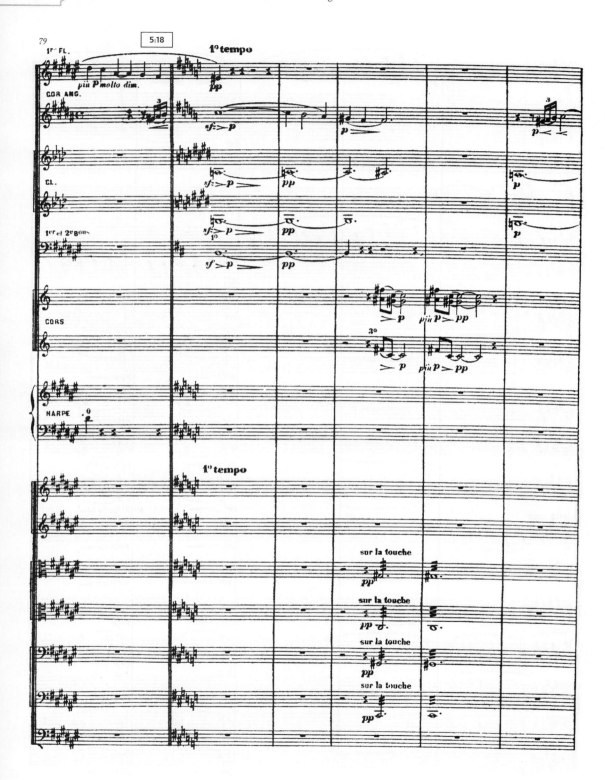

Claude Debussy first conceived his three *Nocturnes* as a set of pieces for solo violin and orchestra for violinist Eugène Ysaÿe, but soon recast them as a suite of symphonic poems. They took him almost three years to complete (1897–99), between work on other projects. The name *Nocturnes* was not meant to evoke the genre Chopin had helped to popularize (see NAWM 135) but was borrowed from a series of impressionist paintings that American artist James McNeill Whistler (1834–1903) titled *Nocturne*. Like Whistler's paintings, Debussy's orchestral pictures evoke scenes that are at the same time ordinary and a bit mysterious: *Nuages* (Clouds), evoking shifting clouds; *Fêtes* (Festivals), depicting evening festivities; and *Sirènes* (Sirens), bringing to life the Sirens of ancient Greece with a wordless women's chorus behind the orchestra. The first two movements were performed in 1900, and the complete piece was published later that year.

Like all of Debussy's orchestral music, *Nuages* is a play of musical images, each characterized by instrumental color, motive, pitch collection, rhythm, and register. In the course of the movement, images are juxtaposed, superimposed, repeated, and altered, creating a kind of musical experience that seems almost visual, rather than following the older literary or rhetorical model of music that presents, develops, and recapitulates themes. In the program for the piece's premiere, Debussy wrote that he sought to capture "the unchanging appearance of the sky with the slow and melancholy progress of the clouds, ending in a gray dissolution gently tinged with white," and he commented to a friend that he was thinking of the play of clouds over the Seine in Paris.

The opening image, a pattern of alternating fifths and thirds, suggests movement without a strong sense of direction, an apt musical representation of slowly moving clouds. Debussy apparently modeled this gesture on a figure in Musorgsky's song *Okonchen prazdnyi, shumnyi den'* (The idle, noisy day is over), from the song cycle *Bez solntsa* (Sunless):

Perhaps Debussy intended an allusion, either to the title "Sunless" (thereby suggesting a cloudy day) or to the text at this point in the song, whose mention of "springtime's passionate dreams" and "a series of hopes, desires, delusions" fits well with the series of dreamy musical ideas in this movement. He may also have been attracted to the figure's rhythmic ambiguity, six beats to the measure that could be heard either in $\frac{6}{4}$ or $\frac{3}{2}$. By changing Musorgsky's sixths to open fifths, Debussy avoids the sense of harmonic progression in the song and gives the gesture an open, empty sound that seems to suggest broad open spaces. This musical idea changes almost every time it recurs: the winds are replaced by strings (measure

11); the oscillations by parallel ninth chords (measure 14), triads (measure 29), or seventh chords (measure 61); and the open fifths and thirds by full triads (measure 21) or seventh chords (measure 43, joined by pizzicato offbeats). Near the end, the pattern is heard only in fragments (measures 94–97), as if the clouds were scattering.

Juxtaposed with or superimposed upon the opening image is a motive in the English horn, set off in a meter of its own ($\frac{4}{4}$ against $\frac{6}{4}$ in the other instruments), that quickly rises and slowly descends through a portion of the octatonic scale, spanning a tritone (measures 5–8). Unlike the constantly changing clouds, this figure changes little. The final notes are sometimes omitted or repeated, but the motive is otherwise the same at each appearance, never developed, transposed, or played by another instrument, and the English horn never plays anything else. After most statements, the horns answer with a tritone (as at measure 23) or another brief gesture, drawing their notes from the same octatonic scale as the English horn (or, in measures 82–87, from a whole-tone scale). At the end, the final notes of the English horn motive echo a couple of times, and then it disappears.

The shifting cloud and steady English horn ideas are interspersed with contrasting episodes: a chordal idea in the strings (measures 15–20) and a unison melody, perhaps derived from the cloud figure, that gradually rises in sequence and crescendos (measures 33–42). A profoundly calm contrasting section (measures 64–79) features sustained strings and a pentatonic tune in flute and harp that evokes the sound world of Asia—perhaps a Japanese flute or *koto* melody, or a Javanese gamelan (gong and percussion orchestra).

The overall form of *Nuages* can be understood in more than one way. If we take the changes of key signature as a guide, the movement consists of three sections in a modified ABA' form, with the opening A section (measures 1–63) far longer than the others. In this view, the Asian-sounding pentatonic episode in the B section (measures 64–79) is the point of greatest contrast, and the final A' (measures 80–102) offers a very partial reprise. But musicologist James Hepokoski has recently argued that the movement is better explained as an example of what he calls "rotational form," in which the music cycles through a series of varied statements of the basic musical material (compare the analysis of Wagner's prelude to *Tristan und Isolde* in NAWM 149). Here, there are four main "rotations" or cycles, each beginning with a variant of the opening "cloud" figure and ending with the English horn motive, followed by a short final rotation that briefly recalls the main ideas.

Here is a chart comparing the two approaches:

Section	A										B	A'			
Rotation	1		2			3			4			5			
Music	a	b	a	c	b'+a'	c'	d	b''+a''	a	c''	e	b'''	(a)	(e)	(b)
Measure	1	5	11	14	21	29	33	43	57	61	64	80	94	98	99

In this chart, the lowercase letters stand for the musical ideas mentioned previously: the oscillating "cloud" figure (a), the English horn motive (b), the parallel chords adapted from the "cloud" figure (c), the rising sequence at measure 33 (d), and the pentatonic Asian-sounding melody (e). If we consider the movement as a rotational form, the four main rotations grow progressively longer (at 10, 18, 28, and 37 measures), and each successive cycle introduces new material. In this view, the pentatonic melody is only the longest of a series of contrasting elements. Such an approach closely fits the idea Debussy had for the movement of an ever-moving yet essentially unchanging sky. The final rotation (measures 94–102) gives us a last glimpse of the "cloud" and the pentatonic melody, but the English horn has already vanished from view, represented only by the tritones in the horns that earlier sounded in response to it.

As in works by Musorgsky (see NAWM 153) and Fauré (NAWM 159), chords in *Nuages* are not used to shape a phrase by tension and release. Instead, each chord is conceived as a sonorous unit in a phrase whose structure is determined more by melodic shape or color than by harmonic movement. Oscillating chords, parallel triads and ninth chords, and sustained chords all serve to create distinctive musical images. However, such a procedure does not necessarily negate a sense of tonal center, which Debussy maintains in *Nuages* through pedal points and frequent returns to the primary tone, B.

Often, Debussy uses different pitch collections to distinguish blocks of sound from one another as they are juxtaposed. The opening cloud figure features a B-minor scale tinged with chromaticism, which contrasts with the octatonic scale in the English horn motive and its accompanying chords. The pentatonic melody in flute and harp inhabits a contrasting tonal world centered on the D♯ Dorian scale (measures 64–68).

Debussy's writing for orchestra is full of striking touches, including the identification of the English horn with a single motive, the use of the horns for only brief gestures, and the bell-like combination of flute in unison with harp. The strings are muted and divided (the violins in as many as twelve parts, the violas and cellos in two), giving a rich but distant sound, and independent lines for solo violin and viola add contrasting colors. Very soft timpani rolls, barely heard near the beginning and end of the piece, underscore the stillness.

Maurice Ravel (1876–1937)

Le tombeau de Couperin: Menuet

Orchestral suite

1914–17

168

From Maurice Ravel, *Le tombeau de Couperin: Suite d'orchestre* (Paris: Éditions Durand, 1919; repr. Bryn Mawr, Pa.: T. Presser, 1919), 35–45. © 1919 Durand S.A. Editions Musicales. Editions A.R.I.M.A. and Durand S.A. Editions Musicales. Joint publication. Reproduced by permission of the publisher. Sole representative U.S.A., Theodore Presser Co.

In a letter dated October 1, 1914, Ravel wrote to his friend and pupil, Roland-Manuel, that he was working on a number of compositions, including a "French suite." His work was interrupted by the outbreak of World War I and his subsequent military service, but after his discharge from the army Ravel finished the suite in 1917 while staying at the home of Fernand Dreyfus and his wife, who was Roland-Manuel's mother. The title *Le tombeau de Couperin* evokes the seventeenth- and eighteenth-century tradition of the *tombeau*, a work that commemorates the death of a notable individual. Modeled on eighteenth-century keyboard suites like those of François Couperin (see NAWM 97 and the Jacquet de la Guerre suite in NAWM 88), Ravel's suite includes six movements: prélude, fugue, forlane, rigaudon, menuet (minuet), and toccata. Each movement is dedicated to the memory of one of Ravel's friends who perished in the war. The menuet honors Jean Dreyfus, the Dreyfuses' son and Roland-Manuel's stepbrother.

At its premiere on April 11, 1919, *Le tombeau de Couperin* was received so enthusiastically that the pianist, Marguerite Long, encored the entire suite. Later that year Ravel began arranging four of the movements as a suite for orchestra: the prélude, forlane, menuet, and rigaudon. They were premiered in Paris by the Pasdeloup Orchestra in February of 1920 under the direction of Rehné-Baton, and the following November they were mounted by the Swedish Ballet at the Théâtre des Champs-Elysées.

In both its keyboard and orchestral forms, *Le tombeau de Couperin* is an early instance of *neoclassicism*, which combines elements from the the musical styles, genres, and forms of the eighteenth century with new sounds and harmonies. In the Menuet, Ravel evokes eighteenth-century music in a number of ways. He follows the Classic form of minuet and trio: a minuet in binary form with each section repeated, a contrasting trio in the same form and a simpler texture, and a reprise of the minuet without repeats. Both minuet and trio are in rounded binary form, with a brief first section of eight measures and a longer second section that repeats the opening material at the end to mark the return to the tonic. The harmonic plan also evokes tradition. The minuet establishes the tonic G major in the first four measures, cadences on a slightly unexpected B major (the dominant of the relative minor substituting for the dominant), meanders harmonically in the second section to a long-delayed cadence on the dominant D major (measure 24), and returns to G. The trio (measure 34), labeled "Musette" in the piano version, features drones and repeating figures on G and D to suggest the drones used in eighteenth-century musettes to imitate peasant bagpipes. The melodies feature rhythms typical for minuets and are primarily in four- and eight-measure phrases, with occasional melodic extensions (as in measures 13–24). The ornamentation is similar to Couperin's and serves a similar function, stressing important notes, maintaining forward momentum, and achieving an elegant line.

Yet these evocations of an older style are combined with several contemporary elements. From the first few measures, Ravel uses much more dissonance than his eighteenth-century predecessors, with many seventh and ninth chords. Parallel minor triads in measures 9–15, including the minor dominant, undermine the sense of key and of tonal function. This intensifies in the trio, where the melody is harmonized exclusively in parallel triads over the G and D pedal points, creating a sound that is as modern as impressionism and also has a medieval air because of the parallel fifths and fourths, but is certainly far from eighteenth-century common practice harmony. Beginning in a G Dorian mode (G minor with E natural and no leading tone), an echo of the modal music of the Middle Ages and Renaissance, Ravel gradually adds flats, starting the phrase at measure 50 on an F minor triad, then reaching A-flat major (measure 54), D-flat major (measure 58), and finally F-flat major (measure 63, third beat), all far removed from the trio's opening tonic of G Dorian.

Even the form departs more and more from Classic models as the movement progresses. The first section of the trio (measures 34–41) is not repeated verbatim but is varied with modified figuration and orchestration (measures 42–49), and the second section (measures 50–73) is heard only once rather than being repeated. Then, instead of a simple repetition of the minuet, Ravel presents a new variation of it (measure 74). It begins with the themes of the minuet and the trio superimposed in counterpoint, so that the parallel triads of the trio accompany the melody of the minuet. Such contrapuntal wizardry is rare among minuets, which were typically lighter in texture than other movements in a suite or symphony. Then, as if to balance the move to the flat side in the trio, Ravel transposes the first sixteen measures of the minuet's second section up a major third to B major (measures 82–97), a key that was foreshadowed by the cadence on B major in measure 8. As the end of the minuet returns one last time (measures 98–105), the harmony moves around the circle of fifths to close on the tonic G major. Then Ravel appends a long coda, quite unusual for a minuet, built from motives in the opening theme. The very end of the piece cadences on a chord that superimposes the dominant over the tonic, which could be heard on the one hand as a tonic ninth chord and on the other as a negation of the very polarity between tonic and dominant on which tonality depends. Nothing could better make the point that this music is *neo*-classical, its every "Classic" gesture given a modernist twist.

In addition to the colorful harmony, Ravel's orchestration provides a variety of instrumental color. Winds and strings alternate taking the lead (as in measures 1–8). The strings constantly shift between playing arco (bowed) and pizzicato (plucked), and use harmonics and mutes in the first section of the trio. The harp and muted brass add distinctive timbres. Melodies often change tone color, as in the shift from oboe to flute and back in the minuet, and from flute to trumpet to strings to full orchestra and back to trumpet in the trio. But perhaps the most charming orchestral touch comes at the very end of the movement (measures 122–29). In the original piano version, Ravel lets the melody tumble gently from the highest D on the piano to a final cadence in the richer middle register. In his orchestration, the melody passes from the highest instrument, the piccolo, to the oboe and then the English horn before concluding with the warm sound of the strings.

Serge Rachmaninoff (1873–1943)

Prelude in G Minor, Op. 23, No. 5

Piano prelude

1901

169

Serge Rachmaninoff composed his Prelude in G Minor in 1901 as a freestanding work, then in 1903 added nine more and published them as his Ten Preludes, Op. 23. Later, he wrote thirteen more preludes for his Op. 32 (1910). These two collections, together with the C#-minor prelude of 1892, constituted a complete set of twenty-four preludes in every major and minor key, following the model of Chopin's Preludes, Op. 28, and of Bach's *Well-Tempered Clavier*. Yet because they were initially conceived individually, Rachmaninoff's preludes are longer than those of Chopin and Bach and are rarely played as a group.

The form of the Prelude in G Minor is relatively simple: ABA Coda, with the A section itself in aaba song form. Yet almost every time an idea repeats, Rachmaninoff introduces new variants, maintaining interest through constant if subtle changes:

Section	A				B			A				Coda
Figure	a	a'	b	a"	c	c'	trans (a)	a'''	a''''	b	a'''''	(from a)
Harmony	i		mod	i	V			i	iv	mod	i	
Measure	1	10	17	25	35	42	50	54	58	64	72	82

The two main sections differ greatly in character. The A theme is marchlike, with repeated sixteenth notes on the offbeats suggesting drumrolls, and builds to a powerful climax. The B theme is lyrical and passionate, over rolling arpeggiations in the accompaniment. Such stark contrasts of material and such strongly etched emotions are quintessential Rachmaninoff.

Rachmaninoff was not the innovator in harmony that his contemporaries Strauss, Debussy, Scriabin, and Schoenberg were. But he developed a highly individual and recognizable style within the musical language of Romanticism, which is perhaps an even more difficult feat. One element that set him apart was his gift for creating melodies that sounded familiar yet fresh, moving in unexpected ways yet always sounding right in retrospect. The opening melody, in the bass, is little more than an arpeggiated G-minor triad followed by an embellished stepwise descent from G to D, but its striking rhythm and the sixteenth-note figures that decorate its main notes make it unique and memorable. The middle-section theme hovers around A, straining to rise and sinking back twice, then climbs almost an octave before falling back into place again. Subtle connections link this theme to that of the first section, including a prominent diminished fourth between F♯ and B♭ (compare measures 36 and 5); echoes in the middle register of a motive from the first theme (the sixteenth-note motive of rising minor third and major second in the middle of measure 3, echoed at measures 36–37 and throughout the middle section); and another bass stepwise descent from G to D (measures 39–40). The second time through (measure 42), a countermelody appears in the tenor, pressing upward and heightening the sense of yearning.

Another factor in Rachmaninoff's individual style was his use of innovative textures on the piano, such as the figuration in the A section, where both hands move constantly back and forth between melody and accompaniment and between higher and lower registers. Even the treatment of harmony is unusual. The music never leaves the key of G minor; instead, Rachmaninoff introduces motion up the circle of fifths (measures 17–21) to suggest a modulation within the A section, then focuses on the dominant seventh chord in the B section, in both cases relying on the major thirds in the chords to create a sense of contrast with the prevailing minor of the opening theme.

The performance on the accompanying recording is by Rachmaninoff himself, recorded in April 1920 on a piano roll that, when replayed on an Ampico reproducing piano, reproduces not only the notes themselves (like the recording of Scott Joplin in NAWM 164) but also the pedaling, the dynamic level, and the emphasis the pianist gave to each note. Recordings of this sort had advantages over audio records of the time because they could go beyond the three- to four-minute limit for 78-rpm records, could be corrected by the artist, and could sound truer than any record because they were played on actual pianos. For the consumer, they brought the thrill of hearing a famous pianist performing on one's own home piano. Rachmaninoff's piano roll shows his dynamic playing, his variety of touch, his use of the pedal, and the fluctuating tempo that was part of the Romantic performing aesthetic. He starts slowly and deliberately, giving room for increasing the pace and excitement on the last few pages. Arpeggiated chords in the middle section and an added note at the end suggest the freedom Romantic pianists took with music, especially their own.

Alexander Scriabin (1872–1915)

Vers la flamme, Op. 72

Tone poem for piano

1914

170

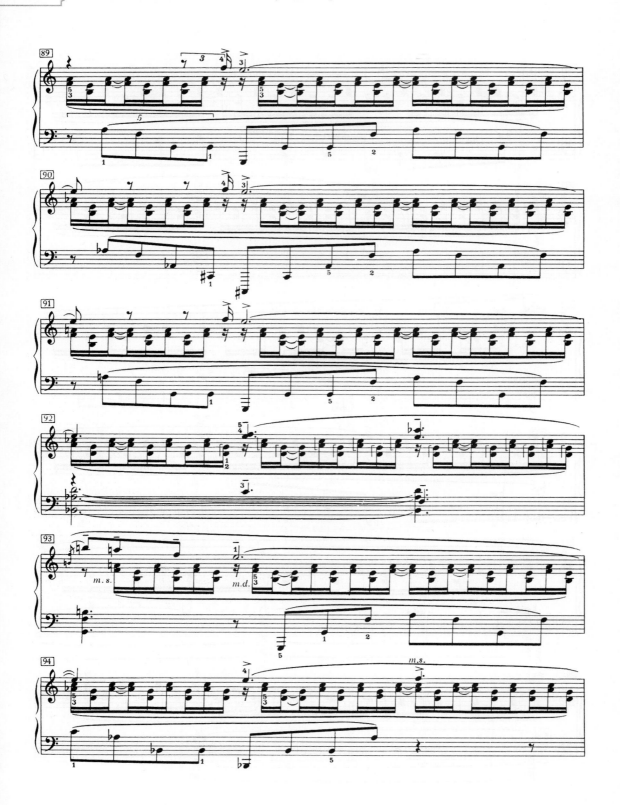

Alexander Scriabin composed *Vers la flamme* (Toward the Flame) in early 1914, conceiving it first as an orchestral work, and then as a sonata, before settling on the novel genre of a tone poem for piano, in emulation of the symphonic poem. In tune with Scriabin's belief that music should offer a transcendent experience leading to ecstasy and communion with the divine, the title suggests a journey toward enlightenment or even immolation, without specifying the course of events. Accordingly, the piece presents a series of abstract ideas, gradually increasing in activity and dynamic level and expanding upward in register until it reaches a transcendent climax at the end.

There are two main thematic ideas that define the form, which may be called theme A (measures 1–6) and theme B (measures 27–34). Theme A always involves two voices moving together in counterpoint, and theme B is a single melody. Both begin with repeated neighbor-note motion, then reach upward, fall back, and rise again, an apt image for the sense of striving implied by the piece's title and overall shape. The piece unfolds as a series of textures, delineating four large sections that place the two thematic elements in new contexts:

Section	Measure	Texture	Theme
1	1	Block chords under melodies	A
	27		B
2	41	Stratified layers, oscillating bass and middle voice in 5 against 9	half-step motive from B
	65	Stratified layers, oscillating middle voice, arpeggios in bass	half-step motive from B, later part of A (measures 70, 74)
3	77	Rapid triplets over chords	A'
	81	Rapid triplets over leaping bass	B (repeats at measure 89)
	95	Rapid triplets alternating with tremolos/high pulsed chords	transition
4	107	Tremolos and high pulsed chords	A
	125		B (beginning only)

The work is not tonal in a conventional sense. Rather, a referential sonority of two interlocked tritones announced at the beginning, E–A♯–G♯–D, often embellished with C♯ or F♯, serves as a kind of tonic chord, transposed and varied over the course of the movement. Variants appear at measures 28, 41, 65, 77, 95, 107, and 125. Several of these substitute B for A♯ or include both, thereby creating a sonority that resembles a dominant seventh chord (E–B–G♯–D) with added notes. At the end the D is raised to D♯ (measure 125), resolving any remaining tension in a climactic apotheosis marked by the widest range and highest pitches of the whole movement. Thus both of the tritones in the initial chord "resolve" over the span of the movement by raising the upper note a half step to form the perfect fifths E–B and G♯–D♯. The closing chord is doubly satisfactory as an ending: as another transformation of the opening chord, it reinforces a sense of closure on the tonic analogue, while at the same time it resolves the dissonances that provided tension in that initial chord. This kind of novel yet completely convincing use of harmony is the secret to Scriabin's evocation of a transcendent ecstasy, reinforced with the great crescendo in dynamics, expansion of range, and increasing pace of attack as the piece reaches its climax.

The sense of concluding "in the tonic" is reinforced by the transpositions of the themes. Although theme B appears in a new transposition each time, theme A returns in sections 3 and 4 at its original pitch, creating a feeling of stability in the second half of the piece akin to a return to the tonic in a piece of tonal music.

Scriabin's use of harmonic relationships by thirds in this piece is characteristic of his work in general. Theme A is almost entirely octatonic (excepting only the F♯), and Scriabin treats it in sequence by minor third (measures 1–12). Theme B highlights a chord of stacked thirds (B–D–F♯–A♯–C♯) that moves by minor third as well (as in measures 29–32). Other passages also feature movement by major third (see the bass line in measures 41–64) or minor third (measures 68–77). Most chords have four or more notes, and the final sonority has six, combining traditional tertian structure in the lower notes with stacks of fourths in the upper register. The many dissonances do not require resolution; instead, as in the music of Musorgsky (NAWM 153) or Debussy (NAWM 167), they provide harmonic color that serves to distinguish one block of ideas from another, while the movement from one complex chord to the next conveys a sense of harmonic progression.

A virtuoso showpiece, *Vers la flamme* poses numerous difficulties for the performer, including rhythms of five against nine (see the passages beginning at measures 41 and 81) and rapid leaps around the keyboard. At the end, Scriabin requires three staves to notate his massive sonorities (measure 125). But the virtuosity is not for its own sake; like Scriabin's harmony, his use of contrasting textures and the gradual acceleration in the density of attacks over the course of the movement create the sense of a spiritual journey and ecstatic release. The expressive markings along the way give signposts on this journey, from "somber" (measure 1) at the beginning, through "with a new emotion" (41), "with a veiled joy" (45), and "with a more and more tumultuous joy" (66), to "sparkling, brilliant" (81). The pianist gets quite a workout, and so do we as listeners.

Erik Satie (1866–1925)

Embryons desséchés (Dried Embryos): No. 3, *de Podophthalma*

Character piece

1913

III: OF A PODOPHTHALMA. Fairly brisk. Out hunting. Mount. Pursuit.

From Erik Satie, *Gymnopédies, Gnossiennes and Other Works for Piano* (New York: Dover Publications, Inc., 1989), 140–43. In the commentary below, the discussion of Satie's uses of borrowed material in the piece draws on Steven Moore Whiting, *Satie the Bohemian: From Cabaret to Concert Hall* (Oxford: Oxford University Press, 1999).

An adviser. He's right! Pause. Slower. In order to cast a spell over the game. Rallentando.

Resume, getting gradually faster. What is it? The adviser.

Cadence obligée *(de l'Auteur)*

ff

4 Juillet 1913

Obligatory cadenza (by the composer). July 4, 1913.

Erik Satie composed his *Embryons desséchés* (Dried Embryos) between June 30 and July 4, 1913, and it was published later that year. The third of the three pieces, *de Podophthalma* (Of the Podophthalma), was dedicated to Jane Mortier, who apparently gave the premiere. In an introduction to the set that Satie drafted but did not include in the publication, he wrote:

> This work is absolutely incomprehensible, even for me. With a singular profundity, it always astonishes me. I wrote it in spite of myself, impelled by Destiny.
>
> Perhaps I wanted to make jokes? That will not surprise me and would be quite my style. However, I will not have any indulgence for those who treat it with disdain. Let them be aware.

Here Satie parodies the Romantic idea that music comes from a divine source, and the composer is merely the unwitting conduit through which it passes. He also spoofs the serious tone of most Romantic music, while insisting that his joke—if it is a joke—be taken seriously. Nothing ruins a joke like explaining it, but by teasing out the strands of his humor, we can see Satie's purpose: to question some of our basic assumptions about music, and particularly to critique musical Romanticism.

The subject of these character pieces—dried embryos of sea creatures—is absurd, and therefore mocks the very notion of program music, character pieces, and representation in music. The absurdity is heightened by the academic airs Satie puts on by using scientific rather than common names for his creatures: in the first piece, *Holothuria*, a genus of sea cucumber, and in the other two, *Edriophthalma* and *Podophthalma*, two classes of crustaceans (no longer used in taxonomy), the former with fixed eyes (such as small shrimp) and the latter with eyes on stalks (like crabs and lobsters). Satie may have been inspired by *Für Darwin* (1864; published in English as *Facts and Arguments for Darwin*, 1869), a book by Swiss-born biologist Fritz Müller that includes chapters on the developmental history of Podophthalma and Edriophthalma, with pictures of their embryos. Satie includes with each piece a short note that combines correct scientific description with a bit of fantasy. Since it is impossible to portray dried embryos in music—which is part of Satie's point—he focuses his note on the living creatures. The note for the third piece reads as follows:

> Crustaceans with eyes placed on movable stalks. They are skillful, tireless hunters. They are found in all the oceans. The meat of the Podophthalma constitutes a tasty food.

The one part of this note that can be suggested in music is the idea of the hunt, and that is what Satie does. He hints at the plot of his tale with marginal annotations in the music, which are translated at the bottom of the page in this edition. (These annotations are themselves a satire of the emotive markings of other composers; compare those of Scriabin, discussed at the end of the commentary for NAWM 170.) He starts with an active rising figure to suggest the chase, creating a sense of growing excitement by moving from low to high on the keyboard and from F major to whole-tone chords and melodies. Then "an adviser" appears, with his own leitmotive that is labeled at each appearance—a satirical jab at analyses of Wagner operas that carefully point out every appearance of a leitmotive. The leitmotive is harmonized with chromatic chords, perhaps another Wagner reference. A hunting call in C major tries to cast a spell on the game being hunted, but it does not seem to work. The adviser leitmotive alternates with the opening music, culminating with a statement of the leitmotive in canon, and then the piece ends with a long triumphant cadence, even though there is no sign that the hunt was successful. Throughout, the sea creatures are anthropomorphized by the stirring music, dialogue with the counselor, and hunting call (imagine the sound of horns played underwater), which makes the entire program ridiculous.

Of course, all these programmatic indications are visible only to the player, not to the audience. It would take longer to explain the program to an audience than it does to play the piece. By designing the work to be fully comprehensible (to the extent that it is comprehensible—see his note above) only to the performer, Satie takes it out of the realm of concert music and places it squarely in the tradition of keyboard music to be played for one's own pleasure. This upends the hierarchy that had developed, in which concert music had become far more prestigious and ambitious than music for amateur performance at home. Also visible only to the performer is the unusual notation: even though the piece is in F major and $\frac{2}{4}$ meter (changing to $\frac{6}{8}$ for the hunting call), Satie notates the music without key signature or barlines, a pointed rejection of convention.

Satie is critiquing the concert tradition in another way as well. Steven Whiting has shown that Satie was drawing elements of the Parisian popular tradition, especially the music sung at the cabaret and café-concert, into the tradition of art music. He does so here in part through musical borrowing. The advisor's melody is taken from the refrain of "The Song of the Orangutan" in Edmond Audran's operetta *La Mascotte* (1880):

En n'trem-blez donc   pas comm' ça   On le rat-tra - pe - ra.
Don't tremble like that, we'll catch it.

Whiting notes that any Frenchman would have recognized the tune and its text, which suggests what the adviser is saying. The hunting call that follows is adapted from one called "La Royale," which was normally played after the hunters had slain the prey; in this context, it suggests a bit of premature celebration or wishful thinking. This hunting call was featured in a musical scene performed in 1900 at the Concert des Ambassadeurs (depicted in the painting on page 706 of HWM), placing it in the context of the café-concert. Moreover, the very ideas of musical humor and parodistic borrowing were common in music of the cabaret and café-concert. By pulling all of these elements into a suite of three piano pieces published in the format of art music, Satie was blurring the categories and thus questioning the hierarchy of prestige that placed art music at the top and dismissed popular music as beneath notice.

Finally, these critiques—which have required some explanation—seem subtle in comparison to the satire of Romantic art music in the piece's ending, which anyone can catch on first hearing. In an "obligatory cadenza (by the composer)," Satie parodies the long cadences at the end of Beethoven's symphonies. The key of F major suggests he is thinking of Beethoven's Symphony No. 8, whose finale needs a long assertion of the tonic after its complex harmonic adventures. But at the end of Satie's brief and light piece, it sounds like a bombastic cliché and thus implies that all of Beethoven is a bombastic cliché.

Satie's piece is irreverent and iconoclastic in mocking the sacred cows of Romanticism, antagonistic in reacting against convention, and nihilistic in negating the traditions of concert music, including the classics of the past. These characteristics place it in the avant-garde, a movement Satie helped to inspire that has had an enduring effect on music ever since.

Arnold Schoenberg (1874–1951)

Pierrot lunaire, Op. 21: Excerpts

Melodrama (song cycle) for speaker and chamber ensemble

1912

(a) No. 8: *Nacht* (Night)

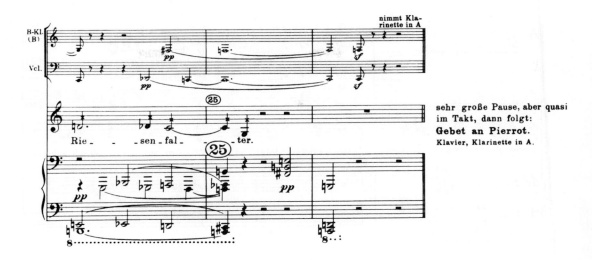

(b) No. 13: *Enthauptung* (Beheading)

folgt: **Die Kreuze**
unmittelbar anschließend.
Klavier (anfangs allein) später
dazu Flöte, Klar. (A), Geige, Vcll.

⌐ ¬ bedeutet Hauptstimme.

NACHT	NIGHT
0:00 Finstre, schwarze Riesenfalter Töteten der Sonne Glanz. Ein geschloßnes Zauberbuch, Ruht der Horizont—verschwiegen.	Dark black giant moths killed the radiance of the sun. A sealed book of magic, the horizon rests, keeping silence.
0:55 Aus dem Qualm verlorner Tiefen Steigt ein Duft, Erinnrung mordend! Finstre, schwarze Riesenfalter Töteten der Sonne Glanz.	From the vapor of forgotten depths rises a fragrance, killing memory! Dark black giant moths killed the radiance of the sun.
1:17 Und vom Himmel erdenwärts Senken sich mit schweren Schwingen Unsichtbar die Ungetüme Auf die Menschenherzen nieder . . . Finstre, schwarze Riesenfalter.	And from heaven earthwards they sink with ponderous oscillations, invisible monsters, down to the hearts of men . . . Dark black giant moths.

ENTHAUPTUNG	BEHEADING
0:00 Der Mond, ein blankes Türkenschwert, Auf einen schwarzen Seidenkissen, Gespenstisch groß—dräut er hinab Durch schmerzensdunkle Nacht.	The moon, a polished scimitar on a black silken cushion, ghostly vast, menaces downwards through pain-dark night.
0:21 Pierrot irrt ohne Rast umher Und starrt empor in Todesängsten Zum Mond, dem blanken Türkenschwert Auf einem schwarzen Seidenkissen.	Pierrot wanders about, restless, and stares on high in mortal terror at the moon, the polished scimitar on a black silken cushion.
0:36 Es schlottern unter ihm die Knie, Ohnmächtig bricht er jäh zusammen. Er wähnt: es sause strafend schon Auf seinen Sündenhals hernieder Der Mond, das blanke Türkenschwert.	His knees knock together under him; swooning, he suddenly collapses. He imagines: in punishment, it is already rushing down on his guilty neck, the moon, the polished scimitar.

—Albert Giraud, translated from
the French by O. Erich Hartleben

Arnold Schoenberg wrote *Pierrot lunaire* in the spring of 1912, after moving from Vienna to Berlin with his family the previous fall. The full title of this cycle of songs translates as "Three times seven poems from Albert Giraud's *Pierrot lunaire*." He composed it at the request of Albertine Zehme, an actress who asked for a piano accompaniment over which she could recite the poetry. As Schoenberg worked on it, he added other instruments, and the result was a piece scored for a speaker and five musicians, some of whom double on a second instrument: flute (piccolo), clarinet (bass clarinet), violin (viola), cello, and piano. By using a different combination of instruments for every song in the cycle, Schoenberg achieves a maximum variety of color. Throughout the cycle, the voice declaims the text in what Schoenberg called *Sprechstimme* (speaking voice), following the notated rhythm exactly but only approximating the written pitches in gliding tones of speech. He indicated this effect—an innovative synthesis of melodrama and song—with an x through the stem of each note. Schoenberg conducted the premiere with Zehme in October 1912, and then they took the work on tour through Germany and Austria. It was well received and helped to establish his reputation as a leading modernist composer of his generation. When *Pierrot lunaire* was published in 1914, Schoenberg designated it Opus 21, the same number as there are songs in the cycle.

For his text, Schoenberg selected poems from a collection by Albert Giraud, a Belgian symbolist poet, translated into German by O. Erich Hartleben. Giraud imagined Pierrot, the stock comic character from the improvised theatrical tradition of *commedia dell'arte*, pursued by fantastic, threatening visions of the moon. The extreme situations and vivid images prompted Schoenberg to use an intense and dissonant musical language in the instruments, heightened by the eerie effect of the gliding, inexact pitches in the voice. Just as certain expressionist painters, such as Oskar Kokoschka and Egon Schiele, distorted representations of real objects to reflect their feelings about their surroundings and themselves, so Schoenberg used exaggerated graphic images and speech inflections in this work to express the feelings conveyed in the poetry.

The poems in the cycle are unrhymed but follow a strict form: each is thirteen lines long, divided in two quatrains and a quintain, and uses the first two lines as a refrain, repeating them as lines 7–8 and stating line 1 again as line 13. In most of the songs, Schoenberg reflected this form by including instrumental interludes after each quatrain and by highlighting repeated lines of text with an allusion to their original music at the same pitch level. As we will see, the two songs included here reflect the poetic form in very different ways.

Pierrot lunaire is *atonal*, meaning that no single pitch serves as a tonal center. Instead, Schoenberg often creates an analogue to a "tonic" region by emphasizing certain motives or chords at the beginning of a song and later restating or varying them at the same pitch level, so that their reappearance signals a return to the opening group of pitches in a way that parallels the return to a tonic in tonal music. He also relies on motivic development to give his music coherence and shape, using the method he called *developing variation*, presenting a basic idea at the outset and then continuously drawing out new variants of that idea. Many of the songs evoke old forms or genres or rely on traditional techniques—such as canons—to ensure unity and give the listener something familiar to grasp.

In No. 8, *Nacht* (Night), Pierrot sees giant black moths casting gloom over the world, shutting out the sun. The basic motive, a rising minor third followed by a descending major third, reappears constantly in various note values throughout the parts, often overlapping itself. At the beginning, for example, the first three notes, E'–G'–$E\flat'$, form a statement of the motive, but the second note initiates another statement (G'–$B\flat'$–$G\flat'$), whose second note in turn initiates another ($B\flat'$–$D\flat'$–A'), and so on, until six intertwined statements appear in the first three measures. (These overlapping statements can be hard to see in the score, since Schoenberg divides each three-note figure between the hands or between instruments. Note that the bass clarinet in B♭ sounds a major ninth lower than written, so that the cello and bass clarinet share a statement of the motive, E–G–$E\flat$.) This three-note motive suffuses the entire piece, in various transformations including inversion and retrograde, and its omnipresence creates a fitting musical image of Pierrot's obsession with the giant moths. The transformations can be subtle and more all-pervading than might be suspected at first; for instance, in measure 8, the bass clarinet has three statements of the motive, whose first notes themselves form another statement of the motive. At one point (measure 10), the voice stops speaking and sings the motive. Even the motive's shape, in original form or inverted, suggests the wings of the moths.

Schoenberg calls this song a *passacaglia*, a set of variations over a repeated bass, but it is an unusual one. The bass ostinato consists of the basic motive on E (E–G–$E\flat$) followed by a chromatic descent that is sometimes concluded by a rising diminished seventh. The ostinato is first stated in measures 4–6 by the bass clarinet and imitated at one-measure intervals by the cello and the two hands on the piano. It reappears varied over ten more times, usually in the piano left hand, returning with particular prominence at measures 11, 16, 23 (in the voice), and 24 to mark the refrains and musical interludes, thus reflecting the poetic structure in a readily audible way. At the end (measures 24–25), the original complex of overlapping statements of the basic motive (from measures 1–3) repeats at pitch, modified to include the chromatic descent that characterizes the bass ostinato. Despite the atonal harmonies, this frequent repetition of the passacaglia ostinato and its opening notes E–G–E♭ creates a sense of tonal location, allowing Schoenberg to establish a home region, depart from it, and return at significant points and at the end, just as in tonal music.

In No. 13, *Enthauptung* (Beheading), Pierrot imagines that he is beheaded by the moon for his crimes. The first five measures encapsulate the poem and include a cascade of notes in the bass clarinet and viola—using both whole-tone scales one after the other—that illustrates the sweep of the scimitar. The next ten measures depict the atmosphere of the moonlit night and Pierrot scurrying to avoid the moon. Even though it may appear to the listener that thematic development has been abandoned for free improvisation shaped by the text, the ideas presented at the outset return frequently in new guises. The poetic structure is reflected by repetitions in the music, though much more subtly than in *Nacht*. When the opening lines of the poem return, they are declaimed using variations of the original rhythm (compare measures 5–7 in the voice to measures 14–16 and 20–21). At the first return, the instruments echo the frenetic texture if not the notes of measures 3–4, and a more explicit though still varied repetition follows immediately: augmented chords in the piano move in parallel in a rhythm and melodic contour taken from the cello and piano parts in the opening measures to evoke the image of Pierrot's knees knocking together (measure 17). As the voice declaims the final refrain, the piano performs the downward runs played by viola and bass clarinet in measures 3–4, at the same pitch level as before, while the other instruments play glissandos. An Epilogue recalls the music of No. 7, *Der kranke Mond* (The Sick Moon).

On the accompanying recording, the vocalist renders the Sprechstimme by touching or approximating each pitch, then slowly gliding to the next one, varying the timbre of her voice in an exaggerated manner to convey the changing moods and images of the text. Schoenberg calls for some special playing techniques; for example, in *Nacht*, the cello bows over the bridge (*am Steg*, measure 10), producing a thin metallic sound, or plays harmonics (*Flag.* for *Flageolet*, measure 11), and the bass clarinet uses flutter-tonguing (measure 13). In some passages, such as the opening of *Enthauptung*, Schoenberg uses brackets to indicate the leading voice, or *Hauptstimme* (here, the cello).

Arnold Schoenberg (1874–1951)

Piano Suite, Op. 25: Excerpts

Suite

1921–23

(a) Prelude

From Arnold Schoenberg, *Complete Works*, part 2, *Klavier- und Orgelmusik*, ser. A, vol. 4, *Werke für Klavier zu zwei Händen*, ed. Eduard Steuermann and Reinhold Brinkmann (Mainz: B. Schott's Söhne, and Vienna: Universal Edition, 1968), 44–45 and 54–56. © 1925 by Universal Edition A.G., Vienna. © Renewed. All rights reserved. Used by permission of European American Music Distributors Company, agent for Universal Edition A.G., Vienna, in the territory of the world exluding the U.S. and Belmont Music Publishers, Pacific Palisades, CA 90272.

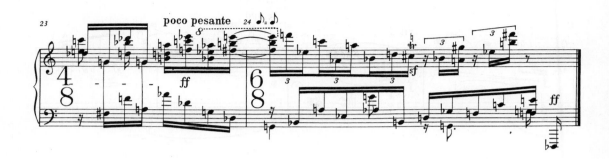

(b) Minuet and Trio

In the late 1910s, Schoenberg became preoccupied with how to recreate what he called "the structural functions of tonality" in his atonal music. In *Pierrot lunaire* (NAWM 172), he created a sense of tonal location by presenting an idea at a certain pitch level and restating it later at the same pitch level (or octave equivalent), paralleling a fundamental procedure of tonal music: the establishment of a tonic, departure from it, and return to it. But he had no analogue to the function of a dominant chord as the opposite pole of the tonic nor an analogue to harmonic progression and resolution, and so could not create extended forms without relying on a text to give a work coherence.

He found the solution in the *twelve-tone method*, which he codified in his Piano Suite. The Prelude was the first twelve-tone piece he composed, in July 1921, and he began the Intermezzo the same month. In February and March 1923, he added the other movements—Gavotte, Musette, Minuet and Trio, and Gigue—to create a suite of dances on the Baroque model. By this time, always obsessed with numbers, Schoenberg was publishing one opus a year, whose number usually matched the year of publication; the Piano Suite, Op. 25, was issued in June 1925.

A twelve-tone *row*, or *series*, consists of all twelve notes of the chromatic scale arranged in an order that provides the sequence of intervals and motives the composer wishes to use. By including all twelve notes, the row avoids emphasizing any one note as the tonal center. Instead, the row itself functions as a kind of tonal region, and its transformations (described below) serve as contrasting regions. Typically, a piece uses the same row throughout, creating both motivic and tonal consistency. The row for the Piano Suite is shown in the example below.

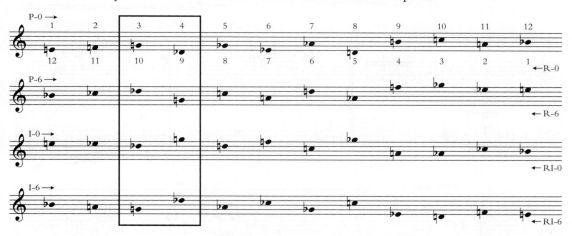

A row can be presented in its original, or prime, form but also in *inversion* (upside down), *retrograde* (backward), or *retrograde inversion* (upside down and backward), and each of these forms may appear in any of twelve possible transpositions. In the Piano Suite, Schoenberg used only two transpositions of each form, as shown in the example: P-0, the untransposed prime form beginning on E; P-6, the prime form transposed up six semitones; I-0, the inversion beginning on E; I-6, the inversion transposed up six semitones; and their retrogrades, R-0, R-6, RI-0, and RI-6 respectively. He had designed the row so that each of these transpositions begins on E and ends on B♭ or the reverse, and that each prime or inverted form has the tritone G–D♭ in notes 3 and 4 (shown by the box in the example). These shared characteristics relate these row forms to each other and distinguish them from all other possible transpositions of the row. In Schoenberg's mind, the use of these eight row forms exclusively was analogous to establishing a key in tonal music, and by using the same eight in each movement he preserved that consistency throughout the suite, just as all the dances in a Baroque suite are usually in the same key. Indeed, in a sketch, he designated P-0 "tonic" and P-6 "dominant," showing that he was thinking of analogies to functional tonality.

Schoenberg often broke the series into smaller units that he used to form motives and chords. Here the most frequent division is into three segments of four notes, called *tetrachords*. The first four notes of R-0, B♭–A–C–B♮, form the letters B–A–C–H in German nomenclature, a salute to the composer whose suites Schoenberg meant to emulate. Variants of this distinctive motive pervade the entire suite, linking Schoenberg's music intimately to Bach's.

The opening passages of the movements included here illustrate Schoenberg's procedures. At the start of the Prelude, P-0 is in the right hand as a melody (measures 1–3) and P-6 accompanies in the left hand, with the second tetrachord (C–A–D–G♯), stated simultaneously with the third (F–F♯–E♭–E). (Enharmonic notes are considered the same, so G♯ and A♭ are used interchangeably, as are G♭ and F♯.) The pickup to measure 4 begins a statement of I-6, with the first tetrachord in the lowest contrapuntal voice (B♭–A–G–D♭, completed on the second beat of measure 5), the second tetrachord in the top voice (A♭–C♭–G♭–C♮), and the third tetrachord in the middle. R-6 follows in measure 5, with the three tetrachords similarly layered in counterpoint (the G and D♭ overlap with the previous row), and then a brief rest marks a cadence. In Schoenberg's analogy, the first phrase moved from "tonic" (P-0) to "dominant" (R-6, the retrograde of P-6).

As the work proceeds, it can be a challenge to locate and identify the rows. Since Schoenberg consistently divides the row into tetrachords, the best strategy is to find one of the tetrachords, figure out what row form it is from, and then search for the other tetrachords from that row form nearby. For instance, the D♭–G–F–E from the end of measure 5 to the downbeat of measure 6 is from R-0, and the other tetrachords of that row appear in the next eight notes. It can be ambiguous whether a retrograde form is being used, because sometimes the order of notes within a tetrachord is reversed or otherwise changed.

The Prelude is somewhat free-form, in the tradition of the Baroque prelude (see NAWM 88a and 102a for examples). Rests and changes of tempo define three sections (measures 1–9, 9–16, and 16–24), with a calmer middle section contrasting with the more active outer sections. By contrast, the Minuet and Trio follows a strict dance form, and it is intriguing to see the ways that Schoenberg has reflected the traditional genre in his new language. It is typical of a trio to be lighter in texture than the minuet that frames it, and that is true here. Schoenberg uses two-part counterpoint in the Trio: P-0 in the left hand (measure 34) is imitated in inversion by I-6 in the right hand, followed by I-0 in the left hand (measure 36) and P-6 in the right. These four measures repeat, and a similar canon constitutes the second half of the Trio. The result cunningly evokes both the spirit of a Bach invention, through a little canon in inversion, and the two-measure phrasing and binary form of a minuet.

At the beginning of the Minuet, the periodic phrasing and the lilting, dance-like rhythms are apparent even without looking for the rows. Each measure-long unit in the right hand is set off from the next by a brief rest. The second two-measure phrase echoes the rhythmic and melodic motives of the first, forming an antecedent-consequent pair. Both of these two-measure phrases end with an allusion to leading-tone motion at a cadence (A to B♭ and D to E♭); the fact that the second ends a fifth lower than the first is a reference to the dominant-tonic relationships of traditional tonality. When we do look for the rows, we find that the first two measures present P-0, using the first tetrachord (E–F–G–D♭) in the left hand as an accompaniment to the other two, which occupy one measure each; measures 3–4 present I-6 in a similar arrangement, with some internal reordering of notes within the tetrachords.

The presentation of one complete row statement every two measures creates a kind of harmonic rhythm. Schoenberg then picks up the pace, completing the next three row statements in four beats (P-6), three beats (I-0), and two beats (P-0) respectively, before settling down to one row statement per measure until the repeat mark at the end of the first section. Once again, rhythmic and motivic repetition on the surface, such as the sequences in measures 5–6 and measures 9–10, articulate the changes of row form. This twelve-tone rhythm is quite a close analogy to the use of chord progressions in tonal music to establish the meter and phrasing through harmonic motion. Thus in many ways, Schoenberg's complex twelve-tone method provided the tools he needed for recreating the functions of tonality in a musical language that did not define a central pitch.

The Minuet follows the standard rounded binary form, except that the second section is not repeated. The first five measures of the second section offer contrasting material derived from the first measure of the movement, then a varied restatement of the first section begins at measure 17. At first it is quite distant, but by measure 21 the motives from measures 5–8 are readily apparent, and measures 29–31 repeat the end of the first section almost exactly. Throughout, Schoenberg marks the ends of important subsections with ritardandos, making it easy to see and hear how he himself envisioned the formal divisions. A brief coda in measures 32–33 ends the Minuet with the same two row forms with which it began, P-0 in the right hand and I-6 in the left, providing an analogy in twelve-tone terms to the closure granted by a V-I cadence at the end of a tonal work.

The question almost everyone asks about twelve-tone music is "Can you really hear the rows?" One response is to observe that the piece can be perfectly coherent even without recognizing a single row form. The canon in inversion in the Trio and the antecedent-consequent phrasing and sequences in the Minuet are evident in the musical contours, without tracing the exact intervals or pitches. In Schoenberg's music, it is less important to hear and identify entire rows than to recognize the motives he draws from the row, like the tetrachords in the Piano Suite, and perhaps to be aware of the harmonic rhythm marked off by successive segments of music containing all twelve tones. These are things listeners can train themselves to hear and performers can quickly locate in the score and represent in performance, without doing a complete analysis of the rows.

Schoenberg meticulously marked the dynamics, articulation, phrasing, and tempo fluctuations, knowing that in such an unfamiliar idiom the performer would have difficulty making choices in such matters without guidance. In some places, such as measure 22 of the Prelude and measures 2 and 4 of the Minuet, he used marks derived from poetry to indicate notes that should be stressed (ʹ) or left unstressed (⌣) in cases where his intended accentuation contradicts the regular meter.

Alban Berg (1885–1935)

Wozzeck, Op. 7: Act III, Scenes 2 and 3

Opera

1917–22

174

(a) Scene 2

2. Szene Waldweg am Teich (Es dunkelt)
2nd Scene *Forest path by a pool (Dusk is falling)*

Marie kommt mit Wozzeck von rechts
enters with Wozzeck from right

Dort links ____ geht's in die Stadt. 's ist noch weit. Komm schneller.
The town ____ lies ov-er there. It's still far, let's hur-ry!

A-ber ich muß fort.
But it's getting late.

Du sollst da-blei-ben, Ma-rie. Komm, setz' Dich.
You must stay a-while, Ma-rie. Come, sit, here,

Komm.
come.

Bist
So

sie setzen sich
they sit down

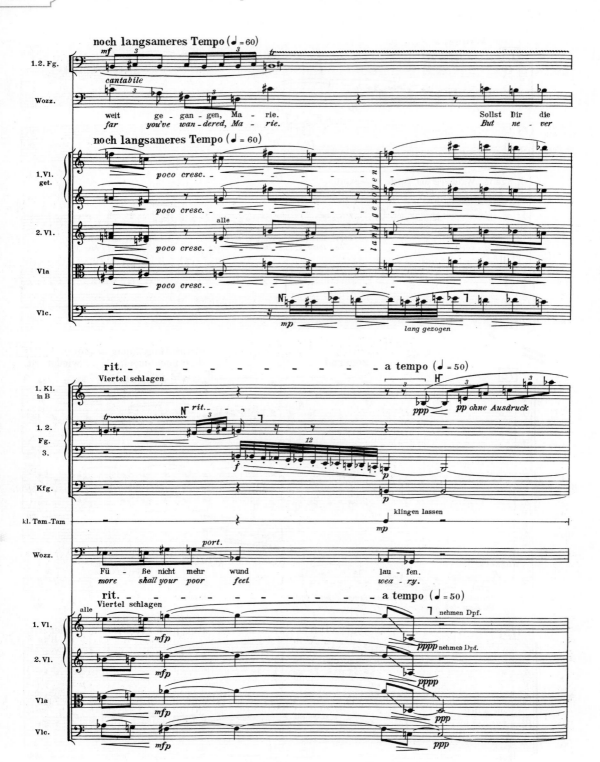

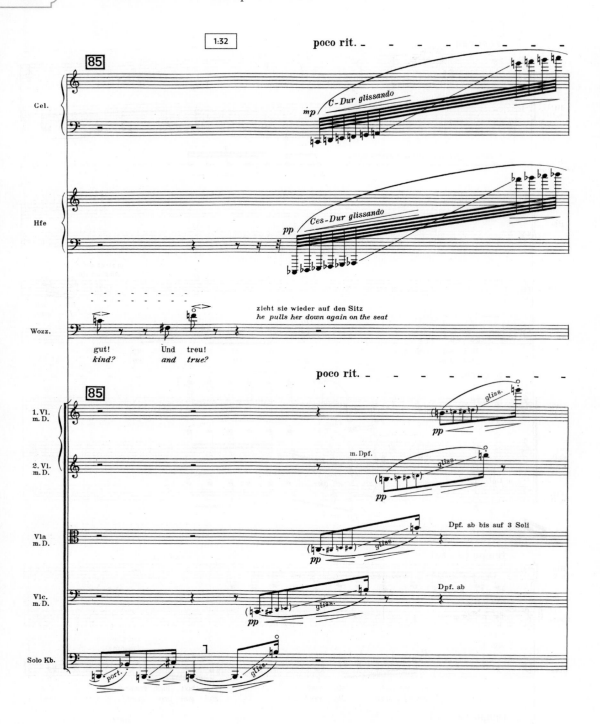

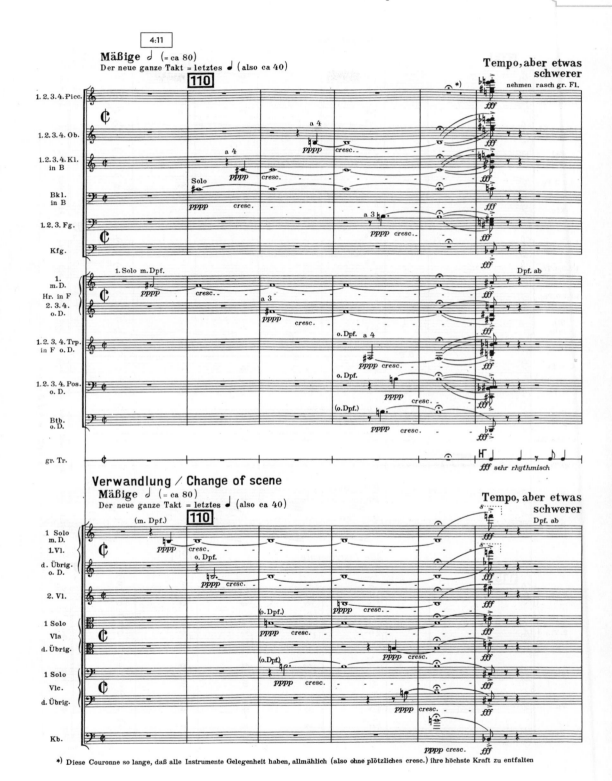

*) Diese Couronne so lange, daß alle Instrumente Gelegenheit haben, allmählich (also ohne plötzliches cresc.) ihre höchste Kraft zu entfalten

(b) Scene 3

*) Triller ohne Nachschlag

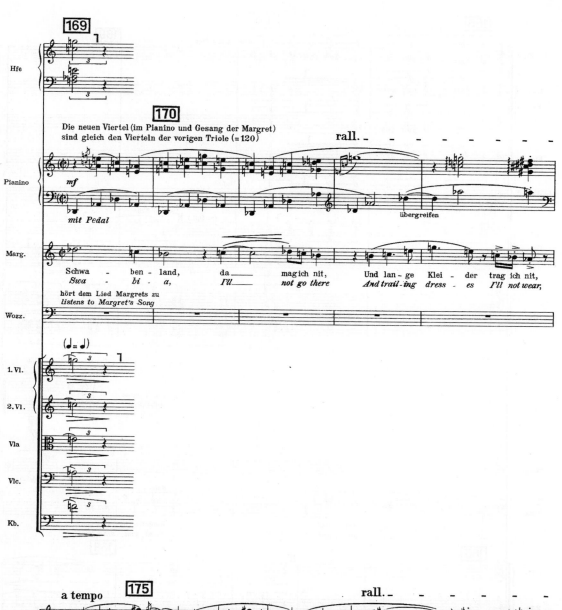

Die neuen Viertel (im Pianino und Gesang der Margret)
sind gleich den Vierteln der vorigen Triole (=120)

Schwa — ben — land, da___ mag ich nit, Und lan — ge Klei — der trag ich nit,
Swa — bi — a, I'll___ not go there And trail-ing dress — es I'll not wear,

hört dem Lied Margrets zu
listens to Margret's Song

Denn lan — ge Klei — der,___ spit-ze Schuh, Die kommen kei — ner Dienstmagd zu.
For point — ed shoes and___ powdered curls: They are no dress for ser-vant-girls!

*If the Chorus encounters insuperable difficulties with pitch, their entrances can be
sounded by the onstage piano (audible only to the singers).

In 1824, Johann Christian Woyzeck was executed for killing the woman he lived with, although many believed he was innocent by reason of insanity. A young doctor and writer, Georg Büchner (1813–1837) wrote a play based on the incident, casting the central figure as a poor soldier who is a powerless victim of circumstances, but Büchner died before finishing it. Decades later, Büchner's play was assembled by a literary scholar (who misread the y as a z and transcribed the name as *Wozzeck*). This version was published in 1879 and, finally, staged in 1913. Alban Berg saw the Vienna production the next year and immediately decided to set the play as an opera, adapting his libretto from the original text (as Strauss had done for *Salome*, NAWM 166) and reordering some of the scenes. His own service in the Austrian military during World War I gave him a sense of Wozzeck's life as a soldier and provided details for the opera. He completed the music in 1922 and had the vocal score printed in order to stimulate interest. He dedicated the score to Alma Mahler, widow of Gustav Mahler. The work was finally premiered in 1925 at the Berlin State Opera, to excellent reviews. Within a few years it became established as one of the most successful modern operas and by far the most popular atonal opera.

The story centers on Franz Wozzeck, a poor soldier, who is mocked by his Captain, has apocalyptic visions, and submits to a Doctor's experiments in order to earn extra money. (The poor characters all have names, but the well-to-do ones have only titles, a symbol of the power they wield in Wozzeck's world.) Wozzeck has a child with his common-law wife Marie, but with his many part-time jobs he has little time for them. When the Drum Major woos Marie, she gives in to his attentions. Wozzeck learns of their affair, and, driven mad by despair, he kills her and then accidentally drowns while seeking to hide the bloody knife. In the heartbreaking final scene, their orphaned child rides his hobby horse, not comprehending what has happened, while other children run to look at Marie's body.

Berg laid out the libretto in three acts with five scenes each. In addition to using leitmotives throughout the opera, he composed each scene as a traditional musical form. These forms help to describe the characters and convey the dramatic situation, but they also show Berg's interest in reflecting on the music of the past, a common theme of modernist composers. The first act introduces the characters, with a Baroque suite to suggest the Captain's devotion to convention; a rhapsody for Wozzeck's visions; a march and lullaby as Marie glimpses the Drum Major and sings to her child; a passacaglia for the Doctor's fixation on his experiments; and a rondo as the Drum Major repeatedly tries to seduce Marie and finally succeeds. The second act is a symphony in five movements, portraying the dramatic developments through a sonata-form movement, a fantasia and fugue, a ternary slow movement, a scherzo, and a rondo, as Wozzeck learns of the affair, ineffectually fights for Marie, and sinks into despair. The third act is a series of six inventions, each on a single element—a theme, a single note, a rhythmic pattern, a chord, a key, and a duration—suggesting Wozzeck's obsessions. The music in each act is continuous, with linking orchestral interludes between scenes. The longest interlude, before the last scene, is like a symphonic Adagio that sums up the tragedy.

The excerpt given here includes scenes 2 and 3 from Act III, the invention on a single note and the invention on a rhythm. As the curtain rises on scene 2, the note B sounds low in the contrabasses, and soft arpeggiated D-major and E♭-major triads create a wash of sound that helps set the scene: dusk, by a pond in the forest. Throughout the scene, dissonant chords and atonal melodies weave around the B, which acts not like a tonal center but like an idea one cannot get out of one's head, reflecting Wozzeck's single-minded focus on avenging Marie's unfaithfulness. With each turn of the conversation, the B takes a new form. Wozzeck and Marie come down the path heading toward town. Marie wants to hurry, but Wozzeck detains her, telling her to sit and rest her feet, as the sustained low B passes among contrabasses, trombone, and bassoons. When he says she has already wandered far (measure 77), hinting at her infidelity, the bassoons add a suspenseful trill to the B. Next a high solo violin takes up the B as a repeated note (measure 80), and he asks her how long they have been together. Harp and horn take over the B in a middle register as she replies, three years. Then, as he asks how long she thinks their relationship will continue (measure 83), the B returns to the lowest register, now embellished by its neighbors, creating greater agitation and instability. Marie is afraid, and Wozzeck asks whether she has been good and true, as glissandos in the strings, harp, and celesta take the B back into the stratosphere.

The violins play the high B in tremolo on the bridge (measure 86), producing an eerie and tense sound as Wozzeck says her lips are sweet, kisses her, and says he wishes he could kiss her often, but the B changes to a weird flutter-tonguing in clarinet and flute as he says he no longer may do so. A trill on B in the timpani and rising octaves in the clarinets sound as he whispers that she will no longer shiver in the morning dew. The moon rises blood red as the B is sustained in seven different octaves in the strings (measure 97). Then, while the timpani pounds out a repeated B, Wozzeck takes out his knife, cries that if Marie will not have him she will have no other man, and slits her throat.

Up to this point, the vocal lines have barely touched the note B, but now Marie screams for help on a high B and low B (measure 103), confirming that her death was the goal on which Wozzeck has been fixated during the entire scene. As she dies, leitmotives associated with her pass by in quick succession, like her life flashing before her eyes: the Drum Major who seduced her (measure 104 in violin I and horn I); the lullaby she sang to her child in Act I (piccolo, middle of measure 104); the military march linked to her first sight of the Drum Major (measures 104–5 in bass clarinets, bassoons, and trumpets); and the motive associated with Marie as a mother and with her child (measure 105, strings).

The scene change that follows (measures 109–21) sums up the invention on a note, with two long crescendos on a sustained B in the full orchestra. It also introduces the invention on a rhythm in the next scene by presenting the principal rhythmic pattern at first subtly, through the entrances on B by the different instruments in the orchestra, and then violently, pounded on the bass drum as loudly as possible. The rhythm of the entrances in measures 109–13 is far easier to see than to hear: compare the durations between successive entrances in the brass and wind instruments to those between attacks in the bass drum in measures 114–15 (which go twice as quickly but in the same rhythmic pattern), and note that the string entrances follow those in the brass and winds a quarter note later.

As the rhythmic pattern emerges from the note B, Wozzeck trades one obsession, revenge, for a new one, his guilt.

When scene 3 begins, Wozzeck is in a tavern. An onstage piano, mistuned to suggest the sound of a cheap barroom piano, bangs out the rhythmic pattern—a series of eight durations—in the form of a fast polka. Throughout the scene, the rhythmic pattern repeats incessantly, in its original values, in augmentation, and in diminution, and in both instruments and voices, often in more than one form at a time. Berg indicates every instance with the sign of an H attached to a bracket, a symbol Schoenberg had invented to designate the main melodic line (H standing for *Hauptstimme*, main voice) but used here to indicate the main rhythm (*Hauptrhythmus*). These constant repetitions envelop Wozzeck, symbolizing his obsession with his guilt.

Wozzeck picks up the rhythm as he watches the dancers (measures 130–41), then briefly frees himself from it by singing a folk song, using a tune from Marie's Act I lullaby (at measure 145). He asks Marie's friend Margret to dance with him, then sits down with her on his lap and asks her to sing a song. But there is no respite for him—even her song is in the obsessive rhythm of the scene (measures 168–79). She notices blood on his hand, singing again in that rhythm (measures 185–93). As others gather around them, Wozzeck says he must have cut himself, but she points out the blood on his elbow and says it smells of human blood, and the others agree. By this point all of them are singing only in the scene's main rhythm, and Wozzeck sings it at twice the speed of the others in a sign of his growing panic (measures 197–207). Throughout this passage (measures 187–211), the orchestra plays its own statements of the rhythm, each on repeated pitches a major seventh apart, rising by whole steps and then half steps as the scene builds to a climax. Surrounded by the emblem of his guilt, Wozzeck flees in a frenzy while overlapping statements of the rhythm sound in the orchestra.

Berg's music is atonal (not twelve-tone), but he frequently imitates the styles and textures of tonal music, as in the triadic accompaniment to the piano polka; the prominent fourths, triadic shapes, and melodic sequences of Wozzeck's imitation folk song; and the rocking accompaniment, balanced phrases, and arching lines of the popular-style song Margret sings. By constantly using familiar elements like these, Berg makes his music both dramatically effective and accessible to a wide range of listeners.

It can be difficult for singers to find their pitches in atonal music. Sometimes the pitches of the vocal lines are contained in the harmonies that accompany them, as in Wozzeck's folksong at measure 145, but that is not always the case. Berg recognized the difficulty, and in measures 202–12 he provided an optional part for the onstage piano that includes a transcription of the parts for the Chorus. This part may be played—audible only to the singers—if they need assistance in finding their pitches.

In the Metropolitan Opera production (which also includes the final two scenes of Act III), the staging is simple. Dusk and the rising red moon are represented through lighting, while a bare stage stands in for the pond, and the tavern's walls and ceiling are only suggested. By contrast, the costumes and props are realistic. The combination of artificiality and realism neatly parallels the similar contrast in the music between the atonal sounds Berg uses throughout—a purely modernist invention—and the imitations of popular music in the tavern scene, which portray the sounds of people playing and singing music in the same way their costumes and gestures portray their clothes and their actions.

▶ Opera video available

Anton Webern (1883–1945)

Symphony, Op. 21: First movement, Ruhig schreitend

Symphony

1927–28

175

*Sounds as notated (i.e., not transposed)

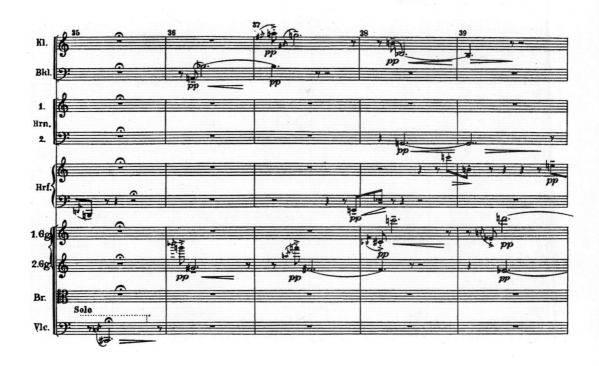

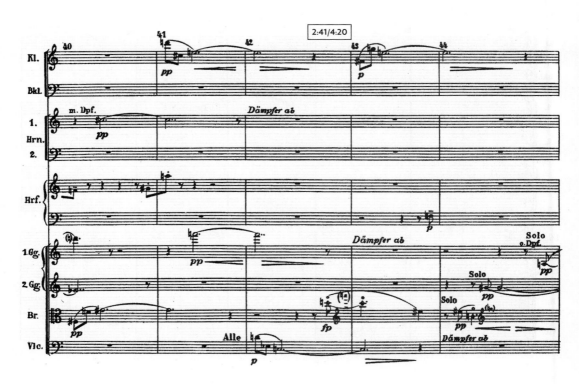

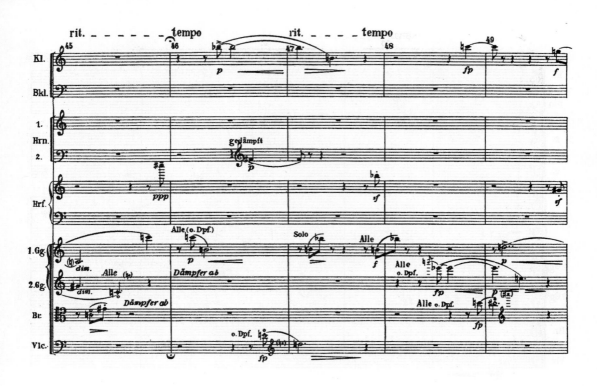

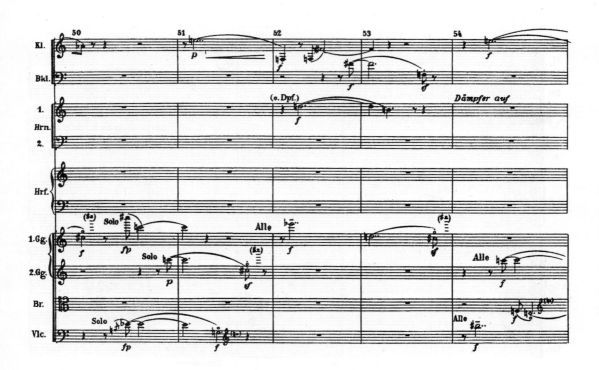

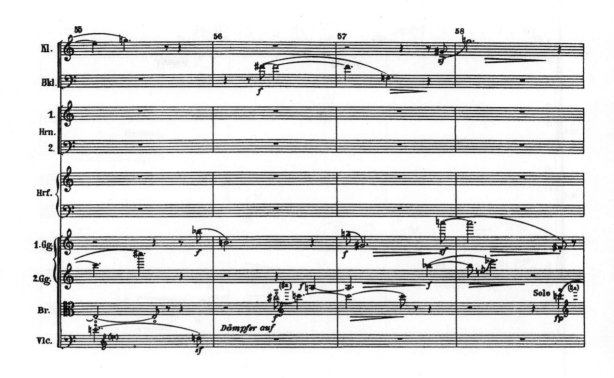

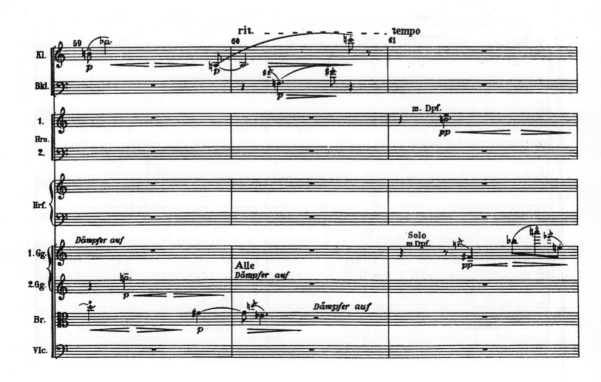

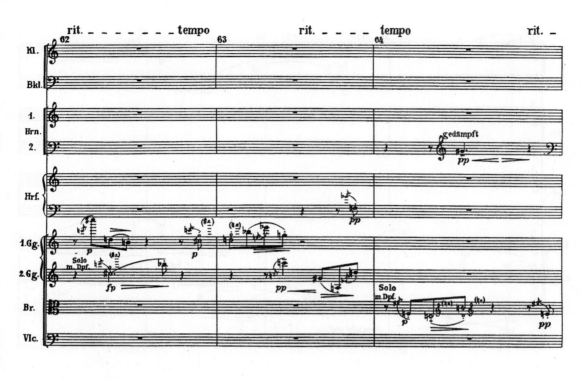

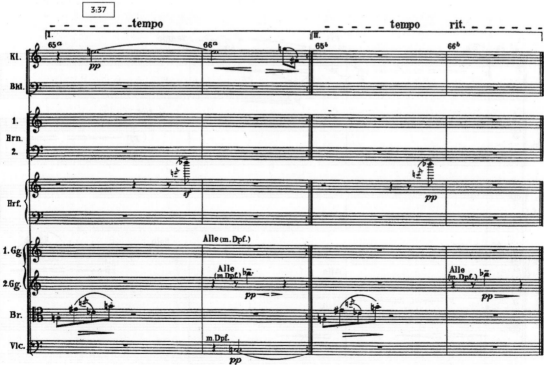

After a decade in which he composed only songs, Anton Webern adopted Schoenberg's twelve-tone method in the mid-1920s, finding in it the solution to writing extended instrumental works in an atonal language. The second such work was his Symphony, Op. 21, scored for a small chamber orchestra in emulation of eighteenth-century symphonies. It has only two movements, the first based on sonata form and the second a theme with seven variations. By invoking these forms and the genre of the symphony, Webern sought to link his modernist twelve-tone language to the conventional forms and tonality of the classical tradition.

To gain an understanding of how he remade past elements in twelve-tone terms requires a detailed look at how he used the rows. Fortunately, Webern made it easier to trace the twelve-tone rows through the music by notating the clarinet, bass clarinet, and horns at actual pitch in the score (rather than in their customary transpositions).

The overall binary form of the first movement is apparent from the marked repetitions, but Webern reconceives the exposition, development, and recapitulation of sonata form in a new way. In the exposition, instead of two contrasting themes, he presents two simultaneous canons in inversion, using statements of his twelve-tone row in the canonic voices (see HWM, p. 830, for a simplified score that shows the beginnings of the canons). Thus he substitutes the Renaissance texture of imitative polyphony for the melody-and-accompaniment texture typical of classical symphonies. However, rather than present any of the canonic voices in a single instrument, he makes the change of instrumental timbre itself part of the melody, an effect Schoenberg called *Klangfarbenmelodie* (tone-color-melody).

The leading voice of the first canon begins in horn 2, continues in the clarinet, and concludes the first row statement in the cello, with each instrument stating one tetrachord (four-note segment) from the row (P–0), as shown here:

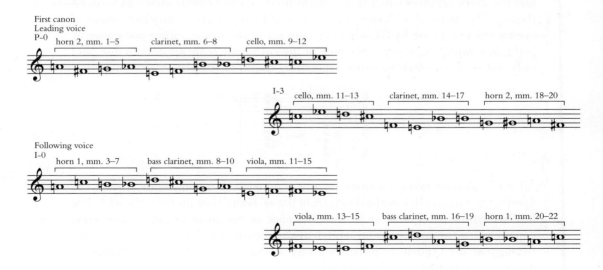

(In order to highlight the row structure, this example omits the rhythms and octave placement for the notes of each row.) The last two notes of the row overlap with I-3, an inverted statement of the row, which moves from cello back to clarinet and horn 2, as shown in the example, again highlighting the division of the row into tetrachords. Webern has so designed the row that this inversion results in the same sequence of tetrachords (allowing for internal reordering of notes) but in reverse order, a symmetry highlighted by the symmetry of timbres.

The following voice of the canon, an inversion of the first voice that starts on the same note (I-0) exactly two measures later, traces a similar path from horn 1 to bass clarinet to viola, then back again, using the same kinds of timbres as the leading voice and in the same order (brass, single-reed wind, and string instrument), as shown in the example. The symmetries of timbre and tetrachord echo a symmetry in the row itself: its transposed retrograde R-6 is the same as P-0, making the row a virtual palindrome (something that is the same backward as it is forward, like "Able was I ere I saw Elba").

The first canon exhibits the short phrases and frequent rests typical of Webern's music. The second canon is even more short-breathed, with sometimes just one note in an instrument. The result is a succession of tiny points, or wisps, of sound, a texture described as *pointillism* that is often the most immediately recognizable aspect of a Webern score. The leading voice in the second canon begins in the harp (measure 2), then moves through plucked and bowed cello (measures 3–5), violin 2 (measure 6), harp (measures 7–8), horn 2 (measures 9–10), harp (measures 11–12, overlapping with a new row statement), horn 2 (measures 12–13), violin 1 (14–15), harp (measure 16), viola (measures 16–17, overlapping with another row statement), and so on. Meanwhile, the following voice, in inversion, begins two measures later and traces a similar path through harp, viola, violin 1, and so on. The use of so many timbres in each canonic voice and the appearance of notes from more than one canonic line in each instrument combine to make the canons very difficult to hear.

In the exposition, the somewhat more lyrical first canon serves as "first theme," and the more rapidly changing and pointillistic second canon serves as "second theme." The sense of a "home key" is created by registration, another source of symmetry. Except for Eb/D♯, which can appear in the octave either just above or just below middle C, every other note of the chromatic scale appears in one, and only one, octave during the entire exposition, sounding the pitches shown here:

All these pitches taken together form a symmetrical arrangement around the opening *a*, ranging in fourths down from the *eb'* above it or up from the *d♯* below it. This symmetrical array is possible because of the strict canon in inversion, equally spaced around the central pitch *a*. The recurrence of these specific pitches throughout the exposition provides a very strong sense of location, although A does not function as a traditional tonic.

The recapitulation reprises the same row forms in the same order as the exposition, but the surface looks and sounds very different, making it hard to hear the return. The recapitulation begins on the last eighth note of measure 42 (highlighted with a *forte-piano* marking), with a statement of the pitches from the first canon's leading voice in viola (through measure 45), cello (measures 46–47), violin 1 (last eighth of measure 47 through measure 53), and again viola (measures 54–55) and violin 1 (measures 55–58). (Some notes in the strings are written as harmonics, and Webern indicates the sounding pitch in small notes.) The following voice of the canon appears exactly two measures later, as it did in the exposition, moving from violin 1 to viola, clarinet, cello, viola, and back to clarinet. The second canon can be traced in similar fashion, beginning with the harp notes in measures 43 and 45.

In the recapitulation, the pitches are again symmetrical, in an arrangement shown here:

Some pitches are in the same octave as in the exposition, others one to three octaves higher, and the axis of symmetry is now *eb″*. This recapitulation resembles traditional ones by restating the material from the exposition, but it does so in a novel way.

The relatively brief development is a palindrome, providing another kind of symmetry. It begins with the clarinet in measure 25b and concludes with the clarinet in measures 43–44, overlapping the beginning of the recapitulation, and measures 34–35 form its center point. The development and recapitulation repeat as a unit, as in many early symphonies (see NAWM 115).

All these canons, symmetries, and palindromes may be difficult or even impossible to hear, reflecting Webern's interest in structural devices that are not necessarily audible. He absorbed this interest, along with his fondness for canons, from his studies of medieval and Renaissance music as a doctoral student of musicology at the University of Vienna. More audible is the subtle progress of the composite rhythm (the rhythm of all parts taken together), which begins by repeating a gentle syncopated figure (quarter note, half note, quarter note) in almost every measure, then gradually introduces an articulation on every quarter note (measure 13), then increases the pace to use eighth notes in the development, and uses more continuous eighth notes in the recapitulation. Webern did not want his performers to analyze the row structure. Instead, he insisted that performers should focus on the musical surface—making each note as expressive as an entire phrase of a Romantic symphony—and he believed that the music's coherence would be clear.

Igor Stravinsky (1882–1971)

The Rite of Spring: Excerpts

Ballet

1911–13

176

(a) *Danse des adolescentes* (Dance of the Adolescent Girls)

From Igor Stravinsky, *The Rite of Spring*, reengraved edition (London: Boosey & Hawkes, 1967), 10–28 and 121–53. © Copyright 1912, 1921 by Hawkes & Son (London) Ltd. Reprinted by permission.

(b) *Danse sacrale* (Sacrificial Dance)

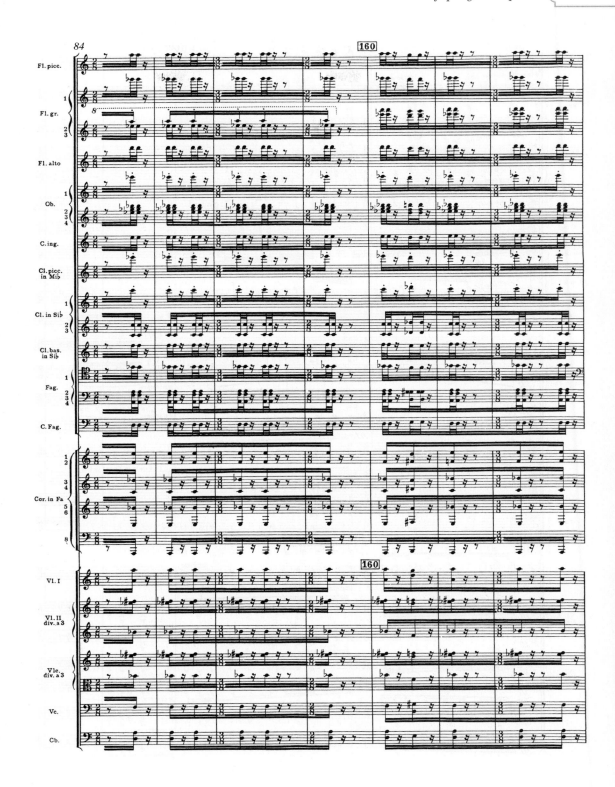

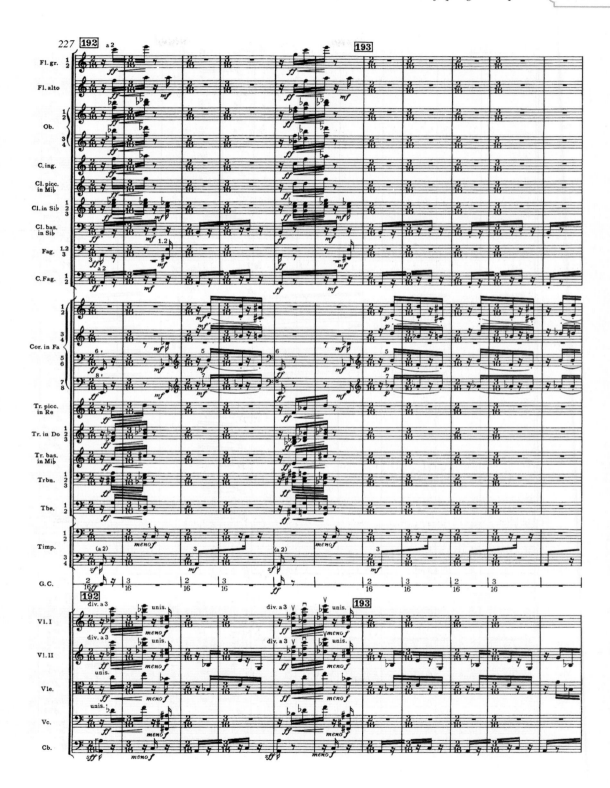

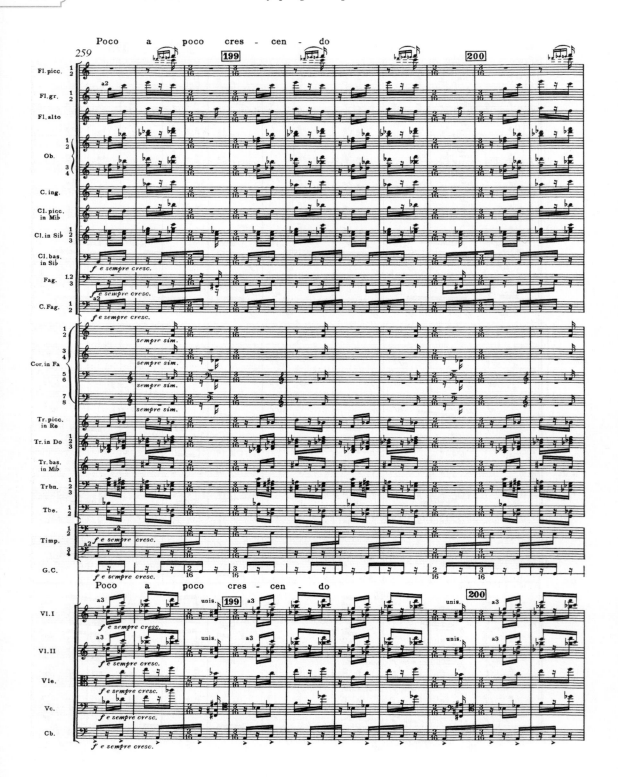

The Rite of Spring was the third ballet Igor Stravinsky wrote for the Ballets Russes (Russian Ballet) in Paris, following his phenomenally successful *Firebird* (1910) and *Petrushka* (1911). The company's impresario, Serge Diaghilev, sought in his productions to fuse the arts in collaborative works drawing on Russian culture. Stravinsky first conceived of *The Rite of Spring* in 1910, imagining a pagan ritual in prehistoric Russia in which an adolescent girl is chosen to dance herself to death as a sacrifice to the god of Spring. He worked out the scenario for the ballet with Nikolai Roerich, an artist and expert on the ancient Slavs.

The goal of the collaborators was not to tell a story, as in previous ballets, but to show a ritual on stage, invoking the spirit of primitive life as a balm for the ills of modern urban society. Roerich designed the sets and costumes, working from Russian peasant designs. Choreographer Vaclav Nijinsky invented deliberately awkward movements for the dancers, the opposite of the refined, graceful motions of traditional ballet. For the music, Stravinsky drew from folk songs, as was his practice, but invented an anti-Romantic, dissonant, and sometimes shocking musical language to suggest primitivism.

At the premiere in May 1913, the audience protested in one of the most notorious scandals in music history (see HWM, p. 834, for Stravinsky's account). Their outrage was aimed more at the choreography than at the music, which was a great success when performed as a concert work in Moscow and Paris in 1914. Ironically, this composition that Stravinsky intended as part of a collective artwork has only rarely been performed as a ballet since, and instead it became one of the most popular and frequently played orchestral works of the twentieth century.

After an Introduction, the curtain rises on the *Danse des adolescentes* (Dance of the Adolescent Girls). The strings, using double stops and downbows on every chord, reiterate a sonority that includes all seven notes of an A♭ harmonic minor scale. The dissonance is intense, but there is no expectation of resolution; the chord is simply a musical object, one of many that Stravinsky juxtaposes throughout the piece, and the striking dissonance evokes a primal feeling. The barring is regular, but because each chord in the first two measures is played in exactly the same manner there is no clear indication of the meter. An unusual pattern of accents, reinforced by eight horns, destroys any feeling of metrical regularity. The effect of the unpredictable accents is to reduce meter to mere pulsation on every eighth note, strongly conveying the idea of primitivism by emphasizing pulse, the most elemental aspect of rhythm.

This texture suddenly breaks off, and we hear another: an ostinato in the English horn, a four-note figure common in Slavic folk music, over arpeggiated triads in bassoons and cellos (measures 9–12). Although this sounds quite different from what precedes it, there is more continuity between these blocks than may be apparent, since all the pitches of the preceding chord appear here as well, with only two new ones (one new note, *c*, and one octave doubling, low *G*). Such combinations of contrast with continuity are typical of Stravinsky's music and occur throughout *The Rite of Spring*.

The pounding chords resume, with an abbreviated form of the accent pattern (measures 13–16 repeat measures 2–5). At measure 17, the English horn ostinato appears over the chords, and other ideas are added, creating a texture of superimposed layers that is characteristic of the entire ballet. Typically, each idea is given its own timbre or group of timbres as well as a unique figuration. The chords break off at measure 23 but the ostinato continues as new ideas are superimposed. Often, blocks of sound are juxtaposed in close succession: for instance, a fanfare figure of stacked fifths in the brass and clarinets at measure 26, repeated in measures 28 and 29, alternates with an embellished running idea in flutes and violin 1 in measures 27 and 30–33, while the other parts play ostinatos. In the original choreography, many of these alternating ideas accompanied motions by different groups of dancers on stage, and the effect is strongly visual, like cross-cutting between shots in a film or music video. The music moves forward by layering, juxtaposing, and alternating ideas in this fashion rather than through motivic development or any of the other sophisticated means of traditional classical music; this is another emblem of the primitive.

The pounding chords return (measure 35), then grow suddenly quieter. Here Stravinsky at last introduces a melody based on a Russian folk tune (bassoons, measure 43), repeating and varying it several times. After a sudden pause (measures 70–71), the English horn ostinato returns, now passed back and forth among other instruments, and it remains a constant presence through the end of the dance. Material heard earlier sometimes returns in new guises (compare measures 78–81 to measures 9–12; measures 99–106 to measures 18–22; and the rhythm in the clarinets at measures 133–40 to the opening rhythm in the horns). But from measure 83 to the end, Stravinsky gradually increases the intensity by building up layers of activity. The leading melody in this section is a folklike tune introduced by solo horn and immediately varied by the flute (measures 89–96). Another folklike melody briefly joins it, presented in cellos and in parallel thirds by the trumpets (measure 119). Then at measure 133 the texture thins suddenly and gradually builds again, adding layer on layer and crescendoing until the next dance suddenly begins. This pattern of building intensity by repeating and overlaying ideas is characteristic of *The Rite of Spring* and appears in almost every dance.

Stravinsky was a master of orchestration, often using special instrumental effects. In *The Rite of Spring*, he includes the unusual timbres of instruments like the low alto flute, the high clarinet in D and E♭, and the trumpet in D, and devices such as mutes and flutter-tonguing. Frequent staccatos and detached playing produce a dry sound, quite far from the lush orchestral sounds of most Romantic composers. Additionally, Stravinsky often divides complex figures between instruments to make them easier to execute, like the piccolo figuration in measures 27–33. At measures 78–81, the violas play a harmonic glissando, moving the finger up and down the C string (without pressing it against the fingerboard) to obtain different notes from the harmonic series, a technique Stravinsky learned from his teacher, Rimsky-Korsakov.

The last dance in *The Rite of Spring* is *Danse sacrale*, the sacrificial dance of the chosen one. Here Stravinsky uses two techniques to undermine meter and reduce rhythm to pulsation: constant changes of meter, as at the beginning, and repeating chords interspersed with rests in unpredictable ways (beginning at measure 34). The dissonant chords, unexpected accents, and loud dynamics convey an atmosphere of violence appropriate to the disturbing events on stage.

The opening section, A, repeats its main idea (measures 2–5) many times, sometimes alternated with other figures of a similar character (as at measures 11–12 and 16). A new section, B (measure 34), begins softly with pulsing chords interrupted by frequent rests; adds a chromatic idea above the chords (measures 47–48); builds to a frightening climax (measures 83–92); then suddenly returns to its opening dynamic level (measure 93) and gradually builds again. The A section returns, transposed down a semitone (measure 116). Then a new section, C, begins (measure 149), signaled by heavy percussion and a whole-tone tune introduced by the horns (measure 154), soon transformed into a folklike melody (measures 160–71). The opening of section A briefly interrupts (measures 174–80). Finally, ideas from A return over an A–C–A–C ostinato in the bass (at measure 203), the music builds to a final climax, and the chosen one collapses to rising chromatic scales in the flutes.

Throughout the ballet, Stravinsky elevates rhythm and tone color to a position equal to pitch and motive as determinants of the form, shape, and progress of the music. His prominent use of ostinatos, changing meters, unpredictable rests and attacks, rhythm and melody reduced to their elements, juxtaposed blocks of sound, layering, discontinuity, and motives identified with specific timbres all had a significant impact on later composers, making *The Rite of Spring* one of the most influential pieces of music ever written.

Igor Stravinsky (1882–1971)

Symphony of Psalms: First movement

Choral symphony

1930

From Igor Stravinsky, *Symphony of Psalms*, rev. ed. (London: Boosey & Hawkes, 1948), 1–15. © Copyright
1931 by Hawkes & Son (London) Ltd. Revised version © copyright 1948 by Hawkes & Son (London) Ltd. U.S.
copyright renewed. Reprinted by permission.

Exaudi orationem meam, Domine, et deprecationem meam:	Hear my prayer, Lord, and my supplication:
auribus percipe lacrimas meas.	give ear to my tears.
Ne sileas.	Do not keep silence.
Quoniam advena ego sum apud te et peregrinus, sicut omnes patres mei.	For I am a stranger to you and a wanderer, like all my fathers.
Remitte mihi, ut refrigerer prius quam abeam et amplius non ero.	Pardon me, that I may be refreshed before I depart and am no more.

— PSALM 38:13–14 (39:12–13)

In late 1929, Serge Koussevitzky, conductor of the Boston Symphony Orchestra, commissioned Stravinsky to compose a symphonic piece for the fiftieth anniversary of the Orchestra, occurring the following year. Stravinsky's response was *Symphony of Psalms*, a three-movement work that set three Latin psalms, combining orchestra with chorus. The first movement uses the last two verses of Psalm 38 in the Latin Vulgate Bible (Psalm 39 in the Protestant numbering).

In this work and others during his neoclassical period (1920–51), Stravinsky applied the trademarks of his mature style, developed in *The Rite of Spring* (NAWM 176), to pieces that echoed the styles, genres, and forms of music from the eighteenth century or earlier. Such works were no longer nationalist, like the early ballets, but were intended as universal statements. Stravinskian traits abound. Just in the opening measures, we hear sudden discontinuities and juxtapositions of material; rapid changes of meter; and unpredictable rhythms and rests that tend to emphasize elemental pulsation rather than meter. Later passages use ostinatos and superimpose multiple layers (as in measures 26–36). Yet the music is less dissonant than the *Rite*, and there are frequent references to the language and styles of the past, including many triads and diatonic scales, an imitation of liturgical chant in the vocal lines, and a fugue in the second movement.

After an introduction, the first movement features two main musical ideas that alternate, A and B, and a contrasting middle section, C:

Music	Intro	A	trans	B1	B2	trans	B1'	A'	C	A''	B1''	B2'	Cadence
Measure	1	15	18	26	33	37	41	49	53	65	68	72	75

Considering only the portion with text (measures 26–78), the form might be described as an arch, with C at the center. Theme A is associated with the most direct appeals to God, at "Ne sileas" (Do not keep silence) and "Remitte mihi" (Pardon me), and section C with the psalmist's description of himself as a wanderer. The juxtaposition of contrasting blocks of material, common in Musorgsky (see NAWM 153) and other Russian composers as well as in Stravinsky's early ballets, is here used no longer as a national characteristic but as a device to articulate an abstract form.

One of the most important aspects of neoclassical music is that it is *neotonal*, establishing a tonal center not through traditional harmony but through repetition and assertion. At the beginning of the first movement, an E-minor chord, repeated irregularly over the next several measures, creates a center on E, but the prominence of G in the chord (G occurs in four octaves, and E in only the lower and uppermost octaves) suggests that the G will be important as well. The A sections are primarily diatonic, using the notes of the E Phrygian scale and sustaining a drone E in the bass. The B sections are largely octatonic, offering a tonal contrast while (at least in the B1 sections) featuring G–B–E sonorities on the downbeats. The transitions and the first B2 section hint strongly at G as an alternate center, and in the closing cadence (measures 74–78) the bass marches down stepwise from E to G while the voices rise from E through F to G. The way Stravinsky juxtaposes E and G as two rival centers, then leads the music from the former center to the latter, is a novel reinterpretation of traditional tonality, the sort of reinvention of past conventions that is at the heart of neoclassicism.

Another aspect of neoclassicism, particularly in Stravinsky's hands, was an attempt to avoid the emotionalism associated with Romantic music. Among the ways the composer avoided Romanticism in this piece were his exclusion of violins and violas from the orchestra, shunning the instruments that most often carry emotional melodies in nineteenth-century symphonies while favoring what Stravinsky regarded as the more objective sounds of wind instruments, and his choice to avoid tempo markings that suggested moods (such as Allegro or Vivace) and to use simple metronome markings instead. Beginning in the 1920s, he often conducted his own works, both as a way to make money and as a model for others of how to conduct his music without indulging in interpretive excess. The performance on the accompanying recording was conducted by Stravinsky himself in 1963, when he was eighty-one, and it exemplifies his preference that the music should speak for itself.

Béla Bartók (1881–1945)

Mikrokosmos: No. 123, *Staccato and Legato*

Étude

1926, 1932–39

A piano teacher as well as a composer, Béla Bartók wrote *Mikrokosmos* to introduce piano students to the techniques and sounds of modern music. The 153 pieces are in six volumes arranged from simplest to most challenging. The collection began to take shape in 1936, when his son Péter began to study piano and Bartók wrote pieces for him to learn. Bartók completed the project during the next three years, incorporating some pieces written a decade earlier. He played excerpts from *Mikrokosmos* in recitals beginning in 1937, performing this piece, *Staccato and Legato*, for the first time in January 1938. The whole collection was published in 1940 by the British publisher Boosey & Hawkes, to which Bartók had switched from his Viennese publisher Universal Edition after Nazi Germany annexed Austria in 1938.

As the title suggests, the entire set represents a microcosm of Bartók's style. *Staccato and Legato* offers both a practical étude for the student—an exercise in playing legato and staccato in alternation within each hand and simultaneously between both hands—and an illustration of Bartók's synthesis of elements derived from peasant music with characteristics of classical music. The synthesis works by emphasizing not only the elements that most distinguish these two traditions but also those elements they have in common.

From the classical tradition, this piece is modeled on Bach, resembling a two-part invention. The two hands are in exact canon, first at an octave and fourth below with entrances a measure apart (measures 1–11) and then, after a sly transition, at an octave and fifth below with entrances half a measure apart (measures 13–22). The subject and answer are both inverted at measure 13. After the cadence in measure 24, Bartók presents a second version of the piece (marked **b**), which repeats the original version but with the counterpoint inverted—that is, with the second voice transposed to be above rather than below the first. Canon, inversion, and invertible counterpoint are all typical of Bach.

The contrast of legato and staccato is also a trait from the classical tradition, and it is used here to point out the canon, as was typical performance practice for playing Bach at the piano; each entrance begins legato, then turns to staccato to make it easier to hear the answer in the other voice.

The tonal structure has a classical shape. The piece starts in a tonal region centered on C, with a subject that spans from C to F and an answer that spans from G to C. The music then repeats, varied, a fifth higher on G (measures 7–12), mimicking a move in tonal music from tonic to dominant. The third phrase is in a region on F, with an inverted subject spanning F to C and an answer that moves from B♭ to F, and the piece closes on C. The overall structure, moving from C to G to F and back to C, is like that of many eighteenth-century pieces that go from tonic to dominant and then somewhere else before returning to the tonic.

But there are folk elements here too. The shape of the opening phrase, rising and falling in the span of a fourth, is common in Hungarian peasant songs. So are several other features in the right-hand melody of the section marked as **a**: the melodic structure of a series of short phrases, each marked off with a rest; the transposition of the first phrase up a fifth (as happens here at measure 6), thereby filling in the rest of the octave; the immediate variation of a phrase rather than repeating it exactly, as we see here with each successive pair of phrases; and the overall contour of the melody, rising from the opening note to the upper octave and then returning. These traits are evident in many of the Hungarian peasant melodies Bartók collected, including this one that he recorded in the Pest region near Budapest in 1907:

In addition to sharing these general characteristics, this Hungarian peasant tune closely resembles Bartók's melody in certain respects: its first measure shares the short-short-long rhythm of measures 2–3 in Bartók's melody, and the melodic contour of those measures of the Bartók is like an inverted chromatic variant of the first measure of the peasant melody. Whether Bartók had this particular tune in mind or not, its similarities to the melody of *Staccato and Legato* show how closely he modeled the latter on Hungarian melodies.

Another feature of *Staccato and Legato*, its chromaticism, may also have a Hungarian source. Several Hungarian peasant melodies mix modes, for instance by shifting between the Dorian and Mixolydian modes (which changes the third of the scale from minor to major). Here the rising gestures suggest the major scale (like the C-major scale spelled out by the first four notes of the subject and answer respectively), and the falling gestures suggest the chromatic scale or Phrygian scale. In the diatonic context established by the opening figure, the chromatic notes sound like ornamental tones, and indeed Bartók observed in his studies of Hungarian folk music that some tunes featured chromatic ornaments within mostly diatonic melodies.

Of course, the contrast of diatonicism and chromaticism is also common in the classical tradition, as are melodies that rise and fall and are formed from phrases that are repeated or varied. We have also seen that both traditions provide a source for the overall motion in *Staccato and Legato* from C to G and back to C. Bartók's synthesis of the two traditions depends upon such common features, even while highlighting what makes each tradition distinctive.

Béla Bartók (1881–1945)

Music for Strings, Percussion and Celesta: Third movement, Adagio

Symphonic suite

1936

179

From Béla Bartók, *Music for String Instruments, Percussion and Celesta* (New York: Boosey & Hawkes, 1939), 66–94.
© Copyright 1937 Universal Edition A.G., Vienna. © Renewed. All rights reserved. Used in the territory of the world excluding the United States by permission of European American Music Distributors Company, agent for Universal Edition A.G., Vienna.

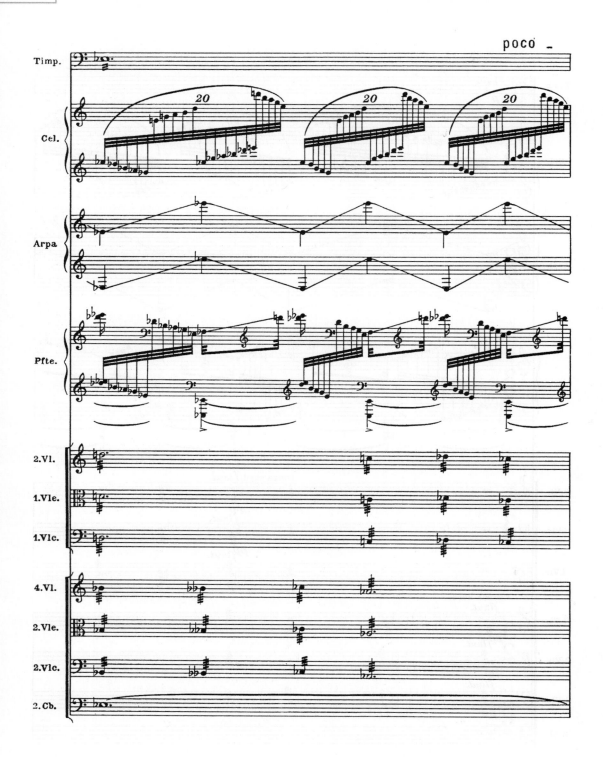

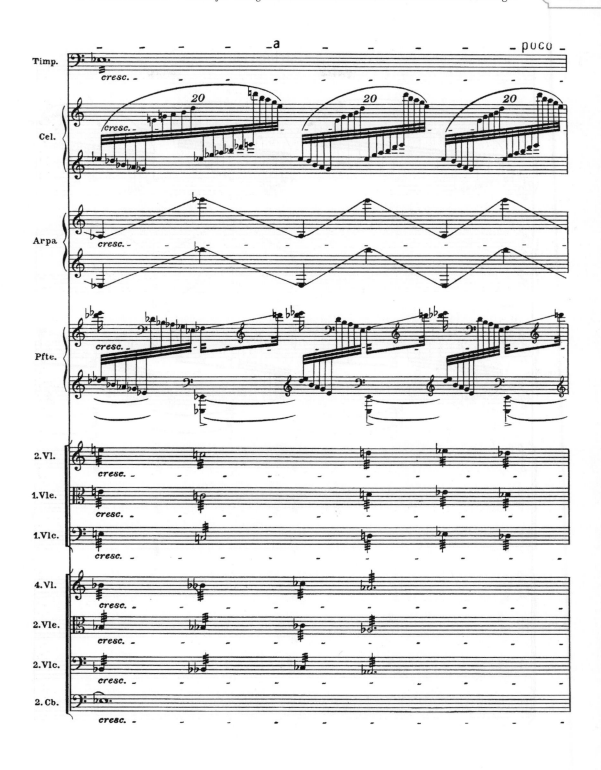

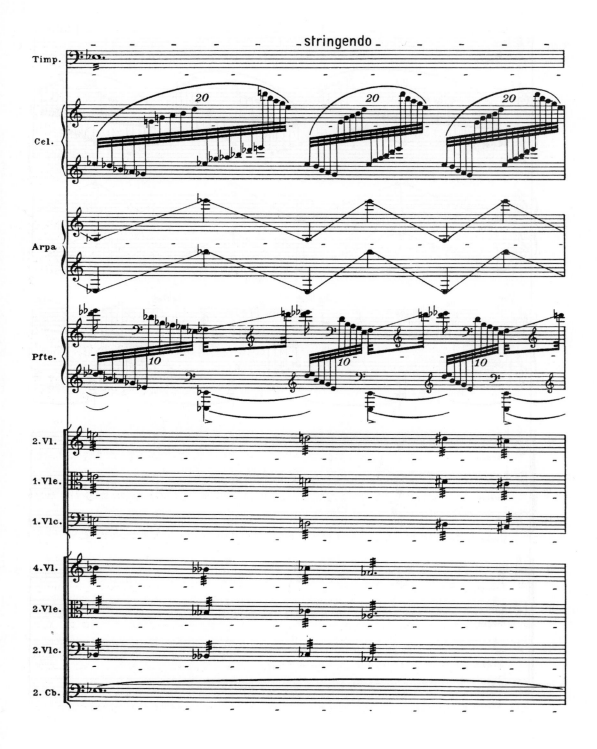

*) kleineres **Instrument** mit höherem **Ton** / *instrument plus petit au son plus clair*
smaller cymbal with higher tone

*) kleineres Instrument / *instrument plus petit*
smaller cymbals

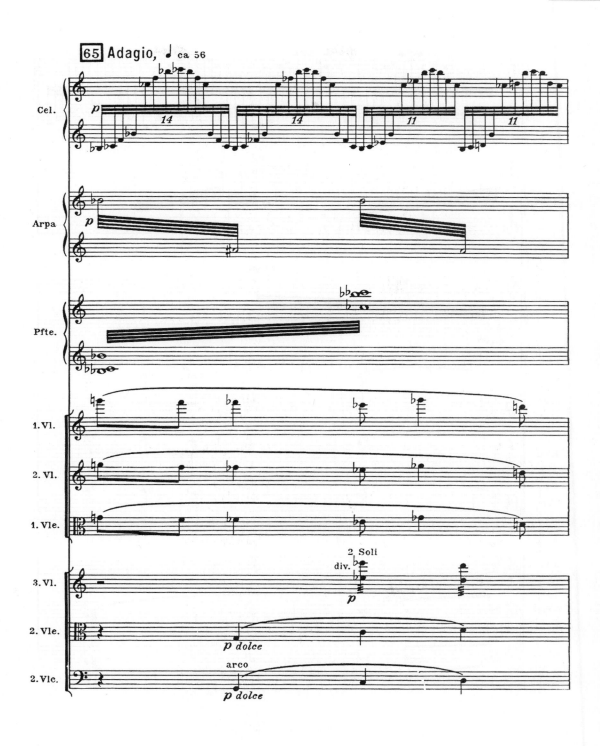

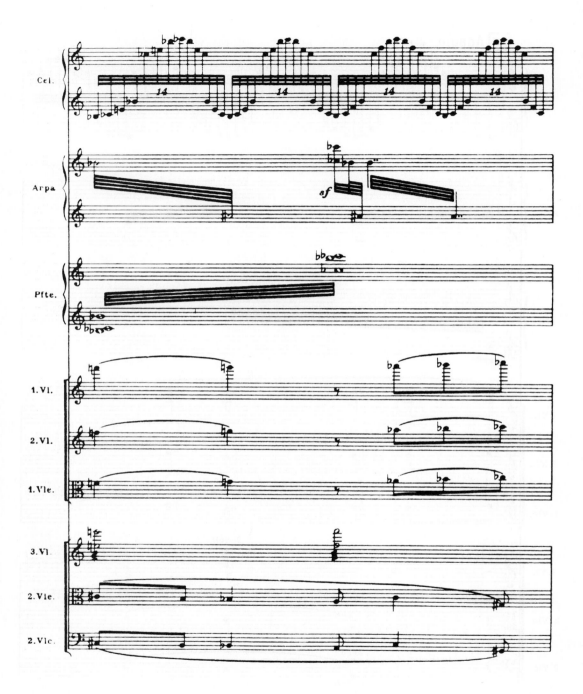

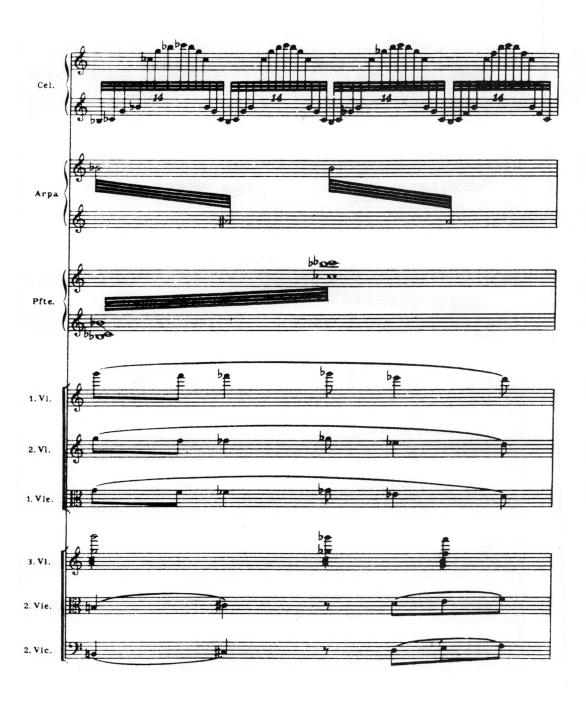

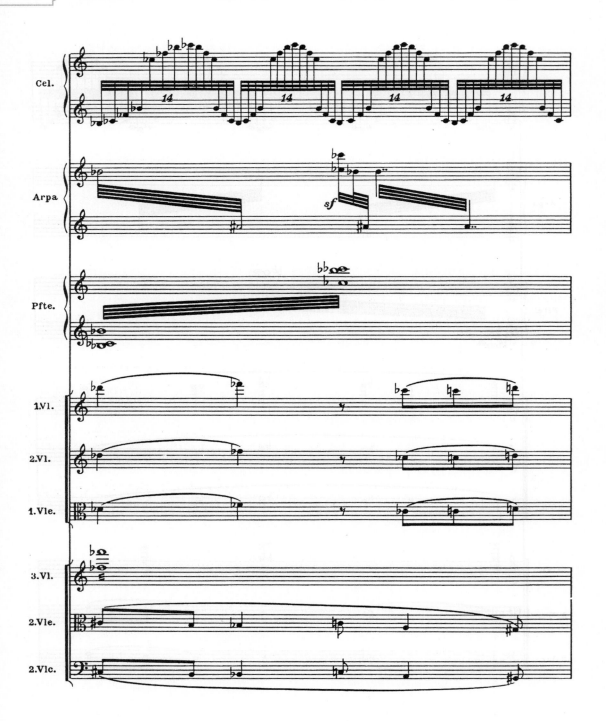

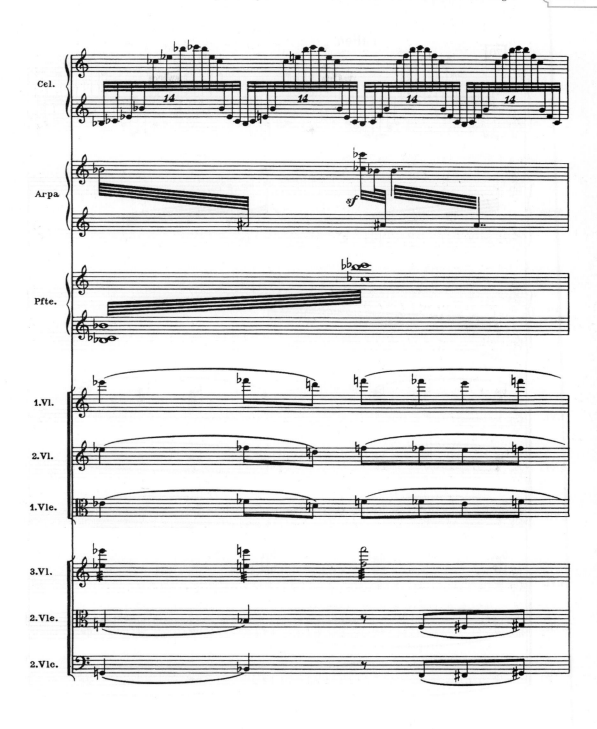

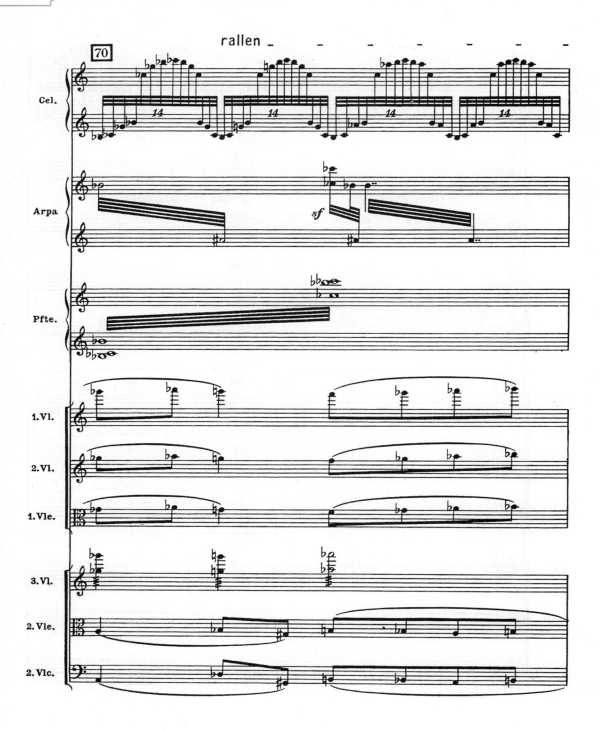

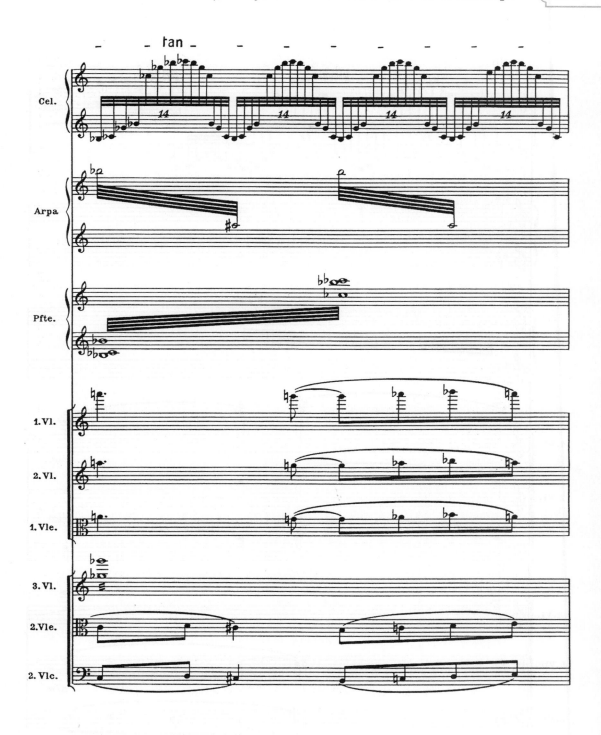

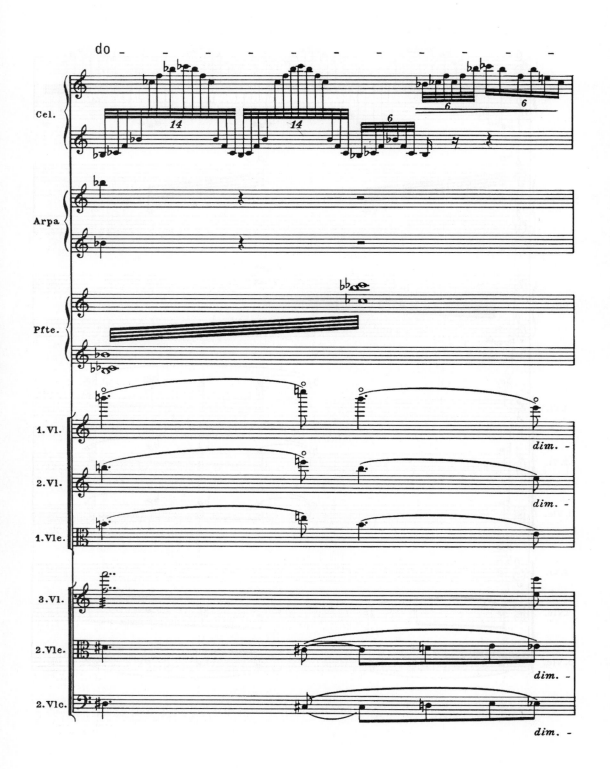

Durée d'exécution: - A ca 1' 45"
(Timings)

A - B	„	1'	12"
B - C	„		55"
C - D	„		57"
D - E	„		58"
E -	„		48"
	ca	6'	35"

Béla Bartók wrote *Music for Strings, Percussion and Celesta* in the summer of 1936 for the Basel Chamber Orchestra and its conductor, Paul Sacher. Bartók's concept for the piece was so clear in his mind that he wrote it out from the start in full score, rather than beginning with a reduced score as composers usually do for orchestral works. It was premiered the next January in Basel, Switzerland, to such great applause that the orchestra played the fourth movement again as an encore.

The work has four movements: a slow fugue, a fast sonata form, a slow arch form, and a rondo finale. The fugue theme is recalled in each later movement. The movements are also linked by a symmetrical scheme of tonal centers—A for the outer movements, with the notes a minor third above (C) and below (F♯) serving as centers for the second and third movements respectively. Like *Symphony of Psalms* (NAWM 177), the piece is neotonal, rather than based on traditional harmony. In each movement, the note a tritone away from the tonal center serves as an opposite pole. Another symmetrical aspect of the music is the layout of the orchestra itself: the strings are divided into two halves (violins 1 and 2, viola 1, cello 1, and bass 1 on the left, curving from front to back, with the others on the right in a mirror arrangement), and the piano, harp, celesta, and percussion are in the middle.

The slow movement, included here, exhibits symmetries on both a minute and a large scale. The opening xylophone solo is a palindrome centered on the first beat of measure 3—that is, the rhythm from that beat is the same going in either direction. The form is also palindromic (though not exactly so), punctuated by the four phrases of the fugue theme (FT) from the first movement:

Section	A	FT1	B	FT2	C	FT3	B'	FT4	A'
Measure	1	19	20	34	35	60	63	74	75

The A section is marked by four striking sounds: the xylophone, which repeats a single pitch (*f'''*); glissandos on the timpani between F♯ and C, the two tonal poles of the movement; low string tremolos on C and F♯; and figures in violas and violins that snake through chromatic space. After the first phrase of the fugue appears (in viola 1 and cello 1 at measure 19), two solo violins and celesta share the B theme, accompanied by an eerie background of trills in the strings and parallel major sevenths articulated by the piano, violin glissandos, and string tremolos.

After another fugue segment, the C section begins with glissandos and two mutually exclusive pentatonic scales played rapidly in the harp, piano, and celesta, over which a twisting theme in parallel octave tremolos gradually rises. This texture has become known as Bartók's "night music," named for the movement *Musiques nocturnes* in his piano suite *Out of Doors* (1926). The twisting theme builds to a climax as celesta, harp, and piano drop out. At the peak, the last segment of the twisting theme is transformed into a transposed, modified retrograde: omitting the bracketed notes, A–A♯–[D♯]–E♯–[F♯]–E–G (violin 1, measures 44–45) becomes C–A–B♭–E♭–D (measure 46). This new motive is itself heard in retrograde in alternation with its original form (measures 48 and 50) or in counterpoint with it (measures 51–53), as if to emphasize the symmetries. The new motive suffuses the texture, imitated in every instrument. Then, as the third phrase of the fugue theme enters (violin 3 and viola 2, measures 60–63), we may hear a hidden connection: the new motive turns out to derive from the last five notes of this phrase of the fugue theme, changing the whole steps into larger intervals (compare D–C–D♭–C♭–B♭ in measures 61–63, from the fugue theme, with the new motive C–A–B♭–E♭–D in measure 46).

A modified reprise of the B theme follows, treated in canon at the tritone and accompanied by a texture reminiscent of the first half of the C section, with tremolos and arpeggios in piano, harp, and celesta and violin tremolos in a high register. The last phrase of the fugue theme appears in piano and celesta, and an abbreviated recollection of the A section closes the movement.

Bartók drew on folk music, not just as a way to evoke a national or folklike style, but as a source of ideas for renewing modern music. That is evident in this movement, which does not sound folklike in the least but draws many elements from folk styles. The string melodies in the A sections borrow their short on-beat accents (as in measure 6) from a rhythm common in Hungarian folk tunes, and take their rapid, snaking figuration (as in measures 7–8) from the ornate, partly chromatic vocal ornaments of Serbo-Croatian folk songs. The B section and the climax of the C section (measures 45–59) both—in different ways—echo a technique of Bulgarian dance orchestras, in which instruments play in octaves against drones and a chordal tapestry of sound is produced by plucked instruments. In the latter passage, the $\frac{5}{4}$ meter suggests the Bulgarian dance rhythm of 2 + 3 (the *paidushko*). Thus, in this movement, and throughout *Music for Strings, Percussion and Celesta*, Bartók has fully assimilated elements of folk music into one of his most original works of art music.

This piece is highly individual in style, form, and even genre. It is clearly related to the four-movement symphony but differentiated from the symphony by its movement structure and prominent percussion and keyboard parts. Paradoxically, such a high degree of individuality is typical of the twentieth century, when composers sought both to follow in the footsteps of the classical masters of the past and to stake out new territory, forging distinctive identities for themselves and for each new piece.

Charles Ives (1874–1954)

General William Booth Enters into Heaven

Song

1914

180

*Both small and large notes in voice part are sung if there is a chorus.

Charles Ives found the poem *General William Booth Enters into Heaven* by American poet Vachel Lindsay (1879–1931) in a 1914 review of Lindsay's first book of poetry. There was probably no poet better suited for Ives's musical idiom than Lindsay, who infused his poems (and his onstage readings of them) with the rhythms and performing styles of hymns, vaudeville, and ragtime. Ives based his song on only the extracts printed in the review: the first, second, and fourth stanzas of the seven-stanza poem. The song remained unpublished until 1935, when Henry Cowell produced nineteen of Ives's songs as an issue of *New Music*, a quarterly journal of works by modern composers.

Lindsay wrote the poem on the death of William Booth, evangelist and founder of the Salvation Army, whom Lindsay pictures entering Heaven beating a bass drum at the head of an army of the souls he had saved. Appropriately, Lindsay drew inspiration from a gospel hymn, indicating that the poem was "to be sung to the tune of 'The Blood of the Lamb.'" He quoted the hymn's refrain line frequently ("Are you washed in the blood of the Lamb?"), and for the other lines he used the hymn's accent pattern of three stressed, three unstressed, and three stressed syllables.

Ives's setting is an art song in the classical tradition, but he incorporates elements from the band music and popular songs of the American vernacular tradition, from Protestant hymnody, and from the experimental music in which he was a pioneer. At the opening, he evokes Booth's bass drum through his technique of imitating drumbeats as dissonant chords on the piano, an experiment from his teen years; the bass notes arrive after the rest of the chord, just as on a bass drum the resonance of the drum head is heard just after the sound of the initial impact. The rhythm here is the "street beat" (measures 1–2), the pattern drummers use to keep marchers moving in step and one of the first things Ives would have learned as a drummer in his father's band. Ives based the vocal melody on motives paraphrased from the hymn "There Is a Fountain Filled with Blood," whose imagery closely matches that of the hymn Lindsay used.

In the second section of the song (measures 19–39), Lindsay describes Booth's followers, and Ives gives each group a different musical characterization, using ostinatos, parallel dissonant chords, and other modernist sounds. At each appearance of the refrain line "(Are you washed in the blood of the Lamb?)," Ives presents a new paraphrase of "There Is a Fountain."

When the marchers arrive at the center of Heaven—depicted as a "mighty courthouse square" like those in county seats across the United States—Ives suggests the milling crowd through a rising and falling whole-tone scale in the voice and repeating ostinatos in the piano (measures 40–51). At the line "Big-voiced lassies made their banjos bang" (measures 52–55), the piano paraphrases *Oh, Dem Golden Slippers* by James A. Bland, a minstrel song about going to Heaven whose second verse begins "Oh my ole banjo." Later Ives adds a bugle call for the line "Loons with trumpets blowed a blare," and a hint of the hymn "Onward, Upward" where the words of Lindsay's poem almost quote it (measures 70–74). All these elements show Ives's affectionate, good-humored approach to depicting the motley crowd, although both Lindsay's poem and Ives's song are entirely serious.

When Jesus appears at the courthouse door and blesses the marchers, Ives states most of "There Is a Fountain," slightly reworked, in the piano (measures 82–88), accompanying a repeating motive in the voice that depicts the crowd still circling around the square. This is the first mostly diatonic passage in the song, and its slow, soft, dignified character reflects Jesus' serenity. Booth does not see Jesus at first (he was blind when he died), and continues to lead the march even as he and all the marchers are cleansed and healed by Jesus' blessing. At the climactic moment of transformations, over the drum pattern in the piano, the singer presents the complete verse of "There Is a Fountain," set awkwardly to Lindsay's words as if to express the force of will it took Booth to motivate his followers. This moment is the culmination of the drama in Lindsay's poem and also of the thematic process of the whole song, a gradual emergence of the hymn tune as the principal theme. The song is thus an example of *cumulative form*, the form Ives used most often, in which the main theme is heard first in fragments and paraphrases and appears complete only at the end.

In the final measures, the action stops, and the closing refrain is set twice, over soft arpeggiated chords and then in the four-part harmony of Protestant hymns. The stark contrasts of style seen here and throughout the song are typical of Ives, who used them to articulate his cumulative form and for expressive purposes, just as Mozart used contrasting styles in his music (see the commentaries for NAWM 121 and 124). In this context, the use of a familiar style amid so many novel sounds suggests the humble devotion of a hymn, and thus brings the message of the song home. The moment quickly passes, and the parade fades away in the distance.

After writing this song, Ives sketched an arrangement for unison choir and chamber orchestra. When he published the song more than twenty years after writing it, he included a number of passages in small notes, indicating that they should be sung if the piece was performed by a choir, and these are sometimes included even when it is sung by a soloist.

George Gershwin (1898–1937)

I Got Rhythm, from *Girl Crazy*

Broadway show song

1930

181

George Gershwin composed *I Got Rhythm*, with lyrics by his brother Ira, for the Broadway musical *Girl Crazy*, which premiered on October 14, 1930, at the Alvin Theater. George typically composed the melody first, and Ira then fitted it with lyrics, the practice also of several other Tin Pan Alley and Broadway songwriting teams. The show introduced Ginger Rogers and Ethel Merman, who became stars on Broadway and in the movies. Merman debuted *I Got Rhythm* in the role of Frisco Kate and later recorded the song in the version heard on the accompanying recordings. The song was published in 1930 in the version reproduced here, arranged with piano accompaniment and with guitar chords and fingerings.

Gershwin laid out *I Got Rhythm* in standard Tin Pan Alley form: verse plus thirty-two-bar chorus with phrases in an AABA' pattern (plus a two-bar tag). Following the trend at the time, the work has only one verse, and the main emphasis in the song is on the chorus, which is immediately repeated. To provide a clear contrast of mood and style, Gershwin set the verse and chorus in different keys. The verse begins in G minor, but modulates to the relative major, B♭, which remains the key area of the A sections of the chorus. The B section of the chorus, called the "bridge," shifts to the mediant, D major, and then travels down the circle of fifths to get back to B♭ in the final A section of the chorus. Ira's lyrics are fresh, modern, optimistic, and slangy, as they are in most of his songs; the opening phrase, for example, is not "I've got" or "I have," but the grammatically incorrect yet catchy "I got." Ira matches George's heavily syncopated rhythm with a punchy text that allows every syllable to be stressed (as in the first four measures of the chorus).

I Got Rhythm was an immediate popular hit, and not only in its original form. Instrumental versions based on the song's chorus began to appear, and soon this song became a jazz standard. However, in jazz performances of the song, it is not the melody that is the focus; rather, jazz performers have valued the harmony, which provided the framework for their improvisations. The "changes" (the jazz term for a specific harmonic progression) of this song became the basis for so many new jazz tunes in the following decades that this particular chord progression came to be known simply as "rhythm changes" (short for "the *I Got Rhythm* changes"). NAWM 184, Duke Ellington's *Cotton Tail*, is one example of a new jazz tune built over this harmonic progression.

Typically, the scores of Tin Pan Alley songs and indeed of most popular songs are merely guidelines for performance. The two-measure introduction can be repeated indefinitely as a vamp to set the stage for the singer. In Merman's recording, the band plays the entire melody of the chorus before returning to the two opening measures as written. Merman then enters with the verse, and follows with the chorus. The recording captures Merman's trademark nasal, chest-voiced performing style, nearly spoken delivery, and textual additions, such as interpolating the words "hanging 'round my front or back door" in the final statement of the chorus. The performance concludes with Merman's signature flourish: punching the final note of the chorus up a fifth and holding it for several measures as the orchestra finishes the melody.

Bessie Smith (1894–1937)

Back Water Blues

Blues

1927

0:00   1. When it rains five days and the skies turn dark as night,
        When it rains five days and the skies turn dark as night,
        Then trouble's takin' place in the lowlands at night.

0:32   2. I woke up this mornin', can't even get out of my door.
        I woke up this mornin', can't even get out of my door.
        That's enough trouble to make a poor girl wonder where she want to go.

0:59   3. Then they rowed a little boat about five miles 'cross the farm.
        Then they rowed a little boat about five miles 'cross the farm.
        I packed all my clothes, throwed them in and they rowed me along.

1:27   4. When it thunders and lightnin', and the wind begins to blow,
        When it thunders and lightnin', and the wind begins to blow,
        There's thousands of people ain't got no place to go.

1:53   5. Then I went and stood upon some high old lonesome hill.
        Then I went and stood upon some high old lonesome hill.
        Then looked down on the house where I used to live.

2:20   6. Back-water blues done caused me to pack my things and go.
        Back-water blues done caused me to pack my things and go.
        'Cause my house fell down and I can't live there no more.

2:48   7. (Moan . . .) I can't move no more,
        (Moan . . .) I can't move no more,
        There ain't no place for a poor old girl to go.

Bessie Smith, known as the "Empress of the Blues," wrote both lyrics and music for her hit song *Back Water Blues*. Columbia Records marketed Smith's recording, made on February 2, 1927, as a response to a flood in Mississippi in April of 1927, and it became one of her best-known records. She had composed the song several months earlier after a flood on Christmas Day, 1926, in Nashville, where she sang in a show a few days after the flood. As is true for much early blues, the text can be understood as a complaint against racial oppression and poverty.

Smith constructed the song in conventional blues form. Each of the seven stanzas shares the same AAB poetic form: the second line repeats the first, followed by a new line of poetry with the same end rhyme. The rhyme is often a near-rhyme, as in the pairing of "go" with "more" in the last two verses; the quality of the vowel is always more important than the ending consonants. The last line of each stanza either completes the thought begun by the first or packs a surprise by offering new information, as in the sixth verse.

Each stanza follows the form of a twelve-bar blues, with four measures for each line of poetry and a general harmonic pattern of tonic chords in the first phrase, subdominant to tonic in the second, and dominant to tonic in the third. After a brief piano introduction, the harmony settles into the tonic for four measures, with the piano moving to the subdominant in the second measure, as sometimes occurs in the form. The next four-measure phrase begins on the subdominant, moving back to the tonic after two measures. For the final line of the stanza, in measures 9–12 of the blues pattern, the harmony moves to the dominant for a measure, then to the subdominant (with added ninth and seventh) before moving back to the tonic for the final two measures. Each phrase of melody lingers around the fifth degree of the scale, decorating or repeating it, and then descends to the tonic. Here, as in many blues, the voice begins just before the first measure of each phrase and cadences on the third measure, allowing space in the third and fourth measures for the pianist to respond, in an evocation of the call-and-response structure typical of African American group singing.

The twelve-bar blues is a flexible harmonic pattern, used as a general framework. Exact adherence to the chords specified here is not crucial; rather, it is the combination of the harmonic framework, use of blue notes (flatted thirds and sevenths, sometimes also flatted fifths), poetic structure, and general mood that together give life to the blues.

The sheet music included here is merely an approximation for the performance, as Smith's recording reveals. Many blues were performed and recorded before they were written down in notation, and there are elements of the performance that the notation is not well equipped to capture. Smith sings a somewhat different melody for each verse, emphasizing the blue notes and altering the rhythm to fit the words of each stanza while following the same basic melodic shape. Pianist James P. Johnson, famed as an exponent of the stride piano style, responds to Smith's phrases with improvised additions of his own. Some of his figurations respond to the text, as when during the fourth stanza he produces a dramatic, downward skipping bass line to imitate the thunder, lightning, and blowing wind. His rocking accompaniment in the left hand throughout most of the song seems to suggest a reassurance that time and life go on and the flood will subside.

King Oliver [Joe Oliver] (1885–1938)

West End Blues, as performed by Louis Armstrong and His Hot Five

Blues

RECORDED 1928

183

(a) Original sheet music [not on recording]

Original sheet music, *West End Blues*, words by Clarence Williams, music by Joe Oliver (New York: Clarence Williams Music Publishing, 1928). International copyright secured. All rights reserved. Used by permission of Hal Leonard Corp.

Folks   in   West End,_____ Folks   in   West End,

Gon – na see some shoot-in'   Like they nev – er have seen be – fore,_____

_____   I mean my   man   and my best friend will   nev – er cheat in West End an – y-

more._____   My   more._____

(b) Transcription of recording by Louis Armstrong and His Hot Five

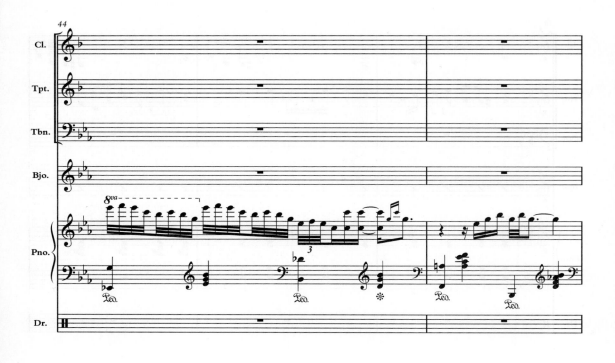

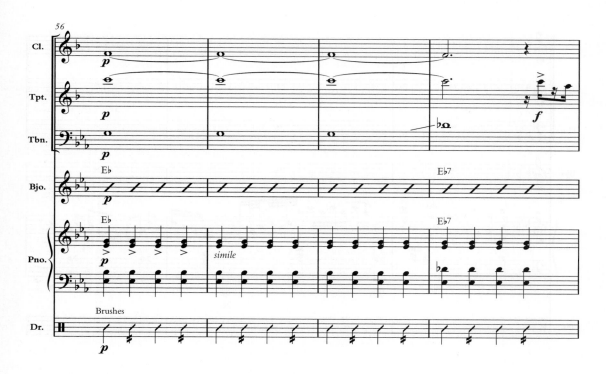

In the period between the two world wars, jazz and other types of popular music were sold both as recordings by star performers and as sheet music for amateurs to play at home or for other musicians to use in their own performances. These two versions of *West End Blues* illustrate the difference between the two formats, as well as the ways jazz performers used the songs they played as the basis for improvisation.

NAWM 183a shows the sheet music for *West End Blues* as composed and published in 1928 by Joe "King" Oliver (music) and Clarence Williams (lyrics). Typical of the popular songs in sheet music of the time, this song begins with a brief piano introduction and is laid out in verse-refrain form. The two bars leading into the first verse are labeled "Vamp," an instruction to the accompanist to keep repeating these measures until the singer joins in. The music for the verse is built over one complete statement of a twelve-bar blues progression (compare NAWM 182). The refrain, to be sung after each verse, presents two successive statements of the twelve-bar blues. Each time through the twelve-bar progression, Oliver writes a different melody and varies the harmony slightly, creating greater variety. The rhythm often features dotted eighths and sixteenths, a written approximation to the swinging rhythms typical of jazz, in which even eighth notes are played in an uneven pattern alternating long and short notes.

The same year Oliver and Williams wrote *West End Blues*, Louis Armstrong and His Hot Five—with Armstrong on trumpet backed by Jimmy Strong on clarinet, Fred Robinson on trombone, Earl Hines on piano, Mancy Cara on banjo, and Zutty Singleton on drums—recorded an instrumental version for OKeh Records in Chicago. This version is on the accompanying recordings, and it is transcribed in NAWM 183b. The parts for the B♭ clarinet and B♭ trumpet both sound a whole step lower than written.

In place of the piano introduction, the recorded version begins with a virtuosic solo by Armstrong that spirals up to near the top of the trumpet's range and then cascades down to end near the bottom. The recorded version has no verse-refrain structure; it has, instead, five statements of the twelve-bar blues pattern, in which members of the group take turns playing solos that are either improvised or in the style of improvisation. In jazz parlance, each such statement is called a chorus (derived from, but different from, the alternate term for the refrain of a popular song). To mark the end of each chorus, the musicians substitute for the tonic chord that usually occupies the last two measures of a twelve-bar blues a quickly moving chord progression known as a *turnaround*, which leads from the tonic to the dominant and prepares for the next chorus (see measures 18–19 for an example).

The entire ensemble plays the first chorus together, with Armstrong taking the melody—a flexible, freely decorated version of the vocal melody of the original song's verse that begins in utter simplicity, becomes more embellished with each phrase, and ends with the rising spirals from the introduction to close on a trilled high C (sounding B♭). The second chorus features Robinson on trombone, beginning with the opening notes of the chorus and then introducing new variations. He is backed by the rhythm section of piano, banjo, and drum set, here played mostly on wood blocks. The third rendition of the blues progression features the clarinet alternating in call and response with Armstrong, who puts down his trumpet and sings in a novelty vocal style that he had made popular: he "scats," singing nonsense syllables to an improvised melody, making his voice sound like an instrument. Hines solos on the piano in the fourth chorus, alternating between two styles of playing in the right hand: (1) rapid, elaborate figurations that resemble the passagework of classical pianists (compare NAWM 136 and 137) and (2) syncopated melody in what has been called his "trumpet style." In the latter style, he often reinforces the melody in octaves (measures 48–51) or embellishes it with tremolos or quickly alternating notes (measures 51–53) that simulate the vibrato, trills, and grace notes of trumpet or clarinet players. The entire ensemble returns for the fifth and final chorus. Once again, Armstrong takes the lead, holding a single high pitch—the high C that concluded his first chorus—for four measures, then filling the next four bars with a virtuosic burst of inventive improvisation, repeating a descending figure five times and then extending and embellishing it. He cedes the stage to Hines for one last brief piano solo, and then the performance ends with a brief cadential tag.

This recording of *West End Blues* exemplifies two of Armstrong's innovative techniques that were seminal to the development of jazz. The first was scat singing, which allowed a voice to imitate an instrument. Scat remains an important technique for jazz singers. Armstrong also quickly became known as an outstanding soloist and paved the way for dynamic, improvised jazz solos, a crucial element of jazz's musical language.

Duke Ellington (1899–1974)

Cotton Tail

Jazz composition (contrafact)

1940

184

184 DUKE ELLINGTON · *Cotton Tail*

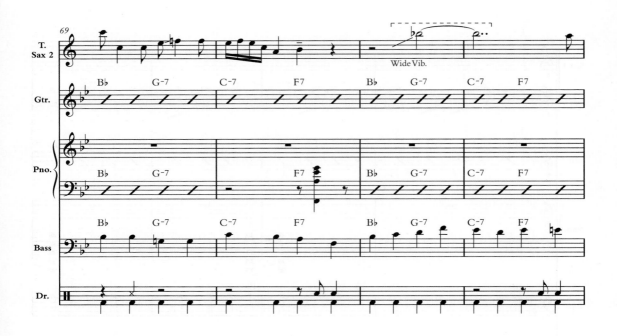

184 DUKE ELLINGTON · *Cotton Tail*

Throughout his career as a band leader and composer, Duke Ellington hired performers more for their individual sounds than for their ability to blend seamlessly into the ensemble, and he wrote music to showcase their particular abilities. In *Cotton Tail*, composed in 1940, Ellington took advantage of the talents of two new members of his band: virtuoso bassist Jimmy Blanton and tenor saxophonist Ben Webster. Both players brought new elements that Ellington incorporated into his own style. Blanton's bass playing is marked by fast-moving lines that reach high into the instrument's range and include many nonchord tones, helping to create contrapuntal textures, especially during the solos. His approach became the foundation for jazz bassists for over a generation and is still widely imitated. Webster began his career in Kansas City and played there with Bennie Moten's band, known for its fast, virtuosic playing and hot improvisation, a style that is evident in his solo in the performance of *Cotton Tail* transcribed here and included on the accompanying recording.

Cotton Tail is a *contrafact*, a new tune composed over a harmonic progression borrowed from another song. Ellington composed a new melody (measures 1–28) to be played over the harmonic progression from the chorus of George Gershwin's *I Got Rhythm* (NAWM 181). Using a familiar harmonic progression was convenient, since players already knew the harmonies and could therefore extemporize with confidence, but adding a new tune and giving it a new name meant that no royalties had to be paid for recording or playing the original song. The harmonic progression from *I Got Rhythm* was used for more contrafacts than any other except the blues, in part because its structure provided interesting possibilities: the A phrases changed chords every half-measure, while the B section lingered on each chord for two measures, offering a strong contrast between rapid and slow harmonic rhythm (the pace of the harmonic progression). Ellington follows Gershwin's harmonies in general outline, but makes many small changes. For example, in measure 5, he underpins the unexpected E natural (equivalent to F♭, the flatted fifth) in the melody with a B♭7 chord with flatted fifth, enriched from a simple tonic B♭ major chord in the original. Later there are several passages in which the harmony is colored by substitute chords, though the overall structure of the progression is maintained.

After the opening statement of the new tune to Gershwin's progression (with its last eight-bar phrase shortened to four bars, measures 25–28), each subsequent statement, or chorus, of the AABA harmonic pattern is given different orchestration. The first two choruses (at measures 29 and 61) feature Ben Webster's blistering, agile solo on tenor sax, punctuated at times by chords from the band. Unlike most big-band solos of the time, which were composed or worked out in advance, Webster's is improvised, built at times from sequences (measures 29–32, 45–52, 61–66, and 77–84) or variation (measures 85–88) and at other times from seemingly free figuration, sometimes highlighted with the growls, rasps, or large vibrato that were among his signature sounds. His lines play off the four-measure phrasing and underlying harmonies but never obscure them, mixing syncopations and nonchord tones with enough notes that are on the beat and in the chord so that we never lose our orientation. Throughout, Blanton's bass line helps to drive the rhythm, adding contrapuntal interest and intensity as it climbs into a high range, even crossing above Webster in measures 31–33 (note that the bass sounds an octave lower than written, the tenor sax a major ninth lower than written).

The third chorus (measure 93) is divided into smaller units: the brass and rhythm sections play the first two A sections; Harry Carney on baritone sax takes the B section (measure 109); and Ellington himself rounds out the final A' with a brief piano solo. The fourth chorus (measure 125) features the reed section (saxophonists Webster, Carney, Barney Bigard, Otto Hardwick, and Johnny Hodges) in block chords (rhythmic unison). The fifth and final chorus (measure 157) is again divided. The first two A sections feature a trademark Ellington technique: brass and reed sections trading short, repeated melodic statements known as riffs, in call-and-response style. The entire band plays the B section, and the final A section returns to the tune from the beginning of the piece, with both reed and brass instruments playing the melody.

The accompanying recording is the first ever of *Cotton Tail*, made on May 4, 1940, and featuring all the original musicians. The score shown here is a transcription from that recording. Thanks to rapid dissemination of the record, Webster's impressive solo became so associated with the tune that later musicians—and even Webster himself—refrained from improvising during the choruses and simply reproduced the solo note for note. In this way, recordings came to preserve performances, even improvised ones, in a form as permanent as notation.

185

Darius Milhaud (1892–1974)

La création du monde (The Creation of the World), Op. 81a:
First tableau

Ballet

1923

From Darius Milhaud, *La création du monde* (Paris: Max Eschig, 1969), 9–21. © 1923 by Editions DURAND. Used by permission.

185 DARIUS MILHAUD · *La création du monde*, Op. 81a: First tableau

During a concert tour to the United States in 1922–23, Darius Milhaud heard African American jazz bands in Harlem and was profoundly affected by their music. Upon his return to Paris he proposed a ballet based on jazz style that would capitalize on the growing French interest in jazz and the continuing fashion for African art inspired by the French colonial presence in Africa. The result was *La création du monde*, written for the Ballets Suédois (Swedish Ballet), a company formed in Paris in 1920 that produced innovative collaborative projects along the lines of the Ballets Russes (see NAWM 176). Blaise Cendrars based the scenario on an African creation story, the cubist painter Fernand Léger designed the sets and costumes using African masks and figurines as models, and Jean Börlin created the choreography, drawing on African dance movements. The ballet premiered on October 25 to mixed reviews, but soon the piece was regarded as a pioneering blend of jazz and classical idioms. In 1926, Milhaud arranged the music as a concert suite for piano and string quartet, and it was published in both versions.

For Milhaud, jazz was an authentic expression of African American experience, with roots in ancient African traditions. But it was also modern, up to date, and chic, in tune with the postwar French admiration for the brashness and vibrancy of American culture. By blending the raw energy of jazz with the classical European tradition, and particularly with the neoclassicism then current in France, Milhaud sought to meld the strengths of both in a fresh, modern idiom.

Milhaud scored the piece for an ensemble that reflects both traditions. It has the typical winds, brass, strings, and percussion of the European orchestra. But the strings are soloists, not orchestral sections, and he includes the sounds of a jazz band, with piano, lots of percussion, and a saxophone substituting for the viola.

The ballet begins with an overture, followed by five tableaux, of which the first is included here. Cendrars's scenario describes the scene:

> The curtain rises slowly on a dark stage. In the middle of the stage we see a confused mass of intertwined bodies: chaos prior to creation. Three giant dieties move slowly around the periphery. These are Nzame, Medere, and N'kva, the masters of creation. They hold counsel, circle around the formless mass, and utter magic incantations.

For this scene, Milhaud wrote a brief fugue in three sections, using a theme inspired by the blues scale and by the rhythms of jazz. The fugue was the quintessential contrapuntal form of the Baroque era, making the blend of jazz and classical traditions hard to miss. In addition, there are many of Milhaud's modernist traits, including *polytonality* (the superimposition of two or more keys at once) and *polyrhythm* (the superimposition of two or more metric or phrase groupings).

The first section (measures 1–23) is the fugal exposition:

- The piano and percussion establish a four-measure-long rhythmic ostinato, with a grouping of 3+3+3+3+4 beats marked by bass drum and piano that works against the notated meter. This evokes similar effects in ragtime (see the first four measures of Joplin's *Maple Leaf Rag*, NAWM 164).

- Over this, the contrabass enters in measure 3 with the fugue subject in D (sounding an octave lower than notated). The subject resembles a jazz riff, featuring short gestures that vary a basic idea. The rhythm includes the upbeats and syncopations typical of jazz, and the melody suggests blue notes on the third and seventh degrees of the scale by alternating minor and major forms and moving chromatically between them (see measures 4–6). The quick arpeggiation in the piano also has the blue third (F–F♯).

- After five measures, the trombone enters with the subject transposed to E (measures 8–13). The piano shifts to that chord, and the contrabass plays the countersubject, which also emphasizes blue thirds and sevenths.

- At measure 13, the E♭ alto saxophone presents the subject transposed to A (it sounds a major sixth lower than notated). The piano moves to A, as does the countersubject in the trombone. The contrabass introduces a second countersubject, which again plays on the blue third and seventh.

- At measure 18, the trumpet enters with the subject back on D, the piano shifts again, the saxophone takes up the countersubject and the trombone the second countersubject, and the contrabass harmonizes with the latter, adding to the mix yet another melody full of blue notes.

The process here is both a very proper fugue and a cunning imitation of the multiple layers of melody typical of group improvisation in New Orleans–style jazz of the early 1920s. The harmonic motion (I–II–V–I) evokes a standard progression in classical music but also hints at the I, IV–I, V–I progression of the twelve-bar blues (see NAWM 182). The rhythms are jazzy but also modern and polyrhythmic. The five-measure-long phrases established by the entrances of the fugue subject overlap the four-measure-long ostinato in piano and percussion, compounding the conflict of beat groupings mentioned above. As we will see, similar conflicts of phrase length appear throughout the tableau, suggesting that they are part of Milhaud's depiction of chaos.

The second section (measures 24–45) is not fugal, but superimposes material in layers:

- The section begins with a melody in D in cello and oboe (measures 24–28) that again features blue notes and derives from the tail end of the fugue subject (compare the contrabass in measures 6–8). It appears over three layers of ostinato with different cycles: (1) a pattern in parallel thirds in D major recurring every six beats (piano right hand, horn, and saxophone); (2) descending parallel triads in C major recurring every five beats (piano left hand, contrabass, trombone, and bassoon); and (3) D major/minor chords in violins and timpani with drum patterns, all recurring irregularly. The superimposition of two keys, C and D, is an instance of polytonality, which Milhaud uses frequently.

- In the rest of the section, the clarinet presents the fugue subject four times, shortened to four measures, in keys that travel up the circle of fifths: F (measure 29), C (measure 33), G (measure 37), and D (measure 41; note that the clarinet is in B♭ and sounds a whole step lower than written). The first and third of these statements reverse the major and minor thirds in the subject. The other instruments accompany with a repeating figuration that recurs in a 6+6+8 beat pattern, thus stretching over five measures, recreating the conflict of five- versus four-measure phrases from the first section. As part of this recurring idea, the bass line works its way down chromatically from F (measure 29) to C (measure 34) to G (measure 39), delaying the arrival on D until the first beat of the third section. Near the end of this progression, the trombone starts to add glissandi, a boisterous, jazzy touch (measures 39–45).

The third section (measures 46–59) returns to the tonic and combines elements from the other two sections. It begins with a varied restatement of the beginning of the second section, with elements rearranged; for example, the parallel triads are now in the D Dorian mode, the parallel third figure in the C Phrygian mode. In measure 50, these two parts of the texture return to their original relationship, and the fugue subject returns in the violins in its original key of D. At measure 54, the two violins are in stretto, with the fugue subject in the keys of A and D, while all the other parts reach a peak of intensity. Then, all of a sudden, the music quiets and moves on to the next tableau.

Throughout the ballet, Milhaud's synthesis of jazz and classical elements is masterful, showing that he understood jazz and blues well and saw how elements drawn from them could be used and reinterpreted in a neoclassical context. He was among the first classically trained composers to draw on jazz or blues, and he inspired many others to follow his example.

Kurt Weill (1900–1950)

Die Dreigroschenoper (The Threepenny Opera): Prelude,
Die Moritat von Mackie Messer

Opera

1928

186

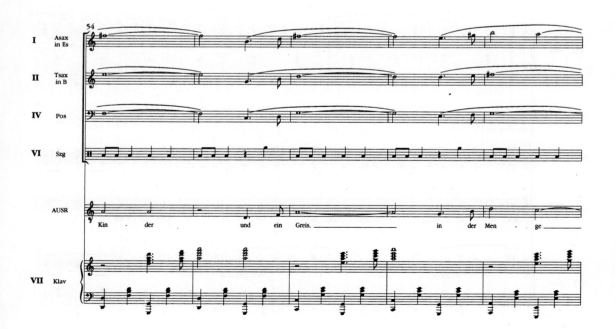

AUSRUFER [TOWN CRIER]

Und der Haifisch, der hat Zähne,   Now the shark, it has teeth,
Und die trägt er im Gesicht,   and it carries them in plain sight,
Und Macheath, der hat ein Messer,   and Macheath, he has a knife,
Doch das Messer sieht man nicht.   but the knife you never see.

An 'nem schönen blauen Sonntag   On a beautiful blue-sky Sunday
Liegt ein toter Mann am Strand,   a dead man lies in the Strand [a London street],
Und ein Mensch geht um die Ecke,   and a man goes around the corner,
Den man Mackie Messer nennt.   the man they call Mack the Knife.

0:55 Und Schmul Meier bleibt verschwunden,   And Samuel Meier has disappeared,
Und so mancher reiche Mann,   such a rich man,
Und sein Geld hat Mackie Messer,   and Mack the Knife has his money,
Dem man nichts beweisen kann.   but no one can prove anything.

1:22 Jenny Towler ward gefunden   Jenny Towler was found
Mit 'nem Messer in der Brust,   with a knife in her chest,
Und am Kai geht Mackie Messer,   and on the wharf goes Mack the Knife
Der von allem nichts gewüßt.   who [says he] knew nothing about it.

1:49 Und das große Feuer in Soho,   And the big fire in Soho,
Sieben Kinder und ein Greis,   [which killed] seven children and an old man,
In der Menge Mackie Messer, den   in the crowd was Mack the Knife, who
Man nichts fragt und der nichts weiß.   no one questioned and who knows nothing.

2:16 Und die minderjähr'ge Witwe,   And the underage widow,
Deren Namen jeder weiß,   whose name everyone knows,
wachte auf und war geschändet,   woke up and was raped,
Mackie, welches war dein Preis?   Mack, was that your prize?

— BERTOLT BRECHT

Die Dreigroschenoper, better known to English-speaking audiences as *The Threepenny Opera*, was modeled on John Gay's *The Beggar's Opera* (NAWM 109), which premiered in London in 1728 and became the most famous and frequently performed ballad opera of the eighteenth and nineteenth centuries. *The Beggar's Opera* was revived in London in 1920 with great success, running for 1,463 performances over three years. German dramatist Bertholt Brecht saw it as a vehicle for a critique of modern capitalist society. He asked his assistant Elisabeth Hauptmann to create a German translation, which he then adapted, adding texts by fifteenth-century French poet François Villon to create a montage of borrowed sources. Kurt Weill provided music that was equally eclectic, incorporating just one of the melodies from the original ballad opera and otherwise combining a variety of sounds and genres, including neoclassicism, operetta, jazz, and popular song styles of the 1920s. Through the variety of references and the ironic distortions of familiar styles, Weill's music combines with Brecht's play to hold up a mirror to modern society and offer a critique.

As in a ballad opera, the dialogue of *Die Dreigroschenoper* is spoken, with musical numbers interspersed. The original cast members were not opera singers but singing actors whose backgrounds were in spoken theater, operetta, or cabaret, including Weill's wife Lotte Lenya. They were accompanied by the Lewis Ruth Band, a seven-member group of European jazz studio musicians, who played on the stage in full view of the audience, exposing the instrumentalists who in traditional opera were usually hidden in the pit. Both the nonoperatic singing and the visible band joined with elements of the play and of the music to create an alienating effect that highlighted the artificiality of opera and thus commented on the genre and its affectations, in a way very similar to *The Beggar's Opera* itself.

The premiere in Berlin on August 31, 1928, was poorly attended. Ernest Josef Aufricht, the young impresario backing the production, even predicted that "the show would close after the first night, if not actually during it." But over the next two years *Die Dreigroschenoper* ran for over 350 performances, and in its first season there were more than fifty new productions all over Europe and overseas from New York to Tokyo. It quickly became the most successful musical theater work of its time.

The opera revolves around the character of Macheath, or Mack the Knife, a notorious gang leader infamous for his gruesome crimes and for seducing and abandoning one woman after another. *Die Moritat von Mackie Messer* (The Ballad of Mack the Knife) is the first sung number in the opera, appearing as part of the Prologue to Act I. The title "moritat" combines the Latin word for "die" (*mori*) with the German word for "deed" (*Tat*) and places the song in the long tradition of murder ballads, narrative songs about a murder. In this case, the song describes several of Macheath's murderous deeds and the impossible task of catching him, because unlike a shark, whose teeth are readily visible and poised to bite, Macheath attacks when no one is looking. The song was a last-minute addition designed to introduce the audience to the violence of the central character before he even takes the stage. Ironically, this song is the most familiar part of the opera, widely performed and recorded as a popular song since the 1950s by artists such as Louis Armstrong and Bobby Darin.

Weill sets the ballad as a strophic song in a mock-popular style, over a light accompaniment that he directs should be performed "in the manner of a barrel organ," an instrument used by street singers in the eighteenth and nineteenth centuries. The whole sixteen-measure melody derives from its opening idea, a simple two-measure phrase with a lilting dotted rhythm leading to two even half notes. The idea repeats and is gradually varied, at first with rising skips and steps and then with falling steps and sevenths. The short phrases, frequent rests, and lilting rhythm give the melody a nonchalant character that is an apt description for Macheath but strongly at odds with the chilling text. The harmony seems simple and tonal, tracing familiar progressions in C major (I–ii$^4_2$–V^9–I, vi–ii^7–V^9–I), but almost every chord has four or five notes, and the tonic chord always has an added sixth on A, making it sound less than final. The melody also generally avoids cadencing on the tonic C and ends phrases instead on A or D. Concluding on A over a C added sixth chord avoids closure and makes the melody sound like it could go on forever; indeed, each verse leads right on into the next one in a seemingly endless cycle that neatly depicts the unending cycle of Macheath's crimes. The melody is virtually unchanged each time it repeats, except that the dynamic level gradually rises, along with the number of notes that are sustained to link one two-measure unit to the next (compare measures 8–11, 25–32, 41–48, 55–64, and 65–88 to see the gradual change from rests between units to sustained tones connecting them). Both the rising dynamic level and the sustained notes increase intensity until, after the final verse, the dynamic level suddenly drops to *piano* as the second half of the melody repeats (measures 81–88).

Under the cycling melody, the accompaniment changes. The first two strophes are accompanied by the harmonium, imitating the barrel organ. For the third strophe, the keyboard player switches to piano, playing a ragtime figure, and is joined by banjo, light percussion (suspended cymbal and snare drum), and the trombone doubling the vocal line. Percussion and trombone drop out for the fourth strophe, as the banjo becomes more active. For the fifth strophe, alto and tenor saxophones and the trombone follow the vocal line in chords, echoed a measure later by the piano, as percussion returns (with tom-tom and cymbal) and the banjo drops out. In the last full strophe the banjo reenters, trumpet and trombone support the voice, soprano and tenor saxophone at first echo the voice and then play a countermelody, and the piano adds parallel minor triads in chromatic motion (measure 66), then diatonic parallel open fifths and octaves—both quite alien to the popular style being parodied here, like an overlay of parallel chords à la Debussy. The percussion now includes bass drum, cymbal, and wood block. The percussion is notated on a single staff (marked Schlagzeug, player VI), with each instrument on its own line or space: suspended cymbal on the space above the staff, wood block on the top space, snare drum on the second line, tom-tom on the third space down, and bass drum on the bottom line.

The choice of instruments, and the constantly changing instrumentation, gradually transform the song, replacing the barrel organ style from the beginning with the sound of 1920s jazz. Piano, banjo, percussion, trombone, trumpet, and saxophones were all prominent in jazz bands of the time (see NAWM 183 and 184). The tempo indication "Blues-Tempo" also alludes to a current jazz style. The gradual change from old-fashioned barrel organ style to a parody of modern jazz neatly captures the whole project of bringing an eighteenth-century ballad opera into the modern age.

Paul Hindemith (1895–1963)

Symphony Mathis der Maler: Second movement, *Grablegung* (Entombment)

Symphony

1933–34

187

From Paul Hindemith, *Sämtliche Werke*, vol. 2, fascicle 2, *Orchesterwerke 1932–34*, ed. Stephen Hinton (Mainz: B. Schott's Söhne, 1991), 114–19. © 1934 by Schott Music GmbH & Co. KG. © Renewed. All rights reserved. Used by permission of European American Music Distributors Company, sole U.S. and Canadian agent for Schott Music GmbH & Co. KG.

While Paul Hindemith was writing the libretto for his opera *Mathis der Maler* in 1933, he decided to compose some of the instrumental preludes and interludes for the opera and assemble them into an orchestral work that could be performed to promote the coming opera. This project had a political dimension. Many of his works had been banned from public performance by the new National Socialist (Nazi) government, because of their radical texts or modernist style, and as a result the opera was unlikely to be staged in Germany. But Hindemith planned to use a more widely accessible idiom in *Mathis der Maler* and saw the instrumental work as a way to attract support for producing the opera. The second movement, included here, was the first to be composed, in November 1933. The other movements—the overture as the first movement, and a finale consisting of the prelude and other passages destined for the opera's sixth tableau—were completed by February 1934, and the three-movement *Symphony Mathis der Maler* was premiered on March 12 by the Berlin Philharmonic Orchestra with Wilhelm Furtwängler conducting. It was a great success with the public and critics alike, and it remains one of the most popular and frequently performed symphonies composed between the wars. The critical reception was remarkable, because writers of differing ideological bents praised the piece for different reasons: to pro-Nazi reviewers, it showed Hindemith's turn away from his more dissonant earlier works, but to supporters of new music, it was a triumph of modernism. Ultimately, Hindemith was condemned by Nazi propaganda minister Joseph Goebbels as an "atonal noise-maker," and his music was banned. The opera was finally premiered in Switzerland in May 1938, and Hindemith moved there that September.

The opera is based on the life of Mathias Grünewald (Mathis Neithardt, ca. 1470–1528), painter of the Isenheim Altarpiece in Colmar, Alsace, and the symphony was linked directly with the altarpiece itself. In a program note for the symphony's premiere, Hindemith observed that "the three movements are related to the corresponding panels for the Isenheim Altarpiece. I tried through musical means to approach the same feeling that the pictures arouse in the viewer." Of the middle movement, based on the panel showing the entombment of Christ after the Crucifixion (shown in HWM, Figure 35.3, page 883), he wrote: "In the 'Entombment,' the still, pale lifelessness of the first theme [measure 1] is contrasted with the warmth and gentleness of the second [measure 16]." This same music appears in the opera as an interlude in the seventh tableau, after the death of Mathis's beloved Regina, and its first and final sections are adapted as the last music in the opera, when Mathis places his few possessions in a trunk, including his paints and brushes, and prepares to die.

The movement flows like a single thought, aided by a pervasive rhythmic figure— quarter note, eighth rest, and eighth note (or its equivalent, dotted quarter and eighth)—that appears in almost every measure. This gently pulsing rhythm, like a very slow heartbeat, captures the cold stillness Hindemith meant to evoke at the beginning, reflecting the lifeless body being lowered into the tomb in Grünewald's painting, but also conveys the feelings of solace that emerge later in the movement. In a variant, heard throughout the opening theme, the eighth note is divided into two sixteenths. The tender theme of the middle section (measure 16) has more rhythmic variety, suggesting life and warmth: a diminution of the original rhythm (dotted eighth and sixteenth), triplets, and pulsing eighths in the accompaniment. The reprise of the opening theme (measure 28) adds regular sixteenth notes in an accompanying line, which combines with the full orchestration and *forte* dynamic level to suggest grandeur. The final section uses rhythmic figures from the first two sections, gradually diminishing in rhythmic variety until only the original rhythm remains, gently rocking between chords.

The form reflects this sense of continuous flow, offering open-endedness rather than closure:

Section	A			B					A'		C	
Motive	a	a'	b	c	c	a"	c'	a'''	a''''		d	e
Tone center	C → G♯	C	C♯	C♯		mod			Bb → F♯		C♯	C♯
Measure	1	6	10	16	20	23	24	26	28		34	39

The opening phrase (a) returns frequently, but it is varied and at a higher dynamic level each time it appears. The first two statements lead in different directions to music we never hear again, giving the first section no finality. The contrasting middle theme (c) is heard twice in oboe and flute over pizzicato strings, then the opening measures of the two themes alternate until the first theme returns for its final appearance. It sounds like a culmination, rounding off an ABA' form. But then the music continues, presenting new material that draws on the rhythmic and melodic figures already heard. Simultaneously new and yet familiar, this added section makes a fitting end to the contemplation of entombment: return is not possible, and one must move on.

The harmony is neotonal rather than tonal. It includes open fifths and octaves, triads, chords built on fourths, and dissonances of a second or seventh, all common devices for Hindemith. These are arranged in phrases according to his theory of "harmonic fluctuation," in which relatively consonant chords move toward greater dissonance and then gradually or suddenly move back to consonance. Most chords are pentatonic or diatonic, and most motion between chords is by step, making the flow from chord to chord sound logical and right, even if it could not be predicted in advance. The fifth- and fourth-chords of the first theme sound stark and hollow, evoking the emotional numbness that often follows the death of a beloved friend, while the third-based chords of measures 10–14 and of the final section (measures 34–45) sound warm and consoling in comparison, even when they are dissonant. Throughout, the orchestration heightens the contrasts between themes and reinforces the mood, from dry muted strings at the beginning to the full orchestra with brass at the grand final statement of the main theme.

Tone centers are suggested through arrival on chords that include a prominent octave and fifth above the lowest note, with or without the third. Thus the movement begins on C, cadences on G♯ in measure 4, returns to C in measure 6, and moves on to C♯ in measure 10. The tone center of the middle section is less clear, but the bass line and the mostly diatonic melody suggest the Dorian mode on C♯. The A' section begins on B♭ and cadences emphatically on F♯. By this point, the harmony has traversed a tritone (C–F♯), echoing the overall progress of the symphony as a whole, which moves a tritone from G in the first movement to D♭ at the end of the third. But instead of ending on F♯ or returning to the opening tone center C, Hindemith begins and ends the final section on C♯, enharmonically the same as the last movement. Like the form, the harmony suggests moving forward, rather than closure, perhaps reflecting the knowledge of anyone viewing Grünewald's altarpiece that the entombment is not the end of the story.

Sergey Prokofiev (1891–1953)

Alexander Nevsky, Op. 78: Fourth movement,
Arise, ye Russian People

Cantata (film score)

1938–39

Two years after moving to the Soviet Union in 1936, Sergey Prokofiev was commissioned to compose the music for *Alexander Nevsky*, the first sound film by the renowned Soviet director Sergei Eisenstein (1898–1948). Alexander Nevsky was a thirteenth-century hero who as a young man led Russian armies to victories over invaders from Sweden in 1240 and from Germany in 1241–42. In the latter conflict Nevsky employed a brilliant strategy that enticed the Germans onto the slippery ice of the frozen Lake Pepius, where Nevsky's foot soldiers overwhelmed the German force and many of the heavily armored German knights drowned after cracking through the ice. Eisenstein's film focuses on this critical event in Russian history, and the epic battle serves as the spectacular climax. Made at a time of growing tensions in Europe just prior to World War II, this film showing Russians' valiant defense of their homeland was a powerful propaganda tool warning of potential invasion by Nazi Germany and of the sacrifices that would be needed to repel them. The film was completed in November 1938 and premiered in December.

As was his frequent practice, Prokofiev subsequently arranged excerpts from the film score as a concert work, which was premiered in May 1939 and published that year. He created a cantata, rather than an orchestral suite, from *Alexander Nevsky* because the film score contains a substantial amount of music for chorus, which takes part in the story and also comments on the events. The cantata contains seven excerpts from the film score. The order of the movements follows the chronology of the film and thus provides a miniature retelling of the story. The music is derived from two types of music in the film: *diegetic music* or *source music*, which is part of the story and is heard or performed by the characters in the film, and *nondiegetic music* or *underscoring*, which establishes a mood, character, or situation (like music in an opera) and is heard only by the audience. Much of the music in the cantata is lifted directly from the film score without extensive alteration other than some minor cuts, extensions through repetition, and rearrangements of material.

Prokofiev's music for the film and cantata reflects the doctrine of *socialist realism*, which called for the arts to help strengthen the Soviet state by celebrating socialism, progress, and the people, using techniques that were directly accessible to the masses. This doctrine required music that was relatively simple, immediately comprehensible, full of melody, and often folklike in style. It did not preclude dissonance or unusual effects if the meaning was clear and appropriate.

The fourth movement of the cantata, included here, is heard in the film when Nevsky gathers his army, underscoring scenes of peasants leaving their farms and their labors to take up whatever weapons they could find to use against the invaders. The text exhorts the people of Russia to fight to the death to defend their homeland. Both of the principal themes recur later in the film, where they accompany the rejoicing of the victorious Russian people. The movement is in ABA' form. Both A sections are also small ABA' forms, although each has different material in the middle section:

Section	Introduction	A			B		A'		
Music		a	b	a'	c	c'	a"	d	a'''
Key	Eb	Eb	Cb → bb	Eb	D		Eb	Cb → ab	Eb
Measure	1	6	14	22	34	50	66	74	82

The brief, clamorous orchestral introduction establishes a mood of fervency with conflicting rhythmic pulses, orchestration that suggests trumpet calls and pealing church bells, and a harmonic clash between a reiterated Bb in the winds and brass and pizzicato second-inversion G-major chords in the strings. The latter imitates the seven-string Russian guitar, which has the same tuning (*D–G–B–d–g–b–d'*), and the sound of plucked string chords continues throughout the A sections. The implied polytonality, double chromatic neighbors in the trumpets, and glissandos in the xylophone are modernist touches that recall Prokofiev's dissonant pre-Soviet style, but they work here as a noisy call to action within a socialist realist idiom.

Once the chorus enters, the music unfolds in regular four-measure phrases. The energetic A section has a folklike character, with its repetitive melody, limited range, and foot-stomping accents. The opening tune (measures 6–13) contains four two-measure units, each beginning with an upward gesture that mirrors the repetitions of the word "arise." The choral writing is homorhythmic, with just two independent lines: the sopranos and tenors present the melody, and the altos and basses provide a supportive counterpoint. The orchestra reinforces the accents in the chorus. Prokofiev's simplified musical language is evident in the diatonic melody and harmony, yet subtle features demonstrate his craft. The tune has modal characteristics, using the notes of the Eb-major scale and concluding on Eb but emphasizing G and C to create a sense of ambiguity between Eb major and C minor. This is reinforced by the harmony, which features traditional triads but unexpected progressions. The repeated Bb in the introduction and the dominant seventh chord on Bb on the last quarter note of measure 5 indicate the key of Eb, but the deceptive resolution in measure 6 suggests C minor, anticipated by the G-major triads in the introduction. Even after a solid V–I cadence on Eb in measures 9–10, the music still sounds modal because it emphasizes the subdominant Ab. Simple it may look and sound, but Prokofiev makes sure that there are enough unexpected touches to keep the listener's interest.

The middle portion of the first section (measures 14–21) moves to Cb major and then Bb minor. The harmony includes occasional dissonances, while the melody, sung by the men of the choir, retains a modal character. The melodic accents are emphasized by drumrolls, harp chords, and rapid arpeggios in the winds. The opening melody returns with greater reinforcement from the orchestra, and the A section closes on a sustained Eb-major chord.

The B section (measures 34–65) is in a different tonal world, an untroubled D major. A mostly conjunct melody is sung by the altos over the warm accompaniment of bowed strings and pulsating horns, then repeated by the basses under ascending scales in the winds. Again, both melody and harmony are unpredictable enough to keep our interest and suggest the modal qualities of folk song. Although the section projects a calm, uplifting mood, the text is no less resolute and warlike.

When the A section returns, the women and men sing antiphonally at first. The middle portion, sung by the women, introduces a new melody and features the striking addition of a scalar figure in triplets played by the xylophone. By changing all these elements rather than simply repeating the first section, Prokofiev conveys a sense of forward progress that fits the film scene and creates a more convincing close.

The result is both effective film music and effective state propaganda, in a language fully adapted to the doctrine of socialist realism. It is also well suited for amateur choirs—it makes more demands on the orchestral players, who are likely to be professionals, than it does on the choir or on the listener—and thus serves another purpose as well. Prokofiev uses a traditional orchestra augmented by some unusual percussion (such as bells and tam-tam, a flat gong) and a saxophone, an instrument that he used often in his Soviet orchestral compositions. In this score, the transposing instruments (English horn, clarinets, saxophone, trumpets, and horns) are notated at sounding pitch.

Dmitri Shostakovich (1906–1975)

Symphony No. 5, Op. 47: Second movement, Allegretto

Symphony

1937

189

189 DMITRI SHOSTAKOVICH • Symphony No. 5, Op. 47: Second movement, Allegretto

189 DMITRI SHOSTAKOVICH · Symphony No. 5, Op. 47: Second movement, Allegretto

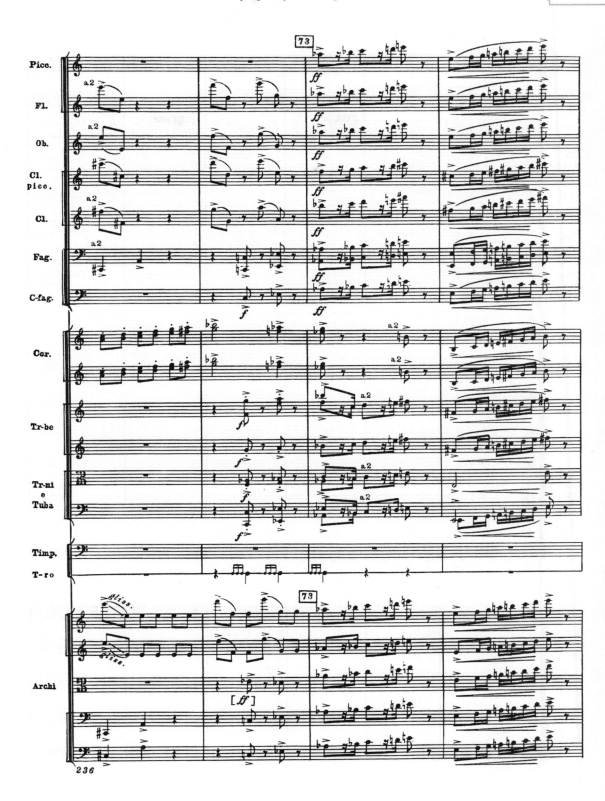

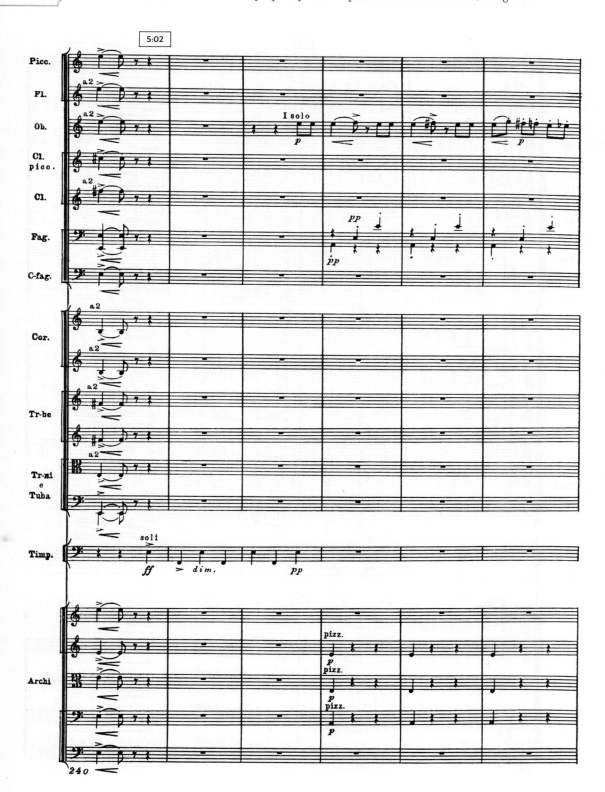

Dmitri Shostakovich earned international recognition at the age of nineteen with performances of his First Symphony (1926) and enjoyed celebrity status in the Soviet Union throughout the next decade. Thus he was stunned when in 1936 the Communist Party newspaper *Pravda*, at the instigation of Soviet dictator Joseph Stalin, suddenly denounced the modernist compositional style of his opera *Lady Macbeth of the Mtsensk District*. Unsure of his future in a time of political purges, Shostakovich shelved his already completed but thoroughly modernist Fourth Symphony and composed his Fifth Symphony in a more moderate idiom. His desire to regain state approval was encapsulated in a critic's description of the piece as "a Soviet artist's reply to just criticism." The work was premiered on November 21, 1937, in Leningrad (now St. Petersburg) by the Leningrad Philharmonic, conducted by Evgeny Mravinsky. The reception by the audience was overwhelming, and Shostakovich was once again viewed favorably by the communist regime.

Compared to many of his earlier works, the Fifth Symphony represents a retrenchment of style, with simpler formal procedures and more direct expression. While this change in approach may be linked to political pressures, it also represents a new idea that Shostakovich had been developing, inspired by studies of Mahler. The symphony, set in a classical four-movement structure, evokes the heroic spirit of the orchestral works of Beethoven and Tchaikovsky.

The second movement, marked Allegretto, is a scherzo in the style of an Austrian Ländler (as are several of Mahler's scherzos). For the most part, Shostakovich follows the form of the dance movement in a classical symphony, as can be observed in the diagram below. The overall form is ternary (Scherzo-Trio-Scherzo), with a trio in written-out binary form (i.e., with the repetitions written out and slightly varied rather than marked with repeat signs) and a scherzo in modified binary form.

Section	Scherzo							Trio				Scherzo							Coda
Music	A			B		B'		C	C'	D	D'	A'			B''		B'		
	a	b	a'	c	d	c'	d	e	e'	f	f'	a''	b'	a'''	c''	d'	c'	d	e''
Key	a			c	F	c	F	C				a			c♯	F♯	c	F	a
Measure	1	11	29	45	56	64	75	87	103	119	138	157	167	185	201	212	220	231	241

(Note that the measure numbers in this score are below the bottom staff rather than above the top staff as usual.)

Mahler's influence can be heard in the orchestration, the jarring contrasts of mood, the occasionally satirical tone, and the use of counterpoint. The vigorous, rather awkward, and tonally ambiguous melody in the low strings at the beginning of the movement introduces a number of motives that will be incorporated in later thematic ideas, such as the rising scale and the repeated notes. The horns (measure 11) usher in a new, playful, or even sarcastic tune played primarily by the E-flat clarinet. The upper woodwinds present another idea with repeated notes (measure 20), and the bassoon follows with an extended solo. In Mahleresque fashion, the bassoon melody obscures the return of the opening low string theme at measure 29, and suggestions of the woodwind figures appear in the violins at measure 37. Thus the first part of the scherzo continually presents and develops ideas, yet it still hints at the structure one would expect at the beginning of a scherzo: a musical period that is stated (measures 1–28) and repeated (measures 29–44), constituting the first half of a binary form.

An abrupt shift to C minor marks the beginning of the second part of the scherzo (measure 45). Two divergent ideas are presented and then repeated: a crude waltz and a boisterous march (at measure 56). The first of these incorporates two $\frac{4}{4}$ measures that comically offset the established triple meter, and the second, with blaring horns, suggests a military fanfare. In the repetition of the waltz, the winds and strings reverse roles. Although the two halves of the scherzo differ in mood and melodic content, several recurring motives link them together. One notable example is the trilled figure in measures 14–15, which returns prominently in measures 52–54.

For those who know of and sympathize with Shostakovich's political situation at the time he wrote this symphony, the comic touches here—such as the rowdy fanfare—may suggest that he was mocking the government that threatened to censor him. Some have interpreted this symphony as a statement of dissent against government control and repression. Yet the circumstances were far too dangerous for anyone to mock Stalin, and we should be cautious about reading into the music meanings the composer may not have intended. More likely, Shostakovich was emulating the jesting, ironic tone of Mahler's scherzos, and leaving it to the listener to decide what the music might mean.

The trio begins with an elegant waltz tune played by a solo violin and accompanied by a harp and pizzicato cello. In the repetition of this sixteen-measure tune by the flute, the delicate mood is enhanced by glissandos in the harp and low strings. Unison strings rudely interrupt with the second half of the trio (at measure 119), which shifts briefly to B major for a phrase from the waltz theme (measures 129–33). On the repetition, the unison figure is given to the woodwinds.

Shostakovich continues to reverse the roles of winds and strings at the reprise of the scherzo. The opening bass melody is now in bassoon and contrabassoon, and pizzicato strings play the themes first introduced by horns and woodwinds. In a nod from one Fifth Symphony to another, Shostakovich's distinctive timbre of bassoon with pizzicato strings recalls the corresponding section in the scherzo of Beethoven's Symphony No. 5. The second part of the scherzo begins a half-step higher than it was originally presented, in C♯ minor, and the march tune, now in F♯ major, is given to the trumpets. Order is restored with the repetition, as the original key areas return and the horns play the march theme one last time. The coda opens with a brief recollection of the trio melody, which is abruptly and forcibly brought to a final cadence.

Although the overall harmonic scheme of the movement is traditional (A minor, with the relative major C in the trio), Shostakovich's harmony is full of modern elements. Alongside the occasional dominant-tonic cadence, there are many moments when the harmony takes an unexpected turn, lurching onto a new chord or into a new key with little or no preparation. Examples include the abrupt shifts of key mentioned above and, on a more local level, the succession in the C-major trio theme of A major, G major, F minor, and G minor chords leading right back to C major (measures 97–102). Ultimately, the tonal centers seem more often asserted than established, as if this were neotonal music pretending to be tonal—an apt metaphor for a modernist composer trying to conform to the restrictions imposed by a totalitarian state.

In writing for orchestra, Shostakovich had an array of outstanding musicians available to him in the Soviet Union, which is reflected in his virtuoso treatment of all sections, including the percussion. With its technical demands and wide range of emotions, this symphony remains popular with audiences and continues to test the limits of modern professional orchestras.

Heitor Villa-Lobos (1887–1959)

Bachianas Brasileiras No. 5: No. 1, Aria (Cantilena)

Vocalise and song

1938

190

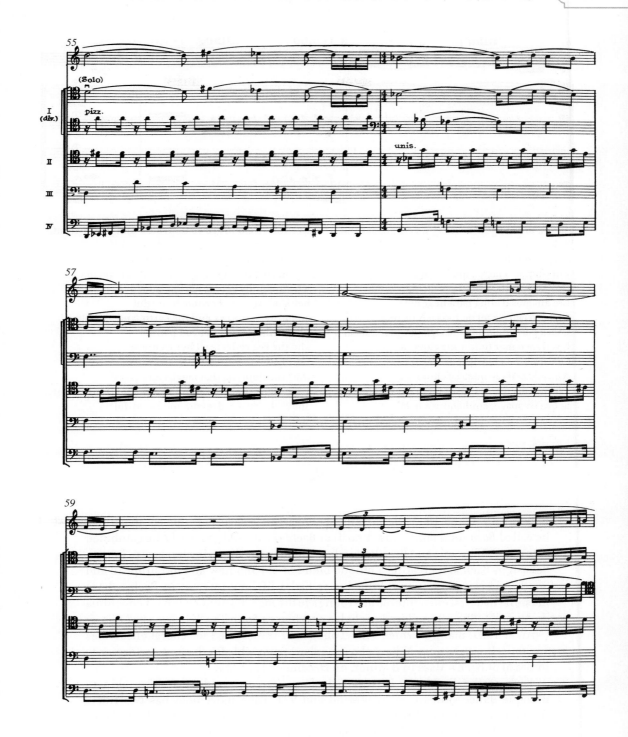

Tarde, uma nuvem rósea lenta e transparente,	Evening, a cloud grows rosy, slow and transparent,
Sobre o espaço, sonhadora e bela!	above the space, dreamy and beautiful!
Surge no infinito a lua docemente,	The moon rises into the infinite, softly,
Enfeitando a tarde, qual meiga donzela	decorating the evening, like a delicate maiden
Que se apresta e alinda sonhadoramente,	who dreamily gets ready and adorns herself,
Em anseios d'alma para ficar bela,	her soul eager to become beautiful,
Grita ao céo e a terra, toda a Natureza!	shouting to the sky and the earth, and all Nature!
Cala a passarada aos seus tristes queixumes,	The birds quiet at her sad plaints
E reflete o mar toda a sua riqueza . . .	and the sea reflects all her richness . . .
Suave a luz da lua desperta agora,	Gently the moonlight now awakens
A cruel saudade que ri e chora!	the cruel longing that laughs and cries!
Tarde, uma nuvem rósea lenta e transparente,	Evening, a cloud grows rosy, slow and transparent,
Sobre o espaço, sonhadora e bela!	above the space, dreamy and beautiful!

— RUTH VALLADARES CORREA

Between 1930 and 1945, Heitor Villa-Lobos wrote a series of nine compositions he called *Bachianas brasileiras* (Brazilian Bachianas). In these works he combined elements of Baroque and Brazilian styles, simultaneously paying homage to Johann Sebastian Bach and creating a unique blend of old and new and of European and South American traditions. Villa-Lobos had a lifelong interest in Bach, whose music he had first encountered at a young age through his Aunt Zizinha (Leopoldina do Amaral). She often played preludes and fugues from *The Well-Tempered Clavier* (NAWM 102), many of which Villa-Lobos later transcribed for choral ensembles and for cello orchestras. Villa-Lobos was also responsible for the first performance in Brazil of Bach's Mass in B Minor, on December 11, 1935.

Each of the *Bachianas brasileiras* is formally conceived as a suite, akin to Baroque dance suites (see NAWM 88 and 97). Each movement has two titles; the first is a traditional Baroque genre (such as aria, dance, prelude, fantasia, or fugue), while the second is a Brazilian national genre (such as *cantilena*, *martelo*, *embolada*, or *desafio*). The double reference is also present in musical style. The recurring pulsations and syncopations of Brazilian popular music seem to share an affinity with the motoric rhythms common in Bach's music. Similarly, throughout the *Bachianas brasileiras* Villa-Lobos uses a harmonic language that is essentially tonal, as in Bach's music as well as Brazilian popular styles, adding color through passing tones and anticipations. Sequences and ornaments recall common devices in Baroque music but become fresh when paired with Brazilian rhythms.

Bachianas brasileiras No. 5 features a soprano and an orchestra of cellos in four sections (Celli I, II, III, and IV in the score), which are often further divided. Villa-Lobos had learned to play cello as a child, studying with his father, and it was one of his favorite instruments. This piece has two movements. "Aria (Cantilena)" was composed in 1938 and features a text by Brazilian writer and singer Ruth Valladares Correa, who sang the soprano solo when the movement was premiered in Rio De Janeiro on March 25, 1939. "Dansa (Martelo)," composed in 1945, sets a text by Brazilian poet Manuel Bandeira. The two movements were first performed together in October 1947 and published that year in New York. Villa-Lobos dedicated the piece to his companion Arminda Neves d'Almeida, whom he called Mindinha.

"Aria (Cantilena)" begins with a descending bass line in celli III, which briefly invokes the sound of a Baroque chaconne, passacaglia, or lament. This descending progression, paired with pizzicato articulations in celli II and IV, also suggests a picked style of Brazilian guitar performance known as *ponteio*. When the bass pattern changes in measure 3, celli IV introduce syncopated rhythms, and the soprano begins the melody, joined by celli I an octave lower. The pairing of celli I with the soprano, who vocalizes on "ah," provides depth and warmth. (The high tessitura for celli I and II requires them to be written in tenor clef, a C clef in which middle C is the second line from the top.) With long, arching phrases, the melody gives the impression of an improvisation that draws simultaneously on influences from Brazilian folk and popular music, from the long cantabile lines of Italian opera (see NAWM 146), and from the highly embellished vocal lines of Bach arias (see NAWM 103b and especially 104d).

The form is also reminiscent of Bach's arias, which usually follow the *da capo aria* form typical of the early eighteenth century, in which the first section (A) repeats after a contrasting middle section (B). Typically the A section of a da capo aria contains two vocal statements framed by instrumental ritornellos that feature the same melodic ideas as the voice. In "Aria (Cantabile)," the main melody appears twice in the A section, at measure 3 in the soprano and celli I and at measure 23 in a solo cello, separated by an interlude in soprano and celli I that spins out ideas from the main melody (measures 14–22). While this shape does not exactly follow the model of an A section for a Baroque aria, it does invoke two of its most prominent characteristics: the alternation of voice with instruments, often stating the same material, and the presence of two vocal statements (here, the main melody and the interlude). The reprise of the A section at measure 51 has only the main melody, now with the soprano humming, joined by half the players of celli I.

The B section (measures 35–50) contrasts in almost every way with the A section. Instead of a vocalise on "ah," the voice sings the poem by Correa, which describes a beautiful midnight scene of clouds and moon reflected in the sea. The moonlight arouses an unexplained nostalgia that prompts both laughter and tears, and in retrospect we understand the yearning, almost lamenting melody of the A section with new insight. (The singing English translation in the score, by Harvey Officer, keeps most of the images of the original Portuguese poem but slightly alters the sense of some phrases.) The texture of the B section is also very different: instead of a long, spun-out, supple melody, the vocal line now mostly recites on repeated notes, tracing a gradual melodic descent from E to A (measures 35–40), climbing back up to E (measures 41–42), then repeating the descent (measures 43–47) and reciting the opening lines of the poem on the tonic A. The accompaniment is no longer contrapuntal as in the A section, but instead features chromatically descending parallel chords over sustained tones in the bass. The more chromatic harmonic language and faster tempo join with the declamation of the poem on repeated notes to create an intensity that resolves with the return of the A material at measure 51.

This aria has become the best-known movement of all the *Bachianas brasileiras*, Villa-Lobos's most familiar piece, and one of the most frequently recorded classical works of the twentieth century. Villa-Lobos himself arranged three other versions of the movement: for nine cellos, for soprano and guitar, and for soprano and piano. Other arrangers have created versions for other mediums, including organ and band.

Silvestre Revueltas (1899–1940)

Homenaje a Federico García Lorca, First movement:
Baile (Dance)

Suite for chamber orchestra

1936

From Silvestre Revueltas, *Homenaje a Federico García Lorca* (New York: Southern Music Publishing Company, 1958), 3–15.

Silvestre Revueltas composed *Homenaje a Federico García Lorca* (Homage to Federico García Lorca) in response to Lorca's assassination on August 19, 1936, in the early weeks of the Spanish Civil War. Lorca (1898–1936), one of the most famous Spanish poets and playwrights of his generation, was an advocate for the poor and disenfranchised and a supporter of the Spanish Republic, the democratically elected government of Spain established in 1931 after the abdication of the king. After years of conflict between left-wing and right-wing parties, five rightist generals organized a military coup in July 1936, precipitating three years of civil war between their coalition of Nationalists and those who sided with the Republic. Because of his liberal views, Lorca was arrested soon after the war began and was killed in secret by a Nationalist militia. Like many Mexicans, Revueltas sympathized with the Republic and was a great admirer of Lorca's poetry and theatrical works. Upon hearing of Lorca's death, he began work on his *Homenaje* for chamber orchestra. Rehearsals began by late October at the conservatory in Mexico City and were quickly followed by performances on November 14 at the Palacio de Bellas Artes in Mexico City and December 5 at the Teatro Degollado in Guadalajara.

The following year Revueltas traveled to Spain as part of a tour in support of the Republican cause organized by a leftist Mexican group, the League of Revolutionary Writers and Artists. *Homenaje* was performed during this tour and received with great enthusiasm. The first performance in Madrid on September 17, 1937, was particularly notable because it coincided with the Teatro Español's production of Lorca's *Mariana Pineda*, a play with revolutionary semtiments. Yet despite its performances in Spain and Mexico throughout the late 1930s, *Homenaje* was not published until 1958.

Homenaje is a masterful blend of popular and classical musical traditions. The unmistakable references to popular styles, both Spanish and Mexican, pay homage to Lorca's sympathy for rural and working-class people. The piece includes three movements: the opening *Baile* (Dance), included here, is followed by *Duelo* (Sorrow) and *Son* (Sound). The combination of serious song and riotous dance in the first movement seems to suggest Lorca's life as poet and dramatist; the mournful second movement, grief at his death; and the vibrant finale, his legacy.

Baile begins with a colorful seven-note chord arpeggiated in the piano, over which a muted trumpet presents a slow, rhythmically free melody marked "like a recitative." This style of melody recalls the flamenco singing tradition *cante jondo* (deep song), which Lorca had celebrated through his *Poema del cante jondo* (Poem of *Cante Jondo*) and his support for the Concurso de Cante Jondo, a flamenco festival in 1922.

At the Allegro, the mood suddenly shifts to a fast dance evoking Mexican mariachi music. Over a repeating pizzicato bass note G and busy accompaniment reminiscent of strumming guitars, the piccolo introduces a catchy tune in G major, then varies the rhythm (measure 16) as the trombone, two trumpets, and tuba play countermelodies. The effect is much like the ensemble improvisations of a mariachi band. The main melody—A in the diagram below—is composed of three ideas (a, b, and c), each based on variants of the same rhythmic pattern. The third idea (c, measure 32) is presented in parallel thirds in E♭ clarinet (sounding a minor third higher than notated) and piccolo (sounding an octave higher), later joined by trumpets an octave lower; melodies in parallel thirds are another characteristic of mariachi music.

Tempo	Lento	Allegro														Lento
Music	Tpt	Intro	A a b c		B	A' a' b' a'		B'	C	A" a" b" c' ext				B"	ext	Tpt
Bass	A♭	G			F♯/G♯	G		F♯/G♯	D	G				F♯/G♯		A♭
Measure	1	2	8 24 32		48	64 80 96		112	128	156 172 180 196 208				224		239

The A melody is answered by the B theme in trombone and tuba, which picks up on the skipping thirds at the end of the A theme and spins them out in a more foursquare, lumbering melody, still in G major. Here the accompaniment changes as well to a much rougher sound, with both chromatic neighbors of G pulsing in the bass—F♯ in the piano and G♯ in the contrabasses—and glissandos in parallel thirds in the first violins, while the second violins arpeggiate an F♯–A–C diminished triad (the triad on the leading tone of G major).

The Allegro cycles through its material three times, like the stanzas of a popular song or repetitions of a dance band, adding new variants and growing more rowdy each time. The second time through (measure 64), the piccolo and E♭ clarinet state the opening idea of the A theme in parallel augmented octaves (or minor ninths) over a rising chromatic line in the tuba, creating a grotesque sound that suggests increasing abandon. Other changes follow: the brass repeats the opening idea, harmonized in mostly dissonant chords (measure 72); the second idea (b) is varied and extended; and the third idea (c) is replaced by a repetition of the first in its grotesque variant (a' in measure 96). The B theme (measure 112) adds more incongruous combinations: tuba and piccolo playing the melody four octaves apart, and then trumpet and tuba in augmented octaves.

Before the third repetition of the main material, a new section appears (C, at measure 128). The melody, passed back and forth between tuba with piccolo and trumpets in parallel thirds, elaborates the skipping thirds and scalar descents of the B theme in a new guise. The melody here is once again in G major, now over a new accompaniment pattern with a pulsing D in the bass and chromatic figures in the piano and violins. This contrasting section between the second and third statements of the main ideas gives the Allegro an overall shape like the AABA form of many popular songs. The quick transition (measures 152–55) back to the final A section is saturated with chromaticism; the pianist executes a glissando on the white notes covering almost the entire range of the instrument while playing clusters on the black notes with his other hand, over an expanding chromatic wedge in the other instruments.

On the final repetition, both the A and B sections are more raucous than ever, building on textures introduced earlier with new dissonances in the accompaniment. Each is lengthened by an extension that further develops the material. A climax of dissonance is reached at measure 196, where the parallel augmented octaves between piccolo and E♭ clarinet (beginning on *d''''* and *d♭'''* in concert pitch) are joined by parallel major sevenths in the trumpets (beginning on *d''* and *e♭'*); another upwelling of dissonance appears at measure 232, where these instruments plus the trombones march a cacophonous chord (*d♭'–b'–d''–a''–e♭''''*) repeatedly down the scale in parallel motion. The dance suddenly breaks off, and after a moment of silence, the movement ends with a repetition of the opening slow melody in muted trumpet, once again contrasting the wild abandon of the dance with the sober lament.

The harmony in this movement is colorfully dissonant, yet ultimately simple in structure. The entire Allegro is centered on G major, colored by chromatic and diatonic neighbor tones. For example, the piano in the A sections constantly sounds the notes of the G major triad but adds E♭, B♭, and E as well, as if decorating G major with the closely related triads of E♭ major and E minor, and in the B sections the key of G is projected primarily by the melody while the accompanying instruments play glissandi or notes that surround and should resolve to the notes of the G major triad. Instead of using harmonic motion to define the form, Revueltas marks his three main thematic areas through their contrasting accompaniments.

The harmony of the Lento sections at the beginning and end of the movement is also colorful. The rolled piano chord is notated as an A♭-major triad in the lower register and an F♯-minor triad with added B in the upper register, so that it combines two triads that are chromatic neighbors to G major. Over this sonority, the slow trumpet melody uses pitches from the key of B major; all but one (A♯) are in the chord below (reading A♭ and E♭ as enharmonic equivalents to G♯ and D♯). The Lento is a perfect frame for the dance, contrasting with it in mood, tempo, style, timbre, and pitch collection, even as the harmony subtly points to a resolution to G major, the central sonority of the Allegro and later the final tonic of the entire *Homenaje a Federico García Lorca*.

Edgard Varèse (1883–1965)

Hyperprism

Work for winds, brass, and percussion

1922–23

From Edgard Varèse, *Hyperprism* (New York: G. Ricordi, 1961). Used by permission of Universal Music MGB Publications.

*) dans le < comme le > la 1ère Trompette legèrement dominante

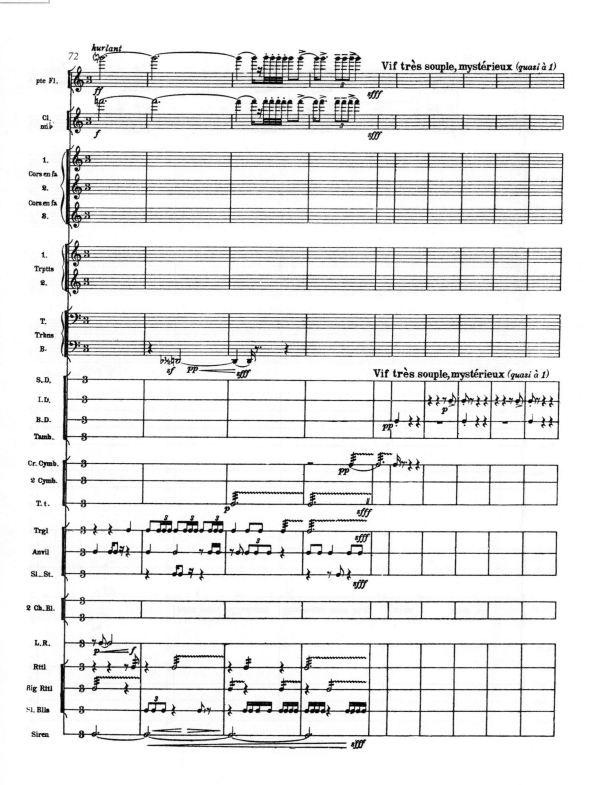

Edgard Varèse wrote *Hyperprism* in 1922–23 and conducted its premiere in New York on March 4, 1923, in a concert of the International Composers' Guild, a group he had cofounded that specialized in presenting new music. The performance sparked catcalls by some in the audience but also drew an offer from London music publisher J. Curwen & Sons to publish the piece, and it appeared the following year.

No doubt *Hyperprism* startled some of its first listeners because it does not do what most music does. Varèse conceived of his music spatially. It is not rhetorical, shaped like a speech or intending to communicate a feeling or experience, as so much music since the Renaissance has been; nor is it organic, each part relating to the others like cells of a living organism, as in a piece by Brahms or Webern. Rather, it is like a dance in sound, in which "sound masses" move through an imagined musical space. Many of the sounds Varèse uses suggest motion, in one or more diminsions: a pitch that rises and falls implies movement up and down, an increase or decrease in volume simulates moving closer or farther away, and a pitch or other sound that changes timbre or moves from one instrument to another seems to move horizontally—and may do so literally in a live concert.

Percussion instruments are well suited to this type of music. Some of the special instruments Varèse uses suggest motion in the very sounds they make, including the siren and the lion's roar (played by pulling on a string attached to a drum head, which makes the drum vibrate with changing pitch and volume, heard near the beginning of the piece in its first complete measure). Moreover, Varèse uses different combinations of percussion instruments to suggest sound masses that move, change, alternate, or interpenetrate. At the beginning, a composite, rapidly changing sound mass is initiated by a cymbal clash and tam-tam (flat gong) and continued by bass drum, moving from metallic to drum sounds. When this sound mass next appears in measure 5, the bass drum initiates it, and other drum and metallic sounds join in: crash cymbal, snare drum, and tambourine. This sound mass repeats in various forms in measures 7, 16–17, and 23, alternating with other ideas in the percussion. One such idea is a beat pattern in the Indian drum that is linked with a constantly changing array of other instruments, including siren, rattles, triangle, sleigh bells, anvil, and Chinese blocks (see measures 3, 6, 8, 11, 18, 20, and 24–25). When this idea repeats and varies, it sometimes merges with the sounds of the first sound mass (as in measures 16–22).

Meanwhile, the nine wind and brass instruments do not play themes and rarely play melodies. Instead, like the percussion, they produce sounds that suggest static or moving sound masses. The tenor trombone introduces the pitch *c♯'* and embellishes it with accents and glissandos, in alternation with the horns playing crescendos, *sforzandos*, and flutter-tonguing on the same note (measures 2–12; the horns are in F and sound a fifth lower than notated). This constitutes a sound mass with a static central pitch, but with a constantly changing timbre—using effects that most listeners in 1923 would have called noise rather than music.

Since the purpose of the pitches in this music is to create sound masses, Varèse avoids combinations that suggest familiar chords or scales. Instead, both melodically and harmonically, he tends to use notes that are next to each other in the chromatic scale but separated by one or more octaves. Such dissonances are prominent throughout the first section (measures 1–29). Thus the *c♯′* in tenor trombone and horns is joined by *D* two octaves below it in the bass trombone. (Interestingly, that low *D* offers Varèse an opportunity to link the brass and percussion sounds directly; it alternates with the lion's roar and siren, and all three are constantly changing dynamic level, giving them somewhat similar sound contours.) At measure 12, when the C♯ shifts up an octave to the trumpets and E♭ clarinet (which sounds a minor third higher than written), it is joined by C in flute and trombone over gentle metallic sounds in the percussion. As the clarinet and flute sustain their dissonance, the other instruments enter to form a chord containing the nine chromatic notes from B♭ to F♯ spread over a range of four and a half octaves (measures 15–16). The instruments do not all begin or end the chord together but enter and exit in groups, staggered in a manner that is typical of Varèse. Having explored chromatic harmonies of from two to nine notes, Varése now turns to melodic chromaticism: the flute melody that follows (measures 19–24) includes all twelve chromatic notes, ending with a minor ninth against the trumpet, which sustains the flute's next-to-last note. The section closes with another major seventh in the high winds (the piccolo A sounds an octave higher than written).

Varèse believed that the form of a work grew out of its material, and typically this results in an episodic structure. What we have examined so far is the first section, unified by the recurring sound masses in the percussion but subdivided into three units by the changing sound masses in the winds and brass: the sustained C♯ (measures 1–11), the chromatic chord (measures 12–18), and the flute melody (measures 19–29).

Everything changes at once at measure 30, launching the second section. Here the texture suddenly becomes homorhythmic, with brass and percussion moving together in the first subsection (measures 30–39). The percussion drop out entirely while the winds and brass engage in counterpoint (measures 40–43), and then all three instrumental families participate in a counterpoint of blocks, layering and juxtaposing figures that each repeat in only one instrument or group of instruments (measures 44–58).

The third section somewhat resembles the first. In the first subsection (59–68), horn 1 and tenor trombone decorate F♯, then the trombone plays a chromatic descending melody with octave displacements, ending over a quarter tone in the bass trombone notated as D half-flat (♭½). Piccolo and clarinet then play angular chromatic figures in rhythmic unison (measures 68–75), sounding together all but two notes of the chromatic scale: D and C♯, the immediate neighbors of that D half-flat. The brief coda (measures 84–89) sounds all twelve notes of the chromatic scale to end the piece.

Varèse's music is very distinctive and original in conception, but he draws on his immediate predecessors. The use of layers, block construction, and juxtaposition are indebted to Stravinsky. The nondevelopmental approach, focus on timbre as an essential musical element, and identification of each musical idea with a particular timbre or with changing timbres are characteristics of both Stravinsky and Debussy. Yet the pitch organization, with its focus on chromaticism and use of chromatic saturation to demarcate sections, relates to Schoenberg's atonal music, which Varèse came to know during his days in Berlin before emigrating to the United States.

In the original score shown here, Varèse laid out the percussion by type, making it easy to track the sounds he was using but leaving it to the players to figure out who plays what when. A revised edition by Richard Sacks distributes the percussion parts to nine players but is essentially the same in sound.

Henry Cowell (1897–1965)

The Banshee

Piano piece

1925

193

The Banshee

Explanation of Symbols

"The Banshee" is played on the open strings of the piano, the player standing at the crook. Another person must sit at the keyboard and hold down the damper pedal throughout the composition. The whole work should be played an octave lower than written.

R. H. stands for "right hand." L. H. stands for "left hand." Different ways of playing the strings are indicated by a letter over each tone, as follows:

(A) indicates a sweep with the flesh of the finger from the lowest string up to the note given.

(B) sweep lengthwise along the string of the note given with flesh of finger.

(C) sweep up and back from lowest A to highest B-flat given in this composition.

(D) pluck string with flesh of finger, where written, instead of octave lower.

(E) sweep along three notes together, in the same manner as (B).

(F) sweep in the manner of (B) but with the back of finger-nail instead of flesh.

(G) when the finger is half way along the string in the manner of (F), start a sweep along the same string with the flesh of the other finger, thus partly damping the sound.

(H) sweep back and forth in the manner of (C), but start at the same time from both above and below, crossing the sweep in the middle.

(I) sweep along five notes, in the manner of (B).

(J) same as (I) but with back of finger-nails instead of flesh of finger.

(K) sweep along in manner of (J) with nails of both hands together, taking in all notes between the two outer limits given.

(L) sweep in manner of (C) with flat of hand instead of single finger.

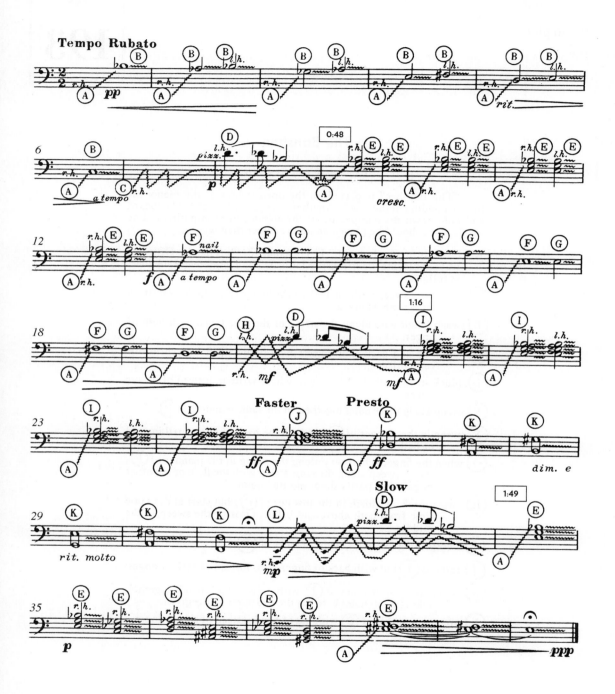

Henry Cowell spent his career exploring new techniques and composing pieces to showcase them. *The Banshee*, which Cowell composed and premiered in early 1925, is typical, presenting sounds made by playing directly on the strings of a grand piano rather than by pressing the keys. With the lid up and the sustaining pedal held down by an assistant or a wedge so the dampers are lifted and the strings resonate freely, the performer stands in the crook of the piano and plays the strings with fingers, fingernails, or the palm of the hand. To show the player how to produce these new sounds, Cowell had to invent a notation, devising one that relies on letters keyed to brief instructions for each playing technique.

There are four types of sound in this piece. With one exception, Cowell uses only the lowest strings of the piano—from B♭ a ninth below middle C to A two octaves lower. These strings are tightly wound with wire, unlike the smooth wire strings in higher registers. (For ease of reading, he notates these strings an octave higher than they sound.) To understand this piece, it will be helpful to find a grand piano and try out these sounds:

1. The simplest sound to produce is a glissando made by sweeping the flesh of the finger across the wire-wound strings. There are several variants: a glissando from the lowest A to an indicated note (letter A); back and forth across the entire range of wire-wound strings (C); back and forth simultaneously in both directions (H); or back and forth with a flat hand rather than a single finger (L).

2. The most striking sound in the piece is created by rubbing along the length of the wire-wound strings with the flesh of the finger, whether on the strings for one note (B), three notes (E), or five notes (I). This is done with the palm facing downward, the hand moving away from the player, and the fingers extended and pressing down on the strings, so the friction of the fingers against the ridges in the wound wire causes the string to vibrate. If done correctly, this creates a howling or moaning sound with varying pitch, strangely similar to a human voice, that must have reminded Cowell of the banshee, a type of female spirit from Irish folklore who wails outside the house of someone who is about to die.

3. A more raspy or zingy sound is made by rubbing along the length of the string with the back of the fingernail, on the strings for one note (F), five notes (J), or nine notes, using both hands (K). This is performed using the same gesture as the finger rubs, only with the fingers curled under so the fingernails contact the strings. Cowell often modifies the one-string fingernail rub in mid-course by adding a flesh-of-the-finger rub in the other hand on the same string (G).

4. The most familiar sound in the piece is made by plucking strings with the flesh of the finger (D), in a descending melodic motive, d'–$d♭'$–$b♭$ (with added g the second time through). This is the one element that is played on the smooth wire strings, in the piano's middle range, and sounds as notated rather than an octave lower.

Of these sounds, the first and last can be imagined from the notation; the plucked pitches are obvious, and the glissandos are notated graphically with a wavy line adapted from the sign for arpeggiating a chord. But nothing in the notation can prepare the ear for the weird sound of rubbing along a wire-wound string with a finger or fingernail. The pitches one hears may be entirely different from those that are notated. At these spots, the notation serves as a kind of tablature, telling the player what to do rather than symbolizing the resulting sound (compare the lute tablatures in NAWM 65 and 87). For this reason, and because of differences among pianos and performers, the actual sounds of this piece can vary a great deal between performances.

With this repertoire of sounds, Cowell organized the piece in four short sections articulated by the plucked motive, which appears at the end of each of the first three sections accompanied by a new variant of the glissando (letters C, H, and L, each of which appears only once in the piece). The first section (measures 1–8), predominantly quiet, introduces the glissandos and finger rubs. The second (measures 9–20) grows louder, adding three-finger rubs and fingernail rubs. Louder still is the third section (measures 21–33), with multi-finger and multi-fingernail rubs. After the plucked motive is heard for the third time, the last section (measures 34–40) is quiet, with only glissandos and three-finger rubs. The overall shape suggests the visit of a banshee, who approaches and begins wailing softly, intensifies her cries, and subsides.

What is the role of the title and implied program in this piece? In the nineteenth century, composers often introduced extraordinary sounds or events to convey a program or scene, such as the flutter-tonguing in brass and wind instruments to imitate the bleating of sheep in Strauss's *Don Quixote* (NAWM 158). One could imagine that Cowell encountered the legend of the banshee and sought musical means to represent it. But given his lifelong interest in new resources, it is far more likely that he was experimenting with sounds that could be made on the piano strings, discovered the banshee-like wailing that resulted from rubbing the wire-bound strings lengthwise, and conceived the piece to demonstrate the techniques he had discovered. In this sense, the piece is a prime example of experimental music, which explores and presents new musical resources for their own sake. The title suggests a possible meaning for the new sounds and makes them easier to accept— and more interesting.

The performance on the accompanying recording is by Cowell himself (he announces the title at the outset), and we can assume that it reveals the sounds he intended to create. Comparing his performance with the score, he takes some liberties, adding some gestures and omitting or hurrying through others, suggesting that the overall shape and effect were most important to him.

Ruth Crawford Seeger (1901–1953)

String Quartet 1931: Fourth movement, Allegro possibile

String Quartet

1931

194

Ruth Crawford composed her String Quartet in 1931 during a year in Berlin and Paris on a Guggenheim Fellowship, the first awarded to a woman. Over the previous year, she had assisted her composition teacher Charles Seeger (whom she later married in 1932 after her return from Europe) in developing ideas of dissonant counterpoint for an unpublished book manuscript, and many of those ideas appear in her quartet. She saw his and her own work as representative of an American tradition in modern music, independent of the European modernists. Accordingly, while in Europe she studied with no one, avoided contact with Schoenberg (who was in Berlin), and met only briefly with Berg and Bartók. Her String Quartet was given the subtitle "1931" when it was published ten years later in *New Music*, a quarterly periodical of new scores by "ultramodern" composers, published by Henry Cowell.

The String Quartet is full of new ideas. Although it consists of four movements in a familiar order—fast, scherzo-like, slow, and fast—each movement is based on a different set of devices, most of which had never been tried in a quartet. The first movement is built on a counterpoint of almost wholly independent melodies. The second movement develops a three-note motive through constant shifts of accent and implied meter. In the third movement, all four instruments play almost constantly but swell to dynamic peaks at different times, and those peaks are heard as a kind of melody passed among the instruments.

The finale, included here, is the most systematic: a palindrome, whose second half is an exact retrograde of the first, transposed up a half step. (The pivot point is at measures 58–59, with the transposition beginning at the second eighth note of measure 60.) The texture consists of two contrapuntal lines. In the first half of the piece, the first violin plays one note, then two, then three, increasing the number of notes in succession to twenty-one, while getting gradually softer. The pitches and rhythms are freely chosen. Meanwhile the other three instruments, muted and playing in octaves, interject phrases of twenty notes, then nineteen, then eighteen, reducing the number of notes to one, while getting gradually louder. In contrast to the varied durations and freely chosen pitches of the first violin line, the lower instruments play only eighth notes (sometimes sustaining the last note in a phrase) and use pitches generated by permutations of a ten-note series. The result is a contrast of opposites: one line (in the violin) of free notes and rhythms, unmuted, that gradually decrescendoes through phrases that grow ever longer, and a second line (in the other instruments) of even notes and rhythms, that gradually crescendoes through phrases that grow ever shorter. After both lines arrive at their last note in measure 57, they sustain it at a soft dynamic level through the pivot point, and then everything reverses.

The series in the lower line is handled in an innovative manner. Rather than invert or retrograde the series, as in the twelve-tone music of Schoenberg, Berg, and Webern, Crawford permutes it through a process called *rotation*, taking the first note and moving it to the end, then doing this again with the second note, and so on:

```
D   E   F   E♭  F♯  A   A♭  G   D♭  C
    E   F   E♭  F♯  A   A♭  G   D♭  C   D
        F   E♭  F♯  A   A♭  G   D♭  C   D   E
            E♭  F♯  A   A♭  G   D♭  C   D   E   F
                F♯  A   A♭  G   D♭  C   D   E   F   E♭     etc.
```

The first phrase, with twenty notes, has the first two statements of this series (measures 3–5), the next phrase has all but the last note of the next two statements (adding up to nineteen notes, in measures 7–9), and so on, until the series has been stated ten times in all possible rotations, ending with the second eighth note of measure 21. At this point, the entire process unfolds again, with the series transposed up a whole step. (One note is missing in one of the rotations—can you find it?) After the second set of ten rotations is complete, the series returns in its original form and transposition (measures 47–54), and the process halts at the pivot point of the palindrome on what would be the first note of the next rotation.

This movement is unique in Crawford's output—no other piece works like this— and is therefore characteristic of Crawford, whose every piece is unique in its language and musical devices. The movement's intense conflicts between elements, such as the opposition in almost every parameter between the two contrapuntal lines, is also typical of her music. Such opposition introduces difficulties for the players in coordinating their parts, which is heightened here by an emphasis on duration and pulse, tending to obscure meter. The slurring in the lower line, which freely alternates groups of four, two, and three notes, also works against the meter, creating a free, rhapsodic interplay of opposing forces—the very embodiment of her and Seeger's notion of dissonant counterpoint.

Aaron Copland (1900–1990)

Appalachian Spring, Excerpt with Variations on *'Tis the Gift to Be Simple*

195

Ballet suite

1943–44, ORCHESTRATED 1945

From Aaron Copland, *Appalachian Spring* (New York: Boosey & Hawkes, 1945), 43–79. Copyright 1945 by The Aaron Copland Fund for Music, Inc. Copyright renewed. Boosey & Hawkes, Inc., sole licensee. Reprinted by permission.

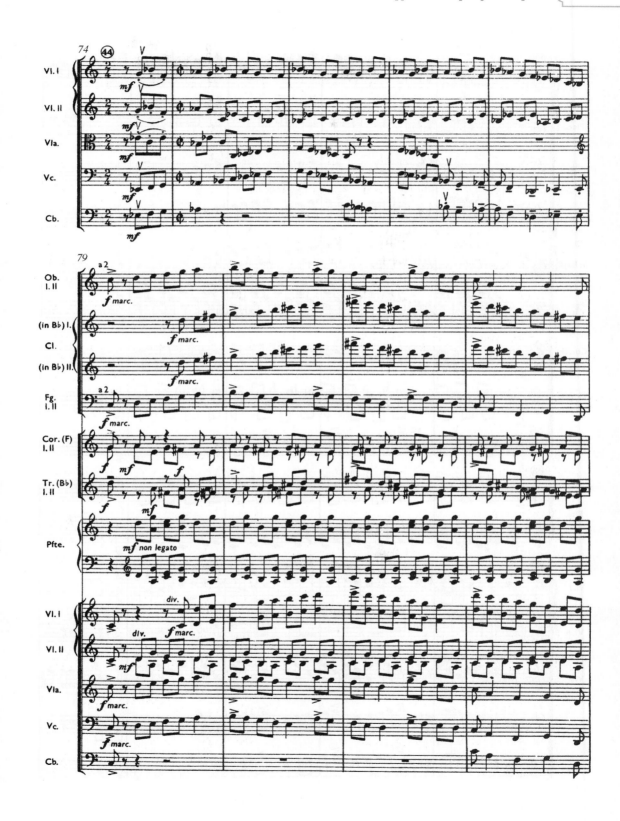

★ Shaker melody "The gift to be simple"

Modern dancer and choreographer Martha Graham used Aaron Copland's dissonant and rhythmically complex *Piano Variations* (1930) as the music for a solo dance in 1931, and the result was so successful that the composer and choreographer looked for an opportunity to collaborate. Their chance came in 1942, when Elizabeth Sprague Coolidge, a prominent patron of modern music, commissioned three ballet scores for Graham, including one from Copland. Graham devised the scenario, which went through many changes even after Copland had begun composing the music. The final version of the ballet centers around a couple about to be married in rural nineteenth-century Pennsylvania, who are feted by a minister and neighbors on the completion of their farmhouse.

In accordance with the commission, Copland scored the original ballet for a chamber ensemble of thirteen instruments. He called the piece simply "Ballet for Martha" while working on it, and only when he arrived in Washington, D.C., for the October 30, 1944, premiere did he learn the title she had given the work, *Appalachian Spring*. He was later amused how often people said to him, "When I listen to that ballet of yours, I can just *feel* spring and *see* the Appalachians," since neither was in his mind as he composed. The ballet was a great success, and the music won Copland the Pulitzer Prize and the New York Music Critics' Circle Award. He later arranged the piece as a suite for full orchestra, premiered on October 4, 1945, in New York, and in that form it has become his most widely known work.

During the 1930s, Copland turned from the astringent modernism typified by the *Piano Variations* to a deliberately simpler, more accessible style, seeking to appeal to a broader public. Without leaving behind the dissonance, counterpoint, motivic unity, and juxtaposed blocks of sound that had marked his modernist works, he incorporated diatonic melodies and harmonies, transparent textures, and recognizable allusions to familiar types and styles of music, including some direct quotations of folk or popular songs. His new style is exemplified in *Appalachian Spring*, which evokes country fiddling, dancing, and singing and captures the spirit of rural America.

In the Allegro and Presto sections that begin the excerpt included here, the shifting meters, offbeat accents, and sudden changes of texture show Stravinsky's influence (see NAWM 176 and 177). But the predominantly diatonic melodies and harmonies, syncopation, and guitarlike chords give this passage a flavor of American folk music. Many passages vertically combine consonant and dissonant notes of the diatonic scale in a technique that has been called *pandiatonicism*. The rapid melodic figuration of the Presto (measure 18 of the excerpt) suggests country fiddling, while counterpoint (as at measures 35–38, 61–65, and 74–87) and motivic links between the Allegro and Presto (the figure from measures 5–6 recurs throughout the Presto) show the heritage of the European classical tradition.

At the Meno mosso (measure 138 of the excerpt), leaps of fourths and fifths in the violin and oboe solos and wide spacing of the chords suggest a sparsely populated landscape. This texture, together with diatonic melodies and lightly dissonant diatonic chords, established a distinctive sound that has been used ever since to depict the open spaces and rugged people of frontier America. A recollection of the opening passage of the ballet ("As at first," measure 151) includes the ballet's characteristic sound, superimposed tonic and dominant or tonic and subdominant triads (measures 152–55 and 158–61, respectively).

At the Doppio movimento (Double time, measure 171), Copland begins a set of variations on the Shaker hymn *'Tis the Gift to Be Simple*, by Elder Joseph Brackett (1797–1882):

The Shakers were a religious sect who practiced celibacy and lived communally, raising their own food and making virtually everything they used themselves. Their hymns were used in religious services, sung in unaccompanied unison while most of the congregation danced. Copland discovered the tune in a published collection of Shaker hymns and thought it ideally suited Graham's scenario because of its links to dance and to rural America, although the people in her ballet were not Shakers (and there never were Shaker settlements in rural Pennsylvania).

Copland's approach to varying this monophonic hymn tune is to change the melody relatively little but to place it in a series of contrasting settings. The one alteration he consistently makes is in the phrasing, treating the first two notes of the hymn's final phrase as if they were the last two notes of the third phrase and thereby emphasizing the long note on "turn" in measure 13 of the tune. The first variation, in A♭ major, is for clarinet, accompanied quite simply by irregularly alternating dominant and tonic sustained tones in flutes and harp. The second variation (measure 191) has a similar texture, a step lower, with the melody in the oboe, paralleled by bassoon a tenth lower, and accompanied by brass and other winds. The third variation gives the melody, half as fast, to trombones and violas, which are later joined in canon by the horns and first violins, but omits the second half of the tune (measures 207–33). The melody passes to the trumpet and to C major in the fourth variation (measure 240), accompanied by trombone, doubled by winds in the third phrase, and joined for the second and fourth phrases by violins and violas fiddling in rapid scales. The final variation presents the two halves of the tune in reverse order: the opening motive in bassoon (measure 272) turns out to be a counterpoint to the second half of the melody in the clarinet, and then the entire orchestra proclaims the first half of the theme over a slowly descending bass (measure 288).

Like many other composers from Berlioz to Stravinsky (see commentary for NAWM 177), Copland often conducted his own works. The performance on the accompanying recording is of the version for full orchestra, conducted by Copland in 1970.

William Grant Still (1895–1978)

Afro-American Symphony (Symphony No. 1):
First movement, Moderato assai

Symphony

1930

196

concise 🔊

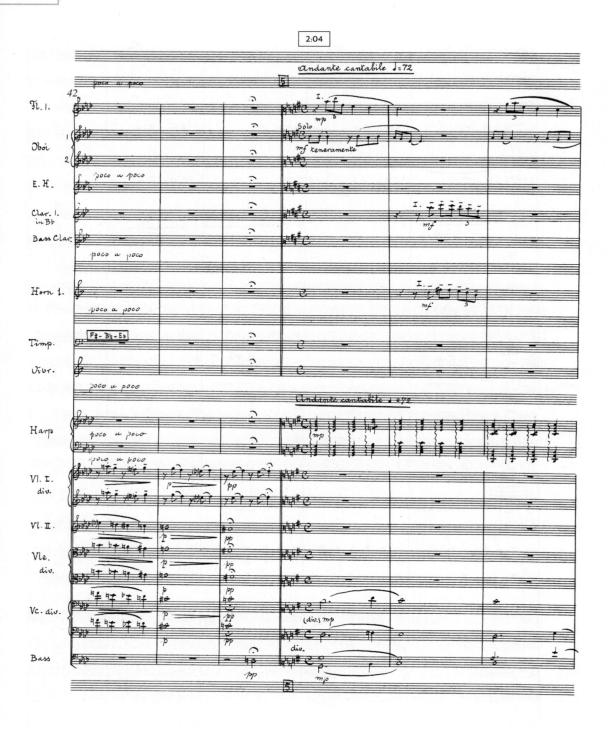

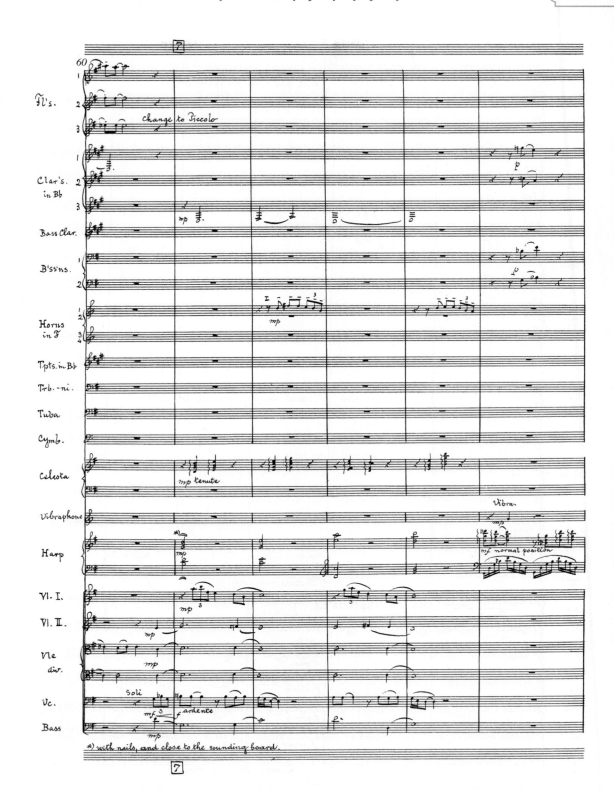

*) with nails, and close to the sounding board.

77
Fl's.
Picc.
Oboi
Clar's. in Bb
staccatos.
Bass Clar.
B'ss'ns.
a4
Horns in F
Tpts. in Bb
mf
Trb.-ni.
f stacc.
Tuba
f stacc.
Timp.
Sn. Dr.
Cymbs
Harp
Vl. I.
arco
pizz.
Vl. II.
arco
pizz.
Vla.
arco
pizz.
Vc.
arco
pizz.
Bass.
(pizz.)

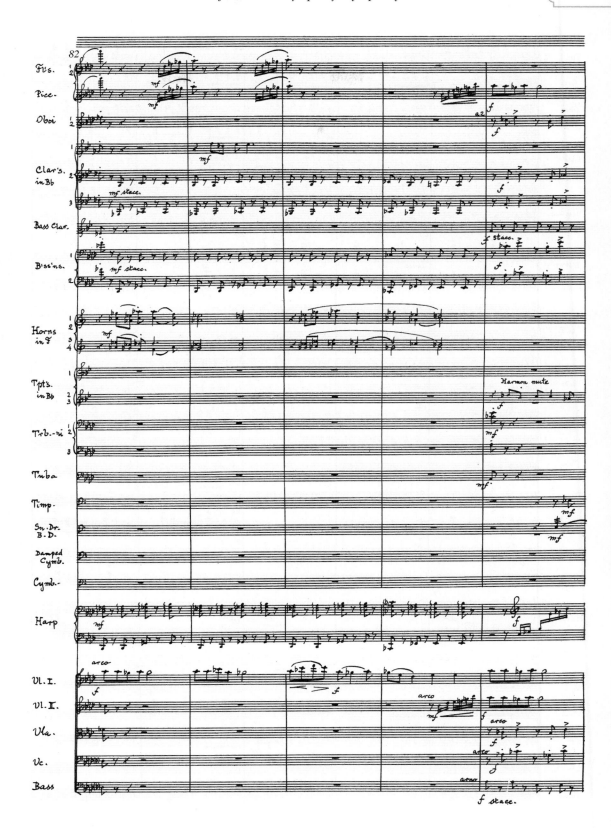

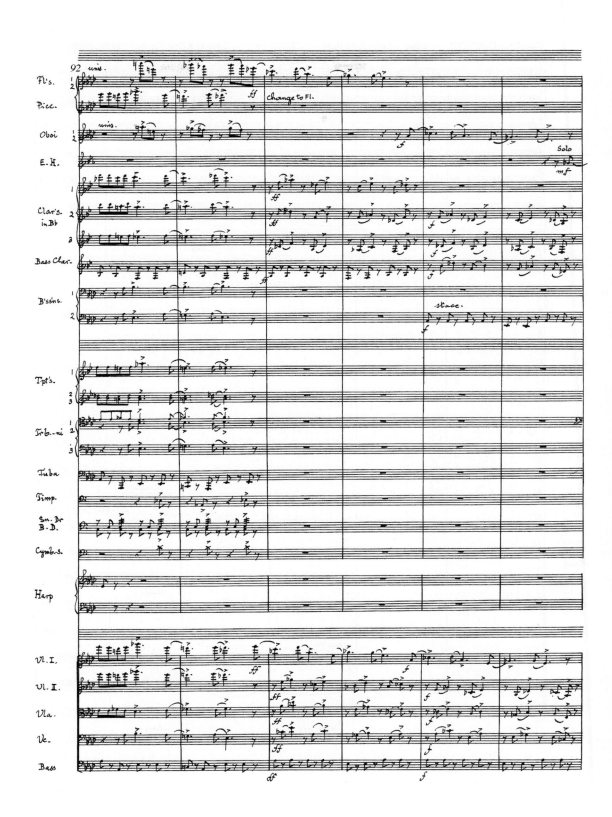

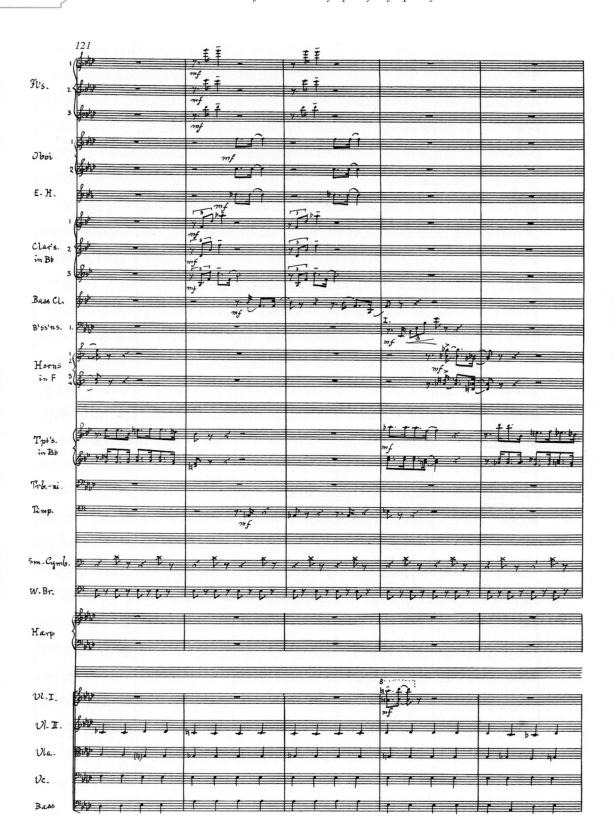

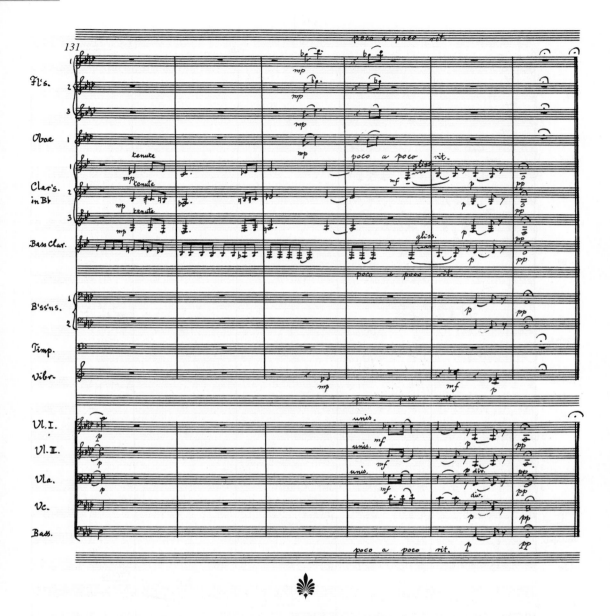

William Grant Still composed his *Afro-American Symphony* in 1930. When it was premiered in 1931 by the Rochester Philharmonic Orchestra conducted by Howard Hanson, it became the first symphony by an African American composer to be performed by a major orchestra. Other black composers followed in Still's wake, including Florence Price, whose Symphony in E Minor was played by the Chicago Symphony Orchestra in 1933, and William Dawson, whose *Negro Folk Symphony* was premiered by the Philadelphia Orchestra in 1934. As a pathbreaker—and one of the most prolific American composers of his era—Still became known as the dean of African American composers. His symphony was published in 1935, and he later revised it in 1969, having written four more symphonies in the interim.

The *Afro-American Symphony* has the traditional four movements, with a sonata-form first movement, a slow movement, a scherzo, and a fast finale. The movements are not explicitly programmatic, but each is a character sketch that is also linked to verses from a poem by Paul Laurence Dunbar (1872–1906), who wrote about African American life in the South, using folk materials and dialects. Originally Still also gave each movement a subtitle appropriate to its content: *Longings; Sorrows; Humor;* and *Aspirations.*

The first movement blends sonata form with an archlike ABCBA form, since the two main themes appear in reverse order in the recapitulation. The movement opens with a brief introductory melody in the English horn, followed by a first theme in the trumpet in the form of a twelve-bar blues in A♭ (measures 7–18; see the blues in NAWM 182 and 183). In addition to the blues melody (in classic AAB form) and harmonic progression, many other elements reflect characteristic features of African American music. Syncopations appear in both melody and accompaniment, and phrases often end just before rather than on a strong beat. The call-and-response structure of African American song is echoed in the frequent interjections by other instruments between the short phrases of melody. Lowered fifth, third, and seventh scale degrees in the melody (as in measures 2–4 and 15–16) imitate blue notes, as do chords that include both major and minor thirds (measures 4–5 and 7). Instrumental timbres are varied and often unusual, including groupings and sounds typical of jazz bands: trumpets and trombones with Harmon mutes, which give a distant, pinched, metallic sound (measures 6–8); steady taps on the bass drum and dampened strikes on the cymbal; winds and brass used in groups of similar sound, like sections in a jazz band, and voiced in chords of four notes (as in measures 7–10); and, later in the movement, a vibraphone (see especially measures 133–35).

The first theme repeats in the clarinet (measure 19) with interjections from other winds, accompanied by strings playing *col legno* (with the wood of the bow) to create a percussive effect. Then the transition begins (measure 33), developing motives from the first theme, as is typical of European symphonies. The second theme (measures 45–67), in the surprising key of G major (a half step below the tonic A♭, rather than the expected dominant, E♭), has the pentatonic contours and melancholy air of a spiritual, which along with blues and jazz was the type of music most widely identified with African Americans. The theme is in ABA' form, beginning in the oboe and moving in turn to violins, flutes, cello, and harp. Once again, interjections by other instruments between phrases of the oboe theme suggest the call-and-response of African American song.

As the second theme concludes, the tempo picks up and the development section begins (measure 68). As in the earlier transition, here the procedures are those of a European sonata-form movement, fragmenting and developing elements from both themes and from the opening English horn melody. After calm is restored, the recapitulation brings back the two main themes in reverse order (measures 104 and 114 respectively), the second in the tonic A♭ minor and the first in A♭ major, with almost no transition between them. This time, the first theme appears in swinging rhythms (alternating long and short notes) rather than even ones; because Still knew that some orchestral musicians might not know what was intended, he marked in a note (at measure 116) that the dotted-eighth-sixteenth rhythms should be played like triplets, the usual ratio of swing. A brief coda (measures 128–36) brings the movement to a close with a reminiscence of the introduction, emphasizing the archlike structure of the entire movement.

The combination of blues and spiritual is appropriate to the sense of longing Still sought to capture in the movement, and to the verses of Dunbar he linked to it:

> 'All my life long twell de night has pas'
> Let de wo'k come ez it will,
> So dat I fin' you, my honey, at last,
> Somewhaih des ovah de hill.'

To a listener today, the way Still uses the orchestra in the *Afro-American Symphony* can sound like movie music. This is neither coincidence nor a sign of unoriginality; in 1934, Still moved to Los Angeles, where he composed for films while continuing to write concert music in classical forms. The manner in which he integrated the string sounds of the symphonic orchestra with the distinctive wind and brass sounds of the jazz orchestra helped to define a style that many other composers and arrangers used for films and popular music.

Charlie Parker (1920–1955) and Dizzy Gillespie (1917–1993)

Anthropology

Bebop tune and solo

1945

(a) Lead sheet

(b) Transcription of Charlie Parker's solo

2:54 [Bud Powell's solo]

3:42 [Trading fours with drummer]

4:29 [Head]

❧

Anthropology is one of dozens of mid-1940s collaborations between Charlie "Bird" Parker and John Birks "Dizzy" Gillespie. The two met in Kansas City, Parker's home town, when Gillespie was on tour with Cab Calloway's big band. In the early 1940s, Parker, Gillespie, and other young jazz virtuosos convened in New York City clubs such as Minton's Playhouse and Monroe's Uptown House to play and improvise together in lengthy after-hours sessions. Out of these jam sessions grew a new musical language known as *bebop*, featuring breakneck speeds, complex chord changes, and angular melodies.

Like many bebop compositions, *Anthropology* is a contrafact—a new tune composed over a harmonic progression borrowed from another song. Specifically, like Duke Ellington's *Cotton Tail* (NAWM 184), it is a contrafact on "rhythm changes," jazz musicians' term for the chord progression from the chorus of George Gershwin's *I Got Rhythm* (NAWM 181). Contrafacts were a major source for new bebop compositions because they constituted a common language for jazz musicians, could easily be molded into a new tune for a last-minute recording session, and did not require payment of royalties to the composer of the original tune. Contrafacts were especially important for Parker: new tunes built over the blues, rhythm changes, and the standard *Honeysuckle Rose* account for much of Parker's output.

The version of *Anthropology* that is included on the accompanying recording is from a live broadcast made on March 31, 1951, at Birdland, the New York jazz club named after Parker's nickname, where Parker was the headliner. The broadcast was recorded and released on LP as *Summit Meeting at Birdland*. The players were all stars, with Parker on alto saxophone and Gillespie on trumpet supported by a rhythm section made up of Bud Powell on piano, Tommy Potter on bass, and Roy Haynes on drums. Through most of the performance, the bass and cymbal keep steady time, and the piano and drums provide irregular punctuations.

The tune begins with the head, a lead melody in AABA form played in unison or octaves by the melody instruments at the beginning and end of the song. The musicians play from a lead sheet, shown here as NAWM 197a, that includes only the head and the chord changes. Everything else is improvised or worked out by ear in rehearsal. In this performance, after the head, Parker plays a solo that fills up three choruses (statements of the AABA harmonic progression), shown here in transcription as NAWM 197b. (The transcription includes the head; the solo begins at measure 29.) Gillespie then solos for three choruses, followed by Powell on piano for two. For the next two choruses, Parker and Gillespie "trade fours" with Haynes, alternating four measures of melody instrument with four measures of drum solo for each eight-measure phrase. The song ends as it began, with Parker and Gillespie leading the way in another statement of the head.

The musicians play at a blistering pace that is characteristic of bebop. The many syncopations (as in measures 8–10) and sudden stops, starts, and silences throughout the tune and Parker's solo keep the rhythm fresh and surprising. The convoluted, highly decorated melody is also typical of bebop: both the head and Parker's solo are full of chromatic notes, and the melody is dissonant with the underlying harmony almost as often as it is consonant. Because the solo is so chromatic, the transcriber has notated it without a key signature.

The solos do not offer variations on the tune, but spin out a constant variety of new ideas that fit within the harmonic progression. In each chorus, Parker uses different material, introduces rests and phrasing at different places, and reconceives his approach to each section, especially the B section (called the *bridge*). The virtuosity is astonishing, as the performers meant it to be. Occasionally, Parker repeats ideas (for example, measures 113–15 repeat measures 81–83), suggesting that at least in some places he is relying on formulas or routines worked out in advance that he can use at will, allowing him to keep up his breakneck speed. At measures 117–21, near the end of his solo, Parker quotes the song *Temptation* by Nacio Herb Brown to lyrics by Arthur Freed, sung by Bing Crosby in the 1933 movie *Going Hollywood*. Such quotations are frequent in Parker's solos, showing his sly wit and his intention to dazzle the listener. With bebop, jazz came to be recognized as an art music worthy of the same attentive listening as classical music.

Leonard Bernstein (1918–1990)

West Side Story, Act I, No. 8, "Cool"

Musical

1957

*Jets snap fingers through bar 171

APPLAUSE SEGUE

The creation of *West Side Story* began in January 1949 when choreographer Jerome Robbins called composer Leonard Bernstein with an idea for a modern version of Shakespeare's *Romeo and Juliet*. Robbins told Bernstein that the inspiration came to him after a conversation with an actor friend who commented that the only way to bring the role of Romeo to life was to conceive it in modern terms. In Shakespeare's play, set in Renaissance Italy, teenagers from feuding families fall in love but are ultimately doomed by their families' enmity. Bernstein, Robbins, and Arthur Laurents, who wrote the book (the spoken text of a musical), began with the idea of recasting the feud as a conflict between Catholics and Jews in the slums on the east side of Manhattan in New York City, titling it *East Side Story*. In 1955, the concept was changed to rival teen gangs on the city's west side: the Sharks, whose families had recently moved from Puerto Rico, and the Jets, descendants of earlier waves of immigrants. With Laurents's book, lyrics by Stephen Sondheim, music by Bernstein, and direction and choreography by Robbins, the show premiered on September 26, 1957, at the Winter Garden Theater on Broadway and was an immediate success. It was nominated for five Tony Awards, the top award for theater in New York, including Best Musical, and it won for Robbins's choreography and Oliver Smith's scenic design.

Bernstein called the work "an out-and-out plea for racial tolerance," addressing not only race and ethnicity but cultural assimilation. In the late 1950s, Puerto Ricans were the most recent and distinctive immigrants in New York City, not yet assimilated, and some both in and outside the Puerto Rican community feared they never would be. Recasting Shakespeare's plot in these terms made the central conflict visceral and up-to-date. The couple at the center of the drama—Tony, a member of the Jets and best friend of their leader Riff, and Maria, sister of Bernardo, the leader of the Sharks—meet on neutral ground at a dance in a school gymnasium and fall in love, but their relationship is ensnared in the conflict between the two gangs. At a rumble (a fight between the gangs, staged as a ballet), Bernardo kills Riff, then Tony kills Bernardo in revenge, setting the stage for the final tragedy. In the end, Tony is killed in turn, and Maria pleads for the violence to end. The tragic effect is redoubled because this all occurs in a Broadway musical, full of soaring songs, jazzy dance numbers, comic moments, and engaging entertainment.

A principal function of the music throughout the show is to suggest the emotional states of the two gangs and the lead characters, using styles and gestures drawn from jazz, Latin music, and modernist classical music. In "Cool," the Jets, led by Riff, attempt to calm themselves before the rumble. (In the 1961 film version, "Cool" was relocated to after the rumble, and another character sang the lead.)

The opening melody is in the disjointed, angular style of bebop, as suggested by the tempo marking "Solid and boppy." The prominent tritones echo earlier uses of that interval in the musical, including the "Jet call" in the prologue and Tony's song "Maria." The tune is introduced in unison by instruments whose timbres are associated with jazz (saxophones, vibraphone, piano, and plucked string bass), accompanying the dialogue, then is taken up by Riff. But the soft dynamic and the persistent swinging rhythm on the high hat (pedal-operated cymbals, marked

HH in the score) suggest cool jazz instead. For Bernstein, jazz styles signified an American sound and conjured a sense of youth and vitality, and in this musical bebop and cool jazz specifically symbolize conflict, appropriate here as the Jets work out their anxiety and tension before the upcoming fight. Cool jazz fits the bill here also as an embodiment of Riff's advice to his gang to keep their cool:

> Don't get hot,
> 'Cause man, you got
> Some high times ahead.
> Take it slow
> And, Daddy-o,
> You can live it up and die in bed!

Riff's phrase "Got a rocket in your pocket" may be sexual innuendo, but it is also a metaphor for anger, a holdover from earlier drafts of the script that were full of references to the Cold War, military jargon, the atomic bomb, and space travel. It is typical of Laurents's attempt to invent "timeless" slang for the show that would not lose its currency as 1950s slang aged and fell out of use.

After Riff's song is a dance for the Jets, choreographed by Robbins in a modern jazz style that expresses energy and anticipates the stylized violence of the rumble to come. For the dance, Bernstein wrote a fugue on a subject full of half-steps and large leaps that encompasses all twelve notes of the chromatic scale. (It is usually described as a twelve-tone subject, although three notes appear twice.) Introduced in three phrases by muted trumpet 1 (measures 43–58) beginning on concert C, it is answered by muted horn 1 and cellos on D♯ (measure 58), muted trombones on F♯ (measure 70), and strings, bass saxophone, and trombone 1 on A (measure 82). The entrances at minor-third intervals avoid the normal tonal associations of a fugue, giving the whole an atonal cast. The answer at measure 58 is joined by a swinging countersubject that begins with the same circle of minor thirds (C–D♯–F♯–[B]–A) and has the character of a bebop solo; subsequent entrances include both this and a second countersubject based on fragments from the "Cool" tune (in winds and vibraphone at measure 70). After the exposition comes a stretto on the countersubject, starting on C and answered on D♯ a half-measure later (measure 94), together with a rhythmic transformation of the fugue subject in the xylophone harmonized by other instruments. The fugue climaxes at measure 104 with unison transformed statements of the three phrases of the fugue subject, trading off with a drum solo.

Variants of the last phrase of the fugue subject lead back to the instrumental introduction of the "Cool" theme at measure 119. An instrumental rendition of most of Riff's vocal melody begins at measure 125, alternating with segments of the fugal countersubject. Then the Jets all sing the final verse of Riff's song (measure 145), and the coda states part of the countersubject once more (measure 163). The overall effect of the ABA' form is to interweave the cool jazz and bebop elements of the song with the neoclassical form of the fugue and the modernist sounds of atonal and twelve-tone music, bringing modern jazz and classical music together on the Broadway stage. Such a blend is typical of Bernstein and also perfectly suited for a tragedy on an operatic scale, set in modern times and in the very diverse city in which the show was first staged.

Vincent Persichetti (1915–1987)

Symphony for Band (Symphony No. 6), Op. 69: First movement, Adagio–Allegro

Symphony for band

1956

94
Picc.
Fl. 1 and 2
Ob. 1 and 2
E♭ Cl.
Cl. 1
Cl. 2 and 3
Alto Cl.
B. Cl.
Bsn. 1 and 2
A. Sax. 1 and 2
T. Sax.
Bari. Sax.
Cor. 1
Cor. 2 and 3
Tpt. 1 and 2
Hn. 1 and 2
Hn. 3 and 4
Euph.
Tbn. 1
Tbn. 2 and 3
Tba.
Perc. 1
Perc. 2
Perc. 3
f risoluto
ff brillante
ff intenso
ff marc.
marc.
cresc.
f cresc.
sfz
Sop. Sn. Dr

199 VINCENT PERSICHETTI · Symphony for Band (Symphony No. 6), Op. 69: First movement

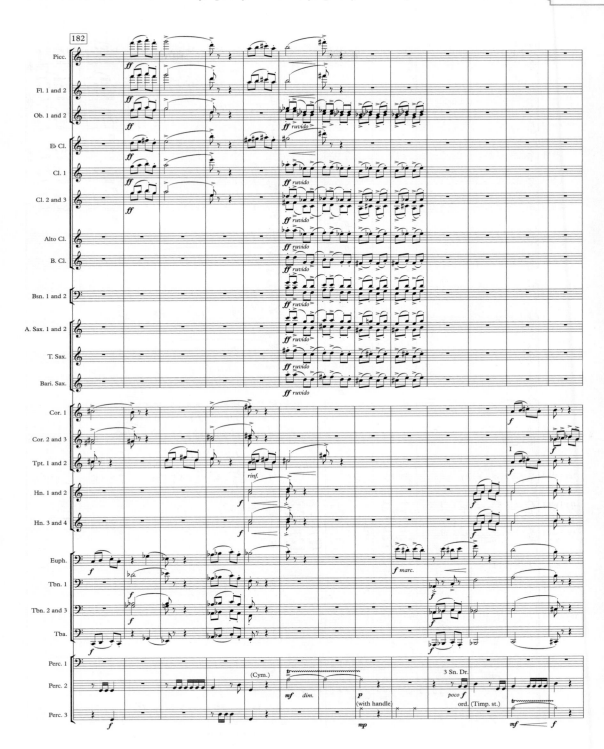

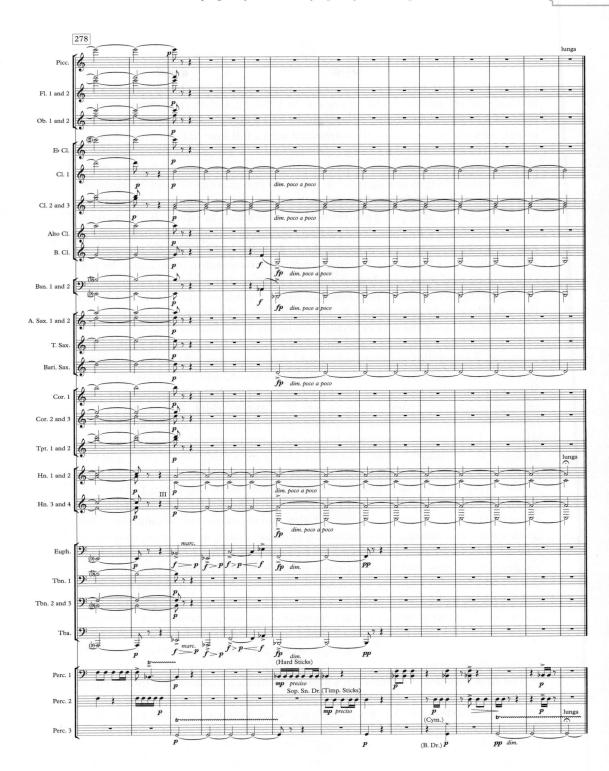

Vincent Persichetti's Symphony for Band (Symphony No. 6), Op. 69, is one of the mainstays of the concert band repertoire. In 1955, Persichetti was commissioned by Washington University in St. Louis to write an eight-minute piece for an ensemble of wind instruments. He responded with a full four-movement symphony for band lasting more than fifteen minutes, on the scale of a Haydn symphony or of Persichetti's own symphonies for orchestra: a first movement with a slow introduction and an Allegro in sonata form; a slow second movement; a quick dancelike movement; and a fast finale. In creating a substantial symphonic work for band, he contributed to an ongoing project of band conductors to establish a permanent classical repertoire for concert bands and wind ensembles. The work was premiered by the Washington University Band, directed by Clark Mitze, on April 16, 1956, at the Music Educators National Conference convention in St. Louis. Its first professional performances, both conducted by Persichetti, were given on August 2 and 3 of the same year by the Goldman Band in outdoor concerts in New York's Prospect Park and Central Park. By the early 1960s, the symphony was regularly appearing on lists of the core repertoire for bands in the United States.

This symphony was successful in part because it is well suited to the band medium. Beyond the standard wind and brass instruments of an orchestra, Persichetti writes for a band that includes soprano, alto, and bass clarinets; alto, tenor, and baritone saxophones; cornets; and euphonium (high tuba). This instrumentation provides a wide variety of timbres, which Persichetti uses in constantly changing combinations, making the music colorful and attractive to listeners. Every instrument gets its turn at the thematic material, making the piece engaging for the players as well, a crucial quality for a piece whose most frequent performers are school, college, and amateur bands.

The symphony focuses heavily on percussion, featuring three players and a variety of instruments, including in the first movement four timpani and suspended cymbal (Percussion 1); tenor, alto, and soprano snare drums, tom-tom, tambourine, and triangle (Percussion 2); and bass drum, tenor drum, suspended cymbal, xylophone, and sizzle cymbal (Percussion 3). The percussion parts are challenging to play and to coordinate, often featuring rapid exchanges among the players (see for example measures 1–10). Persichetti used percussion more extensively here than in his previous music, and his manuscripts for the symphony show his increased interest: they contain lists of percussion instruments, specifications for different kinds of sticks, and a diagram of how the percussion section should be arranged. This symphony set a pattern for many later works for band in which percussion is prominent and full of colorful variety.

The first movement opens with a slow introduction marked by a motto figure in horn 1 (measures 1–2), a premonition of the Allegro's first theme in the low instruments (measure 3), drum exchanges in percussion, and mysterious-sounding counterpoint in the low winds and brass. The opening notes in the timpani (B♭, e, and F), horn (sounding f'–b♭–g'–c', a fifth lower than written), and bass instruments suggest a tonal center of B♭ Lydian, but chromatic notes and rapidly moving harmonies raise uncertainty, as in many slow introductions, and this section closes on an open fifth D–A (measure 19).

A change of tempo and character at measure 21 heralds the exposition, marked Allegro and full of energy. Rising tenths in the low brass underscore a rhythm and contour in the xylophone and snare drums that is immediately taken up by clarinet 1 playing the sprightly, mostly stepwise first theme (measure 25), accompanied by the other clarinets in thirds. The anticipation of this clarinet melody through its rhythm and approximate contour is one sign of Persichetti's close integration of percussion into the thematic fabric of the symphony. After a hint of B♭ Lydian in the opening measures of the exposition, the clarinet presents its melody in F major, followed by a repetition in G major by other woodwinds (measure 33) and then rapidly changing harmonies as the theme is fragmented and developed. A transition leads to the second theme, which is derived from the opening horn motto. It begins at measure 57 with the motto itself, but in a new harmonic environment over an open fifth on A♭–E♭. The leaps in the motto develop into a syncopated, leaping melody that gives this theme a jazzy character and contrasts strongly with the scalar, almost pastoral first theme. The appearance of the second theme in the brass provides a timbral contrast with the woodwind setting of the first theme. Like the first theme, the second is quickly fragmented and tossed among instruments.

A brief closing theme (measure 110) concludes the exposition and leads into the development at measure 120 with sustained chords, a distinct difference from the opening energy of the exposition. Fragments of both themes mix it up, with the second theme most prominent beginning in measure 141 and the first theme taking the lead around measure 173.

The recapitulation begins at measure 220, with the percussion and rising tenths again introducing the first theme. Here that theme appears at three parallel pitch levels, beginning on concert pitches f' in the alto saxophone, a'' a major tenth higher in E♭ clarinet, and g''' a minor seventh higher still in piccolo (measure 226). The simultaneous renditions in F and G telescope the two opening statements from the exposition. Perhaps because both themes are so prominent in the development, the recapitulation is quite short. Material from the second theme returns beginning in measure 237 over the tonic B♭ in the low brass. A brief coda beginning at measure 260 presents the characteristic rhythm from the horn motto in augmentation and ends with a recollection of that motto in euphonium and tuba (measures 280–84) under a final chord that combines a B♭-major triad in the brass with an F-major triad in the clarinets.

Persichetti does not use traditional tonal harmony, yet there are many traditional elements. The themes are mostly diatonic, most chords are based on thirds or fifths, and changes of pitch collection and shades of greater or lesser dissonance create a sense of harmonic motion, tension, and resolution (for example, the relatively consonant final chord emerges from much more intense dissonance on the previous page, created by juxtaposing triads that are dissonant with each other). The recurrences of B♭ as the lowest note at the beginning and end of the movement, at the beginning of the exposition, and at the second theme in the recapitulation establish it as the tonal center. The musical language here is typical of Persichetti's music in any medium, and its combination of modern sounds and techniques with reference to tonal centers was characteristic of many postwar composers in classical genres.

Drawing on musical tradition as well as his own Italian heritage, Persichetti uses a variety of Italian performance indications. Most of these are familiar, from Adagio and Allegro to *dolce* and *semplice*, while others are easy to decipher, like *brillante* and *intenso*. A few such markings are not as common, such as *caloroso* (warm) and *ruvido* (coarse or rough).

The score can be more difficult to read than an orchestral score because of the many transposing instruments. Clarinets, cornets, and trumpets in B♭ all sound a whole step lower than notated; the E♭ clarinet a minor third higher; alto clarinet and alto saxophone in E♭ a major sixth lower; bass clarinet and tenor saxophone in B♭ a major ninth lower; baritone saxophone in E♭ a major thirteenth lower; and horns in F a perfect fifth lower.

Benjamin Britten (1913–1976)

Peter Grimes: Act III, Scene 2, *To hell with all your mercy!*

Opera

1944–45

200

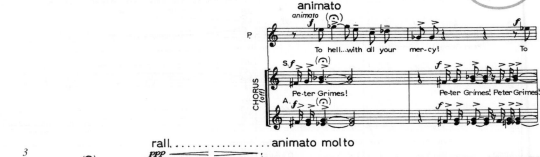

From Benjamin Britten, *Peter Grimes* (London: Boosey & Hawkes, 1963), 491–508. *Peter Grimes*, Op. 33, by Benjamin Britten and Montagu Slater. © Copyright 1945 by Boosey & Hawkes Music Publishers Ltd. Reprinted by permission.

BALSTRODE: *(Crossing to lift Peter up)* Come on, I'll help you with the boat.
ELLEN: No!
BALSTRODE: Sail out till you lose sight of the Moot Hall.   Then sink the boat.   D'you hear? Sink her. Good-bye Peter.

There is a crunch of shingle as Balstrode leads Peter down to his boat, and helps him push it out.   After a short pause, he returns, takes Ellen by the arm, and leads her away.

Dawn slowly begins and the Borough slowly comes to life.   Some stragglers of the manhunt go

End of Opera

Benjamin Britten took his character Peter Grimes from *The Borough* (1810), a narrative poem by English poet George Crabbe about the people of Aldeburgh, a coastal town in Suffolk near Britten's childhood home. The story of Grimes, a fisherman who beat his apprentices, lost them in accidents, and went mad, might seem an unpromising plot for an opera. But for Britten and his life partner, tenor Peter Pears, Grimes's life as an outcast paralleled their own lives as pacifists, as conscientious objectors to all wars (including World War II, then raging), and as homosexuals, hated beyond reason by a society that could not accept them as they were. Grimes himself was neither a pacifist nor a homosexual, nor even a very sympathetic character. Instead, the focus of the libretto, written by Montagu Slater from the scenario Britten and Pears had conceived, was on the crowd's persecution of Grimes simply for being different, and on the way his internalization of their hatred leads to his destruction.

Britten composed the music between January 1944 and February 1945, assisted by a commission from the Koussevitzky Musical Foundation. *Peter Grimes* was premiered at Sadler's Wells Theatre in London on June 7, 1945, just a month after the war ended in Europe, with Pears in the title role. The opera's powerful message about the relationship between the individual and the state resonated deeply in the postwar world, and its emotional, accessible music established Britten's and Pears's reputations as the leading English composer and tenor of their time, respectively. The opera was soon staged throughout Europe and North America and has become one of the most popular postwar operas.

The opera begins with a prologue, an inquest into the death of Peter's apprentice on a fishing trip when they ran out of drinking water. Although Peter is exonerated, the townspeople blame him for the boy's death, and he is advised not to take on another apprentice unless he can get a woman to look after the boy. One solution would be to marry Mrs. Ellen Orford, a widowed schoolmistress and one of the few people friendly to Peter. But Grimes is not ready to marry Ellen, even though he is in love with her, because he feels he must prove himself to the town first by making lots of money. Knowing that Peter cannot handle his boat by himself, Ned Keene, the apothecary, finds him a new boy from the workhouse. Ellen is sympathetic to the boy, but when she discovers a bruise on him, she reproaches Peter for his temper. Peter strikes her and forces the boy to leave with him. This moment, when Peter accepts the town's brutalized image of him, is the crux of the drama, and it begins the downward spiral. Propelled by rumors that he is mistreating the boy, the townspeople come looking for Peter and his apprentice, only to find Peter's home, an old upturned boat beside a cliff, neatly kept but unoccupied. They do not know that their coming spurred Peter to hurry down to his boat and set out to sea, and on the way the boy slipped and fell into a chasm. After a few days with no sign of the boy, rumors fly and the townspeople again come after Peter, unaware that they themselves caused the boy's death. Ellen and the retired merchant skipper Balstrode, who has supported Peter in the past, encounter him wandering in the fog, overcome by grief and stress. Ellen wants to comfort him, but Balstrode advises him to take his boat out to sea and sink with it, which Peter proceeds to do.

The excerpt included here, from the very end of the opera, begins as the offstage chorus of townspeople repeatedly calls Peter's name, and he answers them in a florid and meandering recitative. This tragic scene eloquently displays the remarkable dramatic effects that Britten creates from simple means. Here, the only accompaniment to the chorus's calls and Peter's raving is the foghorn, on the pitch center of E♭. The rest of the scene recalls earlier music, as is appropriate to the final moments of a tragedy. When Peter cries out, "To hell with all your mercy! To hell with your revenge, And God have mercy upon you!," he echoes the motive introduced at the crucial scene when he hit Ellen, to the words "And God have mercy upon me!," which has pervaded the opera ever since. When Ellen comes to take him home, Peter does not respond to her directly, but recalls his song from Act I when he imagined finding a safe harbor in her love (measures 22–38 of this excerpt). When Balstrode helps Peter cast off, there is no music at all; here, Britten recognized that silence is more meaningful.

At the end, what remains are the sea and the townspeople, equally indifferent to Peter's fate. Britten captures that indifference through bitonality, returning to earlier music associated with sea and town, in two simultaneous keys, like two mutually indifferent planes of sound. The calm sea is depicted by sustained tones (e''', c''', and f'') in the upper strings decorated with grace notes, like flecks on the surface, with occasional waves suggested by arpeggiated thirds in harp and clarinet that encompass all the notes of the C-major scale, and a haunting melody in the flute (measures 52–59). Against this backdrop and supported by chords in the brass, the townspeople sing in A major (starting at measure 64) a song in hymn style about their daily routines, first heard at the opening of Act I. Between verses, someone mentions a report of a sinking boat (measures 84–89), but it is dismissed as a rumor (measures 105–9)—ironically, the only rumor in the entire opera that is true. The townspeople sing the final verse of their hymn, about the ceaseless, unpitying motions of the tide, this time inverting the second half of the melody into a majestic descent, and the curtain slowly falls.

In the Metropolitan Opera production on the accompanying video, the contrast between Peter's personal tragedy and the uncaring indifference of the townsfolk is heightened by a shift in staging from stylized realism to abstract minimalism. Peter is costumed in ragged, stained clothing and has unkempt hair, reflecting his distress, and he moves and gestures in ways that express his feelings. He sings in front of two tall structures with realistic wooden siding, representing the buildings of the town. Ellen and Balstrode appear in elevated doorways and look out at us rather than at Peter, conveying a sense of distance between Peter and the town, even those townspeople most sympathetic to him. When Peter acquiesces to Balstrode's command to sail out and sink his boat, he turns and walks down the narrow passage between the two buildings. Then the buildings separate and move to the sides, and the realistic set is replaced by a bare stage whose back wall is lit in shades of blue to suggest the dawn sky. The townsfolk enter, dressed in their work clothes. But instead of going about their business, they stand impassively facing the audience, dwarfed by the size of the stage and nearly unmoving, as if they, like the sea, were a force of nature incapable of understanding or sympathy.

▶ Opera video available

Olivier Messiaen (1908–1992)

Quartet for the End of Time: First movement, *Liturgie de cristal*

Quartet for violin, clarinet, violoncello, and piano

1940–41

Olivier Messiaen wrote his *Quartet for the End of Time* during World War II in the winter of 1940–41 while interned at a prisoner-of-war camp in Silesia. He had been captured by the Germans the previous May as he was serving in the French army. He wrote the piece for performance by himself as pianist, together with a violinist, clarinetist, and cellist who were also imprisoned there. They gave the work its first performance in the camp, in the middle of winter, for their fellow prisoners.

The title refers to the biblical prophecy of the Apocalypse, which will bring the end of time as a progression of finite moments and the beginning of eternity. The score, published in 1942 after Messiaen had been released from captivity, carries the inscription, "In homage to the Angel of the Apocalypse, who raises his hand to the heavens and says, 'There will be no more Time.'" Four of the eight movements are for all four players, but the third is for clarinet alone, the fourth omits piano, the fifth is for cello and piano, and the eighth is for violin and piano, so each performer plays in six movements.

The quartet is a study of time—measured, finite time, and timelessness, or eternity. Although the quartet lacks a text, it is a piece of sacred music, as is a great deal of Messiaen's output. Religion is not so much on the surface of his compositions as it is the motivation and goal for his creative effort.

The first movement, *Liturgie de cristal* (Crystal Liturgy), included here, conveys a sense of ecstatic contemplation of the passage of time. The clarinet and violin each play stylized birdcalls (of the blackbird and nightingale respectively), a type of melody that Messiaen often used to suggest nature as a divine gift. The figures do not develop, but change in unpredictable ways. Like the birds they imitate, each instrument sticks to its own repertoire of sounds. The rhythm of the birdcalls is also that of nature, having a pulse but no clear meter.

The cello and piano lay out complex patterns of duration and pitch that repeat in cycles. The cello constantly repeats a five-note sequence (C–E–D–F♯–B♭) in high harmonics (see below), using a pattern of fifteen durations. New statements of the pattern begin on the second quarter note of measure 8, the last eighth of measure 13, and so on, every five and a half measures. These melodic and rhythmic cycles are like the *color* (repeating melody) and *talea* (repeating rhythm) of fourteenth-century isorhythm (see NAWM 25 and 26a). The durational pattern Messiaen has chosen here combines two *non-retrogradable rhythms*, his term for rhythms that are palindromes, the same forward and backward: the first three notes (respectively 4, 3, and 4 eighth notes in duration) and the remaining twelve (which form the pattern 4–1–1–3–1–1–1–1–3–1–1–4, again counting eighth notes). Such rhythms remain the same whichever direction time runs, and thus suggest the unchangeable, the divine, and the eternal.

The cycles in the piano are more complex, with a series of twenty-nine chords overlapping a rhythmic pattern of seventeen durations. The rhythmic cycle begins again on the downbeat of measure 6 and every thirteen beats thereafter. The second statement of the chord cycle begins on the last eighth note of measure 8, with different rhythms because of the new alignment with the durational pattern. It would take twenty-nine repetitions of the rhythmic pattern and seventeen repetitions of the chord cycle, or a total of 377 beats, to return to the original alignment, and a total of 12,441 beats (4147 measures, or approximately three hours and fifty minutes) if the cello pattern is taken into account. Perhaps Messiaen meant this to imply a very long cycle, of which we hear only a part, as a metaphor for time everlasting, during which we each exist for only a moment.

The combination of the repeating cycles with variable alignment and freer repetition and variation in the violin and clarinet creates music that combines constancy and change. This presentation of ideas is typical of Messiaen, whose works embody a kind of meditation on a few materials that parallels meditative prayer.

The cello harmonics are played on the instrument's highest string, tuned to the A just below middle C. While the index finger of the left hand presses the string against the fingerboard to select the pitch, the smallest finger lightly touches the string at a spot a fourth higher (indicated by a diamond-shaped note), which produces a harmonic two octaves higher than the notated pitch. The ethereal sound, in the same range as the high birdcalls in the violin, lends height and depth to the scene suggested in the music.

202

Pierre Boulez (b. 1925)

Le marteau sans maître: Movement 6, *Bourreaux de solitude*

Chamber song cycle

1953–55

BOURREAUX DE SOLITUDE

Le pas s'est éloigné le marcheur s'est tu
Sur le cadran de l'Imitation
Le Balancier lance sa charge de granit reflexe.

— RENÉ CHAR

EXECUTIONERS OF SOLITUDE

The footstep has moved away the walker is silent
On the dial of the Imitation
The Pendulum launches its load of reflex granite.

Pierre Boulez began *Le marteau sans maître* (The Hammer without a Master) in 1953, intending it for the Donaueschingen Festival in 1954. When the performance had to be postponed, he revised the piece and added the ninth movement. It was finally premiered in June 1955 in Baden-Baden, and it soon became his most famous work. He dedicated the published score to Hans Rosbaud, who conducted the premiere.

Boulez based this piece on texts drawn from René Char's collection of surrealist poetry, *Le marteau sans maître* (1934). He arranged the work in three cycles, each centered on one poem. In two cases, instrumental movements precede and follow the song setting, treating the same basic material in different ways; in the third, there are two settings of the song. But instead of placing these three cycles one after the other, Boulez interleaved them:

Mvt	First cycle	Second cycle	Third cycle
1	Before *L'artisanat furieux*		
2		Commentary I on *Bourreaux de solitude*	
3	*L'artisanat furieux*		
4		Commentary II on *Bourreaux de solitude*	
5			*Bel édifice et les pressentiments*, first version
6		*Bourreaux de solitude*	
7	After *L'artisanat furieux*		
8		Commentary III on *Bourreaux de solitude*	
9			*Bel édifice et les pressentiments*, second version

The second cycle occupies the even-numbered movements. Its focus is the song setting in the sixth movement, included here.

The work is scored for alto voice, alto flute (in G, sounding a fourth lower than written), xylorimba (a large xylophone, sounding an octave higher than written), vibraphone, percussion, guitar (sounding an octave lower than written), and viola (called by its French name *Alto* in the score). The use of low female voice, alto flute, and viola gives the music a darker quality than the more predictable soprano, flute, and violin, while the plucked sounds of the guitar and the percussive sounds of the vibraphone and xylophone offer a lighter texture than a piano. The xylophone and vibraphone are both percussion instruments played with mallets, with bars for different pitches laid out like a keyboard over open tubes that serve as resonators; they differ in that the xylophone's bars are wood while the vibraphone's are metal, and the latter has electrically powered turning wheels in its resonating tubes that create a vibrato or pulsation. As in Schoenberg's *Pierrot lunaire* (NAWM 172), a different group of instruments plays in each movement. All seven performers participate in *Bourreaux de solitude*, although the percussionist plays only maracas.

At this point in his career, Boulez was committed to serial procedures for organizing pitch, duration, and dynamics, but he used them in a very complex manner. In Boulez's view, the rigid patterning in his own early pieces that applied serial principles to duration and other parameters was not the same as composition, which requires the exercise of taste and expressivity. By deploying rows in novel ways, deriving subsidiary series in each parameter from a basic row, and varying his material in many ways simultaneously, he made his music much more diverse, fluid, and expressive, but he also made his path in constructing the music extraordinarily difficult to follow.

Even knowing the basic row for the second cycle is little help:

The row is used in this form only once in this song, in its final measures. The chord on the second sixteenth note of measure 92 contains the first seven notes (with their proper durations and dynamics), and the final chord contains the last five (with the right dynamics, but slightly shortened durations). Elsewhere, Boulez deploys a number of derived series, created using a variety of methods.

Some aspects lie relatively close to the surface. For example, in the first measure, all twelve pitch-classes are sounded once. Each has a different duration, increasing progressively up the chromatic scale from D (one sixteenth note) to C♯ (twelve sixteenths, equal to a dotted quarter note). Each also has a unique dynamic level, increasing as the pitch-classes descend the chromatic scale from A (***pp***) to B♭ (accented ***ff sfz***). The composite rhythm includes an attack on every sixteenth note. The inclusion of all pitch-classes, durations, attack points, dynamic levels, and instruments makes clear that these parameters are systematically organized, while providing a great diversity of sounds for the listener. The rest of the instrumental introduction (measures 1–13) follows similar procedures, although the precise procedures and the underlying pulsation change with each statement of all twelve notes.

When the voice enters at the pickup to measure 14, the sound of the music changes greatly. The singer begins her first phrase on the same note as the alto flute, moves to a note the guitar has just played, and ends on a note shared with viola. When other instruments join in measures 17–18, they play notes she has already sung, or that other instruments have just played, although we have not yet heard all twelve in this section. This duplication of notes between instruments and within phrases gives a very different sound to the main part of the song, in which the voice alternates with short instrumental interludes. The closing section (measures 79–94) is again entirely instrumental, and like the introduction it is marked by twelve-tone saturation and relatively regular rhythm.

While these large-scale factors give shape to the piece, the difficulty of analyzing the particulars of the pitch content, durations, and dynamics in this piece suggests that analysis is really beside the point. Like Schoenberg or Wagner, Boulez does not want us to take apart his music to expose his secrets. Instead, he creates an ever-changing, diverting surface with a highly individual mixture of sounds that can be attractive and engaging. Our very inability to explain his music may allow us to experience it directly, rather than as an example of a complex system.

The difficulty of performing such music is obvious: the rhythms are unusual, the dynamics are constantly changing, the melodies awkward. Clearly, the singer must have perfect pitch. It may seem helpful to the singer to have her pitches matched by other instruments, but that may simply make any errors more obvious. A sign of how difficult the piece is to coordinate is that it needs a conductor, even for an ensemble of only seven—and that Boulez dedicated it to the conductor, not the singer, of the premiere performance.

The performance on the accompanying recording is conducted by the composer himself, who in the decades since this piece's premiere has become more widely known as a conductor than as a composer.

John Cage (1912–1992)

Sonatas and Interludes: Sonata V

Suite for prepared piano

1946–48

203

TABLE OF PREPARATIONS

[MUTES OF VARIOUS MATERIALS ARE PLACED BETWEEN THE STRINGS OF THE KEYS USED, THUS EFFECTING TRANSFORMATIONS OF THE PIANO SOUNDS WITH RESPECT TO ALL OF THEIR CHARACTERISTICS .]

TONE

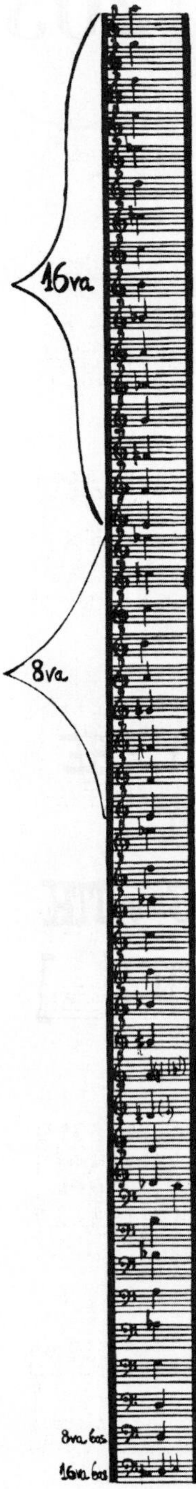
16va
8va
8va bas
16va bas

MATERIAL	STRINGS LEFT TO RIGHT	DISTANCE FROM DAMPER (INCHES)	MATERIAL	STRINGS LEFT TO RIGHT	DISTANCE FROM DAMPER (INCHES)	MATERIAL	STRINGS LEFT TO RIGHT	DISTANCE FROM DAMPER (INCHES)	TONE
			SCREW	2-3	1 1/4 *				A
			MED. BOLT	2-3	1 3/8 *				G
			SCREW	2-3	1 5/8 *				F
			SCREW	2-3	1 13/16 *				E
			SCREW	2-3	1 3/4 *				E♭
			SM. BOLT	2-3	2 *				D
			SCREW	2-3	1 11/16 *				C♯
			FURNITURE BOLT	2-3	2 3/16 *				C
			SCREW	2-3	2 1/2 *				B
			SCREW	2-3	1 7/8 *				B♭
			MED. BOLT	2-3	2 7/8 *				A
			SCREW	2-3	2 1/4 *				A♭
			SCREW	2-3	3 3/4 *				G
			SCREW	2-3	2 15/16 *				F♯
SCREW	1-2	3/4 *	FURN. BOLT + 2 NUTS	2-3	2 1/8 *	SCREW + 2 NUTS	2-3	3 1/4 *	F
			SCREW	2-3	1 13/16 *				E
			FURNITURE BOLT	2-3	1 7/8				E♭
			SCREW	2-3	1 15/16				C♯
			SCREW	2-3	1 1/16				C
(DAMPER TO BRIDGE = 4 7/16; ADJUST ACCORDINGLY)			MED. BOLT	2-3	3 3/4				B
			SCREW	2-3	4 7/16				A
RUBBER	1-2-3	4 1/2	FURNITURE BOLT	2-3	1 1/4				G♯
			SCREW	2-3	1 3/4				F♯
			SCREW	2-3	2 5/16				F
RUBBER	1-2-3	5 3/4							E
RUBBER	1-2-3	6 1/2	FURN. BOLT + NUT	2-3	6 7/8				E♭
			FURNITURE BOLT	2-3	2 9/16				D
RUBBER	1-2-3	3 5/8							D♭
			BOLT	2-3	7 1/8				C
			BOLT	2-3	2				B
SCREW	1-2	10	SCREW	2-3	1	RUBBER	1-2-3	8 1/4	B♭
(PLASTIC (see G))	1-2-3	2 15/16				RUBBER	1-2-3	4 1/2	G♯
PLASTIC (OVER 1 UNDER 2-3)	1-2-3	2 7/8				RUBBER	1-2-3	10 1/8	G
(PLASTIC (see D))	1-2-3	4 1/4				RUBBER	1-2-3	5 7/16	D♯
PLASTIC (OVER 1 - UNDER 2-3)	1-2-3	4 1/8				RUBBER	1-2-3	9 3/4	D
BOLT	1-2	15 1/2	BOLT	2-3	11/16	RUBBER	1-2-3	14 1/8	D♭
BOLT	1-2	14 1/2	BOLT	2-3	7/8	RUBBER	1-2-3	6 1/2	C
BOLT	1-2	14 3/4	BOLT	2-3	9/16	RUBBER	1-2-3	14	B
RUBBER	1-2-3	9 1/2	MED. BOLT	2-3	10 1/8				B♭
SCREW	1-2	5 7/8	LG. BOLT	2-3	5 7/8	SCREW + NUTS	1-2	1	A
BOLT	1-2	7 1/8	MED. BOLT	2-3	2 1/4	RUBBER	1-2-3	4 1/8	A♭
LONG BOLT	1-2	8 3/4	LG BOLT	2-3	3 1/4				G
			BOLT	2-3	11/16				D
SCREW + RUBBER	1-2	4 7/16							D
ERASER (OVER D UNDER C♯ + E♭) AM. PENCIL CO. #346	1	6 3/4							D

* MEASURE FROM BRIDGE.

John Cage was primarily a composer of music for percussion when he invented the prepared piano around 1940. Commissioned to write music to accompany a modern dance work (*Bacchanale*) that was to be staged in a hall too small to fit a percussion ensemble, he discovered that he could create percussion-like sounds on the piano by inserting small objects between the strings. He was inspired by the work of his former teacher, Henry Cowell, who also experimented with producing new sounds on the piano. In Cowell's *The Banshee* (NAWM 193), the performer plays on the strings directly, but all the sounds in a prepared piano piece are produced by playing on the keyboard. Placing material between the strings makes the piano into a one-person percussion orchestra. After writing several prepared-piano scores for dances, Cage began to compose concert works for the instrument as well. His masterpiece for the prepared piano is *Sonatas and Interludes*, composed in 1946–48 and published in 1949 by Cowell's New Music Edition. The score is in Cage's own distinctive handwriting. He dedicated the work to pianist Maro Ajemian, who premiered it at Carnegie Hall in New York in January 1949.

In composing each piece for prepared piano, Cage first settled on what he called a gamut of sounds, the repertoire of sounds he would use in the piece, and on the particular insertions that would produce those sounds, which he had learned by experiment over several years. The Table of Preparations in the score for *Sonatas and Interludes* shows the forty-five preparations required for the piece, indicating what material to use and exactly where to place it, since the exact position affects the sound. Each piece in the set of sixteen sonatas and four interludes uses only some of the prepared sounds, giving it a distinctive palette. Some use unaltered piano sounds as well. The notation is in most respects like standard piano notation, but the sound that comes out when a key is pressed may be on a different pitch and may not sound like a piano at all. Thus the notation becomes like tablature (see the lute tablature in NAWM 65 and 87), telling the player where to place the fingers and how long to play each note, but not what sound will result.

Sonata V is an ideal example to demonstrate how the material inserted between the strings affects their sound, because each hand plays repeatedly on a small group of keys in a limited range, making it easy to compare the effect of each insertion. At the outset, the "melody" in the right hand goes down and up a segment of the chromatic scale from *b'* to *eb"*. As shown in the Table of Preparations, the strings for these notes have had different materials inserted in them:

- a metal bolt between the second and third strings for *b'* and *c"*
- a piece of rubber in *db"*
- a metal furniture bolt between the second and third strings for *d"*
- rubber *and* a metal furniture bolt and nut in the strings for *eb"*

Listen to the "melody" as the right hand goes back and forth through this gamut of sound. What sounds do you hear, and how do those sounds relate to the material inserted between the strings?

Adding a metal bolt between the strings creates a gonglike sound: the string vibrates freely but in a different way because of the additional mass, and there may be more than one pitch because the tension on the strings holding the bolt may differ. Adding weight to the strings also lowers the pitch. Indeed, in the performance on the accompanying recording, the pitch obtained by playing *d″* sounds lower than the pitch made by playing *c′*, because the furniture bolt in the strings of the former is heavier than the normal bolt in the latter.

In all three cases in which only a bolt is inserted, it is placed between the second and third strings for each note. This leaves the first string unaltered, so that it resonates at the usual notated pitch. When the *una corda* ("one string") pedal on the piano is pressed, indicated by a dashed line under the music, the hammers that strike the strings are all moved slightly to the right, so that they do not strike the first string. In the first half of the piece, when the *una corda* pedal is held down, we hear only the gonglike sound of the strings with the bolts inserted between them. But in measures 21–27 and 37–40, when the *una corda* pedal is not pressed, the hammers hit the unaltered strings as well, and we hear two different sounds, the gong and the piano tone.

Adding a piece of rubber has a very different result: it deadens the sound, so we hear a sharp attack and little sustain. This makes the *eb″* and *db″* sound like small drums or woodblocks rather than a piano. The combination of rubber with a bolt on the *eb″* sounds particularly woodlike in the accompanying recording. As the "melody" goes up and down in the right hand, we hear an alternation between woodlike and metallic sounds.

Meanwhile, the notes in the left hand move quickly up and down between *b* and *eb′*, an octave below the right hand as notated, although the sounds are far from exact octaves apart. Here the preparations are different:

- two metal bolts plus a piece of rubber for *b*, *c*, and *db′*
- a piece of plastic plus a piece of rubber for *d′* and *eb′*

Because of their similar preparations, these five notes are fairly consistent in sound, suggesting a series of tuned log drums.

Most of the piece focuses on these ten sounds, but later on Cage introduces four more. The *ab* in the right hand in measures 28–29 is prepared with a piece of rubber and two bolts, one somewhat larger ("medium bolt"), and produces a sound like a tin can with a spoon in it that is immediately damped. The *g′* and *ab′* in the left hand in measures 32–33 are prepared with plastic and rubber, so sound similar in timbre to the *d′* and *eb′* below them. And the high *g″* grace note in measure 37 is entirely unaltered, so it sounds like a piano note. In each case, the new notes are grouped with other notes that have similar sounds. Even the pure piano tone of the *g″* is combined with the *b′*, *c″*, and *d″*, which include unaltered piano strings, and Cage allows the sounds to mingle by keeping the sustaining pedal down for two measures (indicated by the solid bracket under the music).

Given this gamut of sounds, how does Cage shape the piece?

Thirteen of the sixteen sonatas in *Sonatas and Interludes*, including this sonata, are in simple binary form, in two sections with a marked repeat of each section. This invokes a comparison to the keyboard sonatas of Domenico Scarlatti (see NAWM 113), a deliberate reference to a historical model that is unusual for Cage, although as we have seen such references are quite common for other twentieth-century composers such as Schoenberg (NAWM 172a and 173), Webern (NAWM

175), Stravinsky (NAWM 177), and Bartók (NAWM 178). Sonatas IX, X, and XI add a third, unrepeated section, respectively at the beginning, at the end, or between the two repeated sections. There are also four interludes, the first two through-composed, the last two in four repeated sections. The first interlude falls after Sonata IV, the second and third after Sonata VIII, and the fourth after Sonata XII, breaking the sonatas into groups of four in a symmetrical arrangement.

In addition to these outward forms based on repetition, each movement also uses a type of structure based on duration that Cage first devised for his percussion pieces, in which the proportions within the whole piece are reflected within each unit. The units are marked off by double barlines and grouped into larger sections. In Sonata V, the first section has two nine-measure units, and the second section has two and a half (the last measure, in $\frac{3}{2}$, counts as one and a half measures of $\frac{2}{2}$). When each section is repeated, the overall structure is $2+2+2\frac{1}{2}+2\frac{1}{2}$. The same proportions can be seen within each unit, demarcated by the musical material. Cage sometimes referred to this structure as *square root form*, because it features the same number of units as there are measures in each unit—in this case, nine complete units of nine measures each—so that the total number of measures in each piece is the square of the number of measures in each unit (here, 9 x 9 = 81), and thus the number in each unit is the square root of the total.

Having examined the sounds and the durational structure Cage uses in this piece, we are ready to see how they interact to create the piece's overall shape:

· The first unit (measures 1–9) is characterized by an ostinato in the left hand and varied "melody" in the right. The longest notes—the dotted quarter notes in measures 1, 3, 5, and 7—demarcate the sub-units of $2+2+2\frac{1}{2}+2\frac{1}{2}$ measures. These are also particularly distinctive sounds: the striking woodlike sound notated *eb″* and the more drumlike sound on *db″*, both quite different from the metallic sounds on the other notes.

· The second unit begins like the first but quickly changes to emphasize long gonglike sounds. The $2+2+2\frac{1}{2}+2\frac{1}{2}$ proportion is less clearly articulated; there is no change at measure 12, the gong changes at measure 14 together with the accompanimental ostinato (now five quarter notes long), and only the ostinato changes in the middle of measure 16 (back to its original form). Then the first two units repeat as a section.

· The third unit (measures 19–27) begins the second section. It continues the long gongs of the second unit, now softer, and the ostinato figure is varied and stated only once within each sub-unit. Because the *una corda* pedal is released, the gong sounds are joined for the first time by pure piano tones. The $2+2+2\frac{1}{2}+2\frac{1}{2}$ measure groupings are very clear, articulated by gong sounds and the re-initiation of the ostinato figure.

· The fourth unit (measures 28–36) is the loudest and most active, returning to the opening material and varying it while also introducing three new sounds on *ab*, *g′*, and *ab′*. The $2+2+2\frac{1}{2}+2\frac{1}{2}$ measure groupings are marked by changes of material.

· The last unit—really half a unit (measures 37–40)—drops the ostinato entirely and features only the gongs and piano tones. Thus overall the piece moves from a mixture of wood and gong sounds to gong and piano tones, even creating the sense of a cadence at the end. As a half unit, these measures have just a 2+2½ grouping of measures (half the usual length), delineated by releasing the sustaining pedal and all notes but *c"* on the downbeat of measure 39.

As Cage discovered in playing his prepared piano pieces on various pianos and hearing them played by a number of pianists, the variability beween pianos and pianists means that the exact sounds created by the preparations will differ as well. This can be heard by comparing several recordings. His inability to precisely determine the sounds of the prepared piano was one factor that led Cage to take up indeterminacy in his later music. Yet the general move from woody to metallic timbres described here will be true of any performance, and so will the rhythm, so the shape of the piece will remain the same.

John Cage (1912–1992)

Music of Changes: Book I

Chance composition for piano

1951

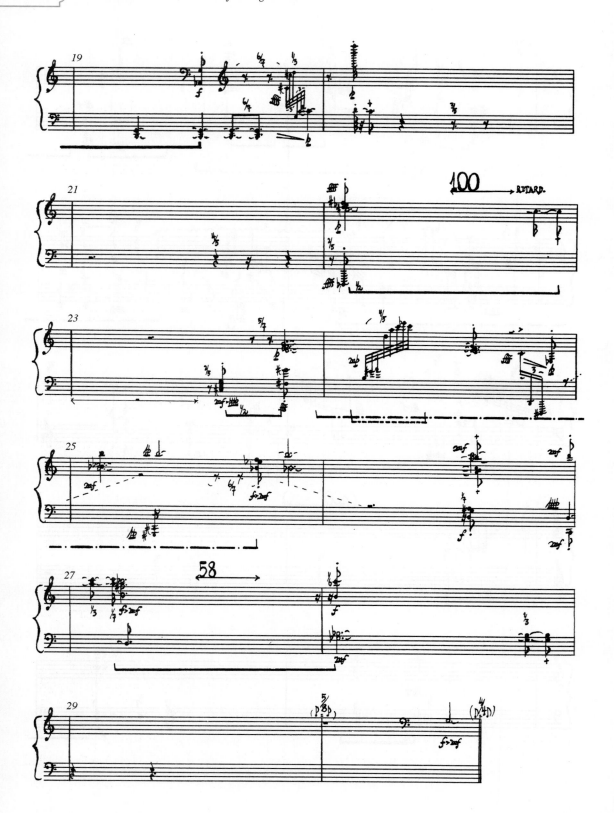

Music of Changes was one of the first pieces in which John Cage explored the possibility of determining aspects of the music by chance operations. He composed the work in four sections he called "books." Book I, included here, was composed in May 1951 and premiered that August by pianist David Tudor at the University of Colorado in Boulder; the other three books were completed later that year, and Tudor premiered the entire work in New York in January 1952.

The form of the piece was designed in advance. Cage used forms based on duration, particularly square-root form, in which the large-scale divisions of the work as a whole are reflected within each unit (see explanation in NAWM 203). A simple version might have seven units of seven measures each, but *Music of Changes* is far more complex, with a structure of durations based on a total of $29\frac{5}{8}$ durational units, each $29\frac{5}{8}$ measures long. Both the piece as a whole and each unit are divided into segments defined by the ratios 3–5–$6\frac{3}{4}$–$6\frac{3}{4}$–5–$3\frac{1}{8}$. Book I contains the first three units (measures 1–30, 31–60, and 61–90); in each, the last measure is only $\frac{5}{8}$ as long as the others, for a total of $29\frac{5}{8}$ measures. The divisions within each unit—of 3, 5, $6\frac{3}{4}$, $6\frac{3}{4}$, 5, and $3\frac{1}{8}$ measures respectively—can be seen in the score, delineated by indications of tempo (see the tempo markings in the first unit, at measures 4, 9, 15, 22, and 27) and by changes of musical material and density.

Once Cage designed the durational structure, he filled it using chance operations. The title of the work refers to the ancient Chinese book *I-Ching* (Book of Changes), which contains a method for consulting an oracle by tossing coins six times to determine an answer from a list of sixty-four possible outcomes. For *Music of Changes*, Cage set up a series of charts, each with sixty-four elements that he chose using the same system. One chart determined how many events would occur during a particular segment; another determined the tempo (there were thirty-two tempos and thirty-two blanks, which if chosen maintained the previous tempo). Then there were eight charts each for sounds, dynamics (including accents), and durations. In the charts for sounds, half the possibilities were silences; the rest ranged from single notes to chords to "constellations" (several quick notes in a row) to noises (such as striking or slamming the lid of the keyboard). All these sounds were also designed in advance, so that only their selection for a particular position was determined by chance.

The result, as Cage noted, is a piece whose sequence of sounds is determined neither by the taste or psychology of the composer, nor by the traditions of past music. Neither the composer, the performer, nor the listener needs to make any value judgments, and no message is being communicated. The sounds are simply themselves, to be listened to attentively and appreciated for their own sake.

The notation (in Cage's own hand) is unusual, but what the performer plays is completely determined. The "beat" set by the tempo is the quarter note, or one-fourth of a measure, shown by a line (2.5 centimeters long in the original score, here reduced). The notation is proportional: a note's place in time is shown precisely by its position in the measure, reading the length of the measure as an exact timeline. Diamond-shaped notes indicate keys (sometimes a single key, sometimes a range of keys, as at the beginning) that are depressed silently to raise the dampers, which are then kept off the strings by the sostenuto pedal (marked with a dash-and-dot line under the notes), so that the strings resonate with harmonics generated by other notes. Other indications include using the sustaining pedal (marked with a solid line under the notes) and *una corda* pedal (which shifts the hammers to strike one instead of three strings for each note, marked with a dashed line, as in measures 33–34) and releasing a key to stop the tone (a plus above the note). Full of unusual techniques and rhythms, the piece is quite difficult to play, but the performer can take comfort from Cage's comment about this and other pieces generated by chance: "A 'mistake' is beside the point, for once anything happens it authentically is."

George Crumb (b. 1929)

Black Angels: Thirteen Images from the Dark Land:
Images 4 and 5

Electric string quartet

1970

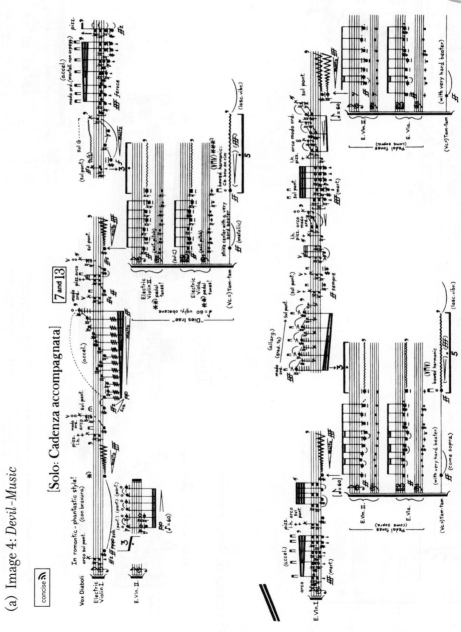

From George Crumb, *Black Angels (Images I)* (New York: C. F. Peters, 1971), 3–4. Copyright 1971 by C. F. Peters Corporation, New York. All rights reserved. Used by permission.

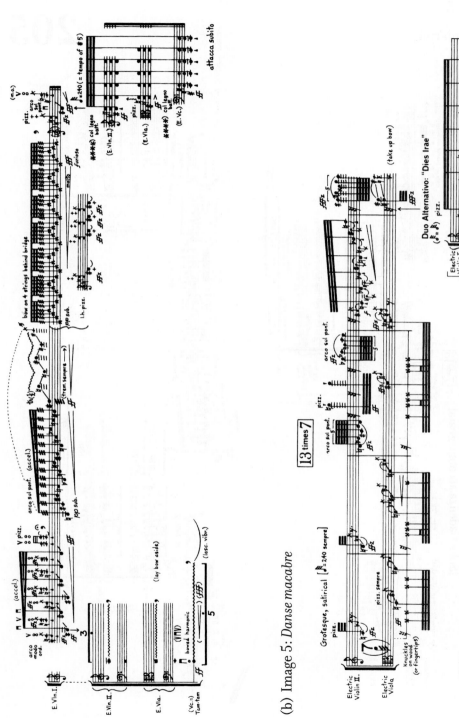

(b) Image 5: *Danse macabre*

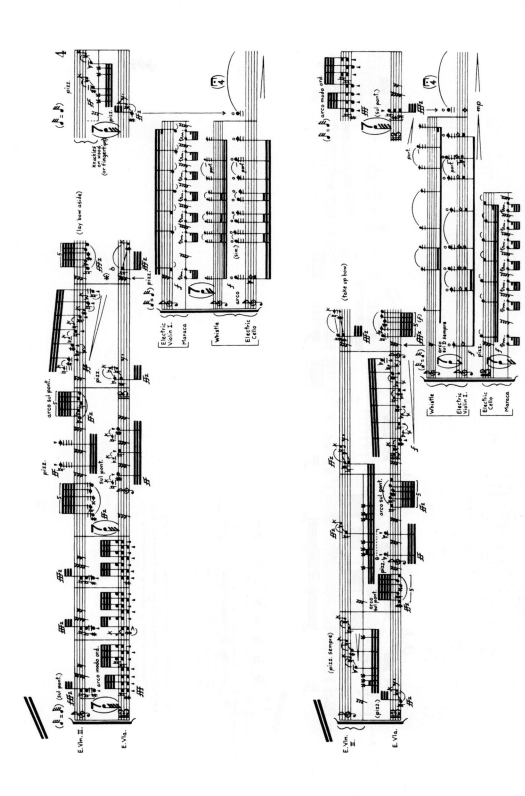

* ♢ = a percussive pizzicato (string rebounds from fingerboard)
** The Hungarian numerals one through seven. Pronounce: *ehᵭy*, Keh-tuh, hah-rohm (trilled r), *naydy, aht (ö like German), haht, hate.*

The late 1960s and early 1970s were turbulent years in the history of the United States. The Vietnam War and other issues were vehemently debated, especially on college campuses. George Crumb, a professor at the University of Pennsylvania, was deeply affected by this strife, as were many of his artist colleagues across the country. For a commission from the University of Michigan, Crumb composed *Black Angels* in 1970, inscribing at the end of the score "in tempore belli" (in time of war). The work is both a protest against the Vietnam War and a reaction to the troubled world of the late 1960s. The premiere by the Stanley Quartet in Ann Arbor, Michigan, on October 23, 1970, received a standing ovation.

A black angel is a conventional image used by painters to represent a fallen angel. According to the composer, the work represents three stages in the journey of the soul: fall from grace (the section marked "Departure," including Images 1–5), spiritual annihilation ("Absence," Images 6–9), and redemption ("Return," Images 10–13). The subtitle *Thirteen Images from the Dark Land* suggests the pervasive numerology underlying this work. The score contains numerous references to the numbers 7 and 13, which Crumb characterized as "fateful numbers"—numbers that are considered to be lucky or unlucky. These numbers affect duration, pitch, harmony, and melody. Several of the movements, for example, are based on a prominent chord with $d\sharp'–a'–e''$; counting downward in semitones from the e'', these pitches represent the numbers 0–7–13. At the conclusion of the work, Crumb duly noted: "finished on Friday the Thirteenth, March 1970."

Crumb creates a surrealistic, dreamlike character through his imaginative use of color. An electronically amplified string quartet can produce a variety of unique sounds, and Crumb explores unusual means of bowing, such as striking the strings near the pegs with the bow, holding the bow underhand in the manner of viol players, and bowing between the left-hand fingers and the pegs, along with glissandos, *sul ponticello* (on the bridge, creating a thin, metallic sound), and percussive pizzicato. In addition, the performers are asked to play a variety of percussion instruments, including maracas, tam-tams, and water-tuned crystal glasses, and to make vocal sounds, such as clicking, whistling, whispering, and chanting. The spoken words involve ritualistic counting focusing on the numbers seven and thirteen in German, French, Russian, Hungarian, Japanese, and Swahili. These effects are not mere striving for novelty; the composer employed them to create a nightmarish atmosphere as a substrate for his poetic message.

Image 4, *Devil-Music*, and Image 5, *Danse macabre*, should be considered as a pair. There is no break between them, they share a common theme, and they have similar structures. Indeed, one can hear *Devil-Music* as an improvisatory introduction to *Danse macabre*. The titles of both movements refer to medieval artworks in which the devil is shown playing the violin and leading various dancing figures to their deaths. These images were also treated in two celebrated compositions from the nineteenth century, Franz Liszt's *Totentanz* for piano and orchestra, and Camille Saint-Saëns's *Danse macabre* for violin and orchestra. The titles of both can be translated as "dance of death." Images 4 and 5 share several characteristics with these orchestral works. As in *Totentanz*, Death is associated with the Gregorian chant melody from the Requiem Mass, *Dies irae*, first used with such association in the finale of Berlioz's *Symphonie fantastique* (NAWM 138). As in Saint-Saëns's *Danse macabre*, Death plays the violin, and the tritone involving an open string is emphasized. For Saint-Saëns, the sound of open strings and a tritone represented the devil tuning his violin. In the medieval era, the tritone was called *diabolus in musica* (devil in music).

In both Images 4 and 5, the first three phrases of *Dies irae* alternate with contrasting material. In *Devil-Music* the principal line, labeled *Vox Diaboli* (devil's voice), features an intense solo cadenza for the first violinist. Virtuosic effects include triple-stopped chords, pizzicato notes plucked by the left hand (normally used only for fingering), and harmonics. In several instances, the soloist is instructed to press with the bow on the strings until "pitch becomes pure noise." Throughout the cadenza, perfect fifths and diminished fifths can be heard, often incorporating open strings; the $d\#'-a'-e''$ sonority, which uses two open strings (a' and e''), predominates. Interspersed in the brief breaks of the cadenza are the phrases of the *Dies irae* played by the second violin and viola in pedal tones—pitches an octave lower than notated (and lower than the instruments can normally play), produced by moving the bow slowly while exerting great pressure. The cellist accompanies with the tam-tam. For the final cadence, all of the instruments present a version of the principal three-note chord. The bottom three string parts employ the percussive effects of pizzicato or *col legno* (hitting the strings with the wood side of the bow).

Danse macabre alternates material played by the second violin and viola with the phases of the *Dies irae* in the first violin and cello. The second violin and viola lines rely heavily on pizzicato and other unusual effects, such as tapping on the viola with knuckles. Embedded in the second and fourth statements of these two instruments are brief quotations from Saint-Saëns's *Danse macabre*. The *Dies irae* is also presented with unusual timbres, involving pizzicato, harmonics, maracas, and whistling. At the conclusion of this Image, the first violinist and cellist whisper the numbers one through seven in Hungarian.

A performance of *Black Angels* demands considerable technical skills, creativity, and theatricality. Because a string quartet plays without a conductor, Crumb requires each performer to play from the score (rather than from a single part, as customary) so that the coordination of the parts is every player's responsibility. As an aid to the musicians, Crumb simplified the notation by omitting unnecessary rests, and he created oversized scores that can be read easily from a distance (but which had to be reduced to fit into a book this size). The score is in his own neat, very distinctive handwriting. In addition to numerous explanations and suggestions, Crumb includes a chart showing a preferred arrangement of percussion instruments. This work has become a staple in the repertory of several young professional quartets, including the Concord String Quartet heard in the recording.

Edgard Varèse (1883–1965)

Poème électronique

Electro-acoustic tape piece

1957–58

Edgard Varèse's *Poème électronique*, although now available as a self-contained sound recording, was originally part of a modern *Gesamtkunstwerk* involving architecture, sculpture, projected images, and two pieces of music. In 1956, the Philips Company, at the time a leading manufacturer of electronic light and sound equipment, commissioned the architect Le Corbusier to create a pavilion for the 1958 World's Fair in Brussels, Belgium. The structure, later named the Philips Pavilion, was to demonstrate the most modern electronic technology available. Le Corbusier, working as an impresario, hired architect and composer Iannis Xenakis to design the pavilion and to write a two-minute interlude that would play between performances, titled *Interlude Sonore* (later renamed *Concret PH*). Le Corbusier then hired Varèse to compose an eight-minute electronic piece to be played inside the pavilion on an estimated 350 speakers along with visuals selected by Le Corbusier. This project would allow Le Corbusier to create, together with Varèse and Xenakis, a totally synthetic work of art, which Le Corbusier called an electronic poem. Yet unlike Wagner's meticulously aligned vision of *Gesamtkunstwerk*, Varèse was to compose his music without knowing what visuals would be playing at the time.

Poème électronique differs from other pieces in this anthology in that it has no score. Instead, Varèse composed the piece out of sounds recorded on audiotape. Although he occasionally sketched ideas in standard notation, often they would on the same sketch page be recast into minute and second timings, showing his process of turning ideas from traditional notation into the medium of recorded sound. Other sketches suggest sounds with wavelike signs or squiggles that resemble early medieval neumes, showing the sounds as continuously moving entities rather than as fixed pitches.

The new technologies of electronic sound generation, sound manipulation, and recording on tape gave Varèse new ways to explore his compositional philosophy of music as sound moving through space, which he had worked out in the 1920s and 1930s in pieces for acoustic instruments (see NAWM 192). Varèse sought to create new sounds utilizing old and new intruments. Accordingly, he included in *Poème électronique* pure electronic sounds, nontraditional sounds such as sirens, and traditional sounds such as voice in new sonic environments. These sounds

Poème électronique was composed on audiotape, and there is no score. This commentary is based primarily on Marc Treib, *Space Calculated in Seconds: The Philips Pavilion, Le Corbusier, and Edgard Varèse* (Princeton: Princeton University Press, 1996), with further information from Vincenzo Lombardo et al., "A Virtual-Reality Reconstruction of *Poème Électronique* Based on Philological Research," *Computer Music Journal* 33 (Summer 2009): 24–47.

are often altered by electronic means, providing an even greater variety of timbre and pitch options. Varèse's intent was to have these sounds collide in ways that suggested either penetration or repulsion, creating a work defined not by melody or counterpoint but by a continuous ebb and flow. He realized the spatial nature of his musical vision in a spectacular way in this piece, by recording the sounds on three separate tracks and directing those tracks through complex wiring schemes into hundreds of speakers distributed around the Philips Pavilion, creating the impression of sounds literally moving through space. In this way, *Poème électronique* was part of a structure that realized its own music.

Time, which in music of the past was measured in tempos and beats, is in *Poème électronique* measured in seconds, which have no particular character or heirarchy and cannot be changed like metronome markings. Since there was no established meter or tempo to govern the occurrence of heirarchical beats, Varèse could place his musical events whenever he chose. Thus, the musical events are not related to a meter but to each other, which helped Varèse realize the continuous flow of music he sought.

Dynamics of *Poème électronique* are different from those in music of the past as well. Due to electronic technology, which allows for numerically measured levels of volume, a *forte* does not just mean "loud," but a specific level of loudness measured in decibels. Electronic technology also allowed Varèse to separate dynamic from timbre. For example, at 6:45 into the piece a female voice sings a textless line. Toward the end of the line, the singer sings notes that are much higher in her range than what immediately preceded them. These notes sound as if they should be louder by the timbre of the sound, but grow gradually quieter until they are overtaken by a choir of male voices. As the dynamic decreases, Varèse also adds more reverberation to the voice, making it sound as if it is growing increasingly distant. Whereas at 6:49 the female voice sounds close to the listener by virtue of being louder and having less reverberation, the higher voice toward the end sounds as if it is being magically whisked away as it grows softer and has increased reverberation.

The visual elements that accompanied *Poème électronique* were organized by Le Corbusier into seven sections and labeled with vague but spiritual sounding titles: "Genesis," "Matter and Spirit," "From Darkness to Dawn," "Manmade Gods," "How Time Molds Civilization," "Harmony," and "To All Mankind." Their timings and corresponding visual and musical events are given in the table on page 689. With the exception of "Genesis," each section shows a collection of images that provide a loose progression from prehistorical objects and ideas, through various forms of civilization and religion, into cultural and technological modernity. Rather than suggesting specific meanings, these images are open to many interpretations and were perhaps meant to evoke idiosyncratic reactions. Along with Varèse's music and the other visual and structural elements, Le Corbusier's *Gesamtkunstwerk* presented its audience with many opportunities to find meanings in a variety of media.

Poème électronique premiered when the Philips Pavilion opened on May 20, 1958. From then until late September, when the Brussels World's Fair closed, it was heard by fifteen thousand people a day, almost two million people in all. It was probably heard in its performance space by more people than any other serious

Time	Section	Colors	Images	Music
0:00	Genesis	Horizontal rainbow, black, horizontal collection, vertical collection with organic shapes, rust, blue, black with white circle	Bull and bullfighter, shell, animation of a woman looking over her shoulder, four men	Bell toll, blips, ticks, siren, stereo buzzes, metallic ringing, "string" glissando
1:01	Matter and Spirit	Blue, design with circle, similar design with circle, green and red with red circle, green with red circle	Dinosaur skeleton, chimpanzees, masks, tribal sculpture	"String" glissandi, drill pitches, rattling chains, "bassoon," distant "string" glissandi, low-pitched blips, "seagulls"
2:01	From Darkness to Dawn	Black with organic shapes, red with organic shapes, red, purple, green, purple, black, black with lightning bolt, red and blue, pink, purple, yellow, purple and blue	Owl head, guinea fowl, female eyes, god of war statue, head of Christ, children's toys, skeletal hands of a Cro-Magnon man, rows of bodies, statue	Timpani, drills, "ooh-ahh," snare rolls, sirens, cymbal roll, electronic glissandi, bell toll, static tones, low ambient crescendo
3:25	Manmade Gods	Vertical assortment, horizontal black and white	Easter Island, four cubes, a statue of Buddha cropped to hands, shells, African statues	Shakers, digital tom, gong, "ahh-oh," "ooh-gah" utterances
4:01	How Time Molds Civilization	White, green, dark blue, purple, green, blue-purple, yellow, purple, orange, red, red-violet, red, pink and grey	Children in a classroom setting, machinery, satellite dishes, airplane, mushroom cloud explosion, Charlie Chaplin	Distant "ooh," sudden octave with sustained "ah," tom-tom, snare, shaker, "you oughtta know" utterances, tambourine, bass drum, cymbal, shuffling feet, low rumbles
5:01	Harmony	Horizontal green orange white, horizontal purple green white, horizontal blue orange white	Mechanical parts, owl eyes with mechanical eyebrows, swaddled baby, mirrored swaddled baby, Charlie Chaplin with mechanical part, Laurel and Hardy with mechanical parts, baby, eclipse	Reverb utterances, digital noises, shuffling feet, distorted voices, tom-toms, "grand pause" silence, crescendo drone, high pitch, multiphonic clangorous tone
6:01	To All Mankind	Grey, black, pink, light blue red with white shapes and dot, yellow green with white shape and dot, green red with white shape and dot, blue red with white shape and dot, pink red with dot, grey with red dot, rainbow with orange dot	Harbor photograph, city sketch, humanoid next to double helix, "the child as hope," "open hand," baby, baby with woman	Soft rhythmic drum, low tones, snare, static pitches, crescendo pitches, ticks, jet sounds, bells, female voice, male polyphonic voices, metallic rings, drums, organ, "string" glissandi, soft jets

work of electronic music in concert performance. Since then, it has become a classic of electronic music, one of the most widely available and often heard tape pieces. Seperated from its architectural environment and visual imagery, it can be heard as a piece of absolute music or as music that suggests a wide range of associations and potential meanings.

Milton Babbitt (1916–2011)

Philomel: Section I

Monodrama for soprano, recorded soprano, and synthesized sound
1964

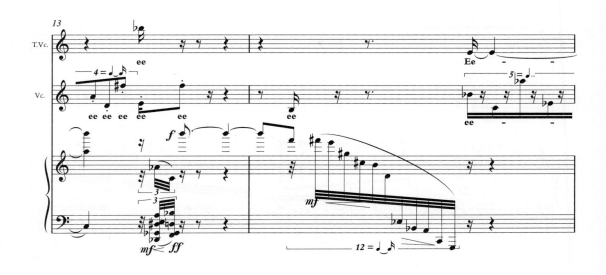

INTERLUDE (Tape)

Not true tears — Not true trees —

INTERLUDE

2:26

I feel ____ trees ____ in my ____ hair and on the ground, ____

Hon - ey - mel - ons foul - ing My knees and feet

Sound-less - ly in my Flight through the for - est; ____

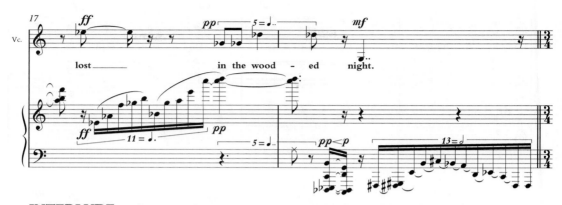

INTERLUDE

TAPE VOICE: Pillowing melody, honey unheard —

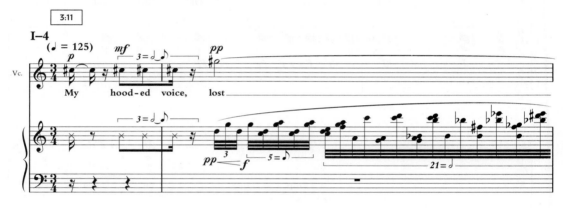

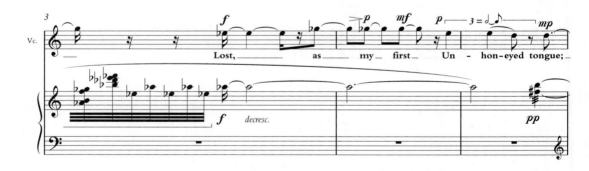

INTERLUDE

TAPE VOICE: Feeling killed, Philomel stilled, Her honey unfulfilled.

3:52

TAPE
(Recorded Soprano)
(Eeeeeeeeeeeeeeeee)

PHILOMEL
Eeeeeeeeeeeeeeeeeee!
Eeeeeeeeeeeeeeeeeee!
Feeeeeeeeeeeeeeeeeee!
I feel
Feel a million trees
And the heat of trees

TAPE
Not true trees—

PHILOMEL
Feel a million tears

TAPE
Not true tears—
Not true trees—

PHILOMEL
1:35   Is it Tereus I feel?

TAPE
Not Tereus: not a true Tereus—

PHILOMEL
Feel a million filaments;
Fear the tearing, the feeling
Trees, of ephemeral leaves
Trees tear,
And I bear
Families of tears
I feel a million Philomels

TAPE
Trees filled with mellowing
Felonous fame—

PHILOMEL
2:26   I feel trees in my hair
And on the ground,
Honeymelons fouling
My knees and feet
Soundlessly in my

Flight through the forest;
I founder in quiet.
Here I find only
Miles of felted silence
Unwinding behind me,
Lost, lost in the wooded night.

TAPE
Pillowing melody,
Honey unheard—

PHILOMEL
3:11   My hooded voice, lost
Lost, as my first
Unhoneyed tongue;
Forced, as my last
Unfeathered defense
Fast-tangled in lust
Of these woods so dense.
Emptied, unfeeling and unfilled
By trees here where no birds have
    trilled—
Feeling killed
Philomel stilled
Her honey unfulfilled.

TAPE
Feeling killed
Philomel stilled
Her honey unfulfilled

PHILOMEL
3:52   What is that sound?
A voice found?
Broken, the bound
Of silence, beyond
Violence of human sound,
As if a new self
Could be founded on sound.
The trees are astounded!

PHILOMEL AND TAPE
(*simultaneously*)
What is this humming?
I am becoming
My own song . . .

— JOHN HOLLANDER

Milton Babbitt's *Philomel* was commissioned by the Ford Foundation for the soprano Bethany Beardslee and premiered by her in 1964. Probably Babbitt's most popular work, it combines live performance with prerecorded tape and synthesized sounds. The soprano soloist is heard against a tape that incorporates an altered recording of her own voice, a kind of distorted echo, together with electronic sounds. The "score" shown here includes the complete part for voice and—with exceptions—a total representation of the rhythmic and pitch content of the synthesized and recorded accompaniment in all those sections of the work in which the singer participates. The exceptions occur when, to avoid notational complexity, the rhythmic representation is only closely approximate, and registral relations are simplified. Such a score is unusual for electronic music, in which "composition" typically happens on tape rather than on paper, but is useful for the singer. The tape interludes, in which the singer does not participate, are not notated.

The poem, written expressly for this setting by John Hollander, is based on a fable by Ovid (*Metamorphoses* 6:412–674). Procne, wife of Tereus, king of Thrace, is eager to see her sister, Philomela, after an absence of many years, and sends Tereus to fetch her. On the return trip Tereus rapes Philomela in a Thracian wood and cuts out her tongue to prevent disclosure, but his guilt is exposed nevertheless by a tapestry in which Philomela weaves her story. Procne, horrified, avenges herself against her husband by killing their son and feeding Tereus from the butchered corpse. In a rage, Tereus pursues the two sisters, but before he can catch them the gods transform him into a hoopoe bird, Procne into a swallow, and Philomela into a nightingale. In the metamorphosis Philomela regains her voice. The sung text begins at this point.

Babbitt's composition, like John Hollander's poem, is in three sections. In the first, excerpted here, Philomel screams as she recalls the pain of violation; dazed, she expresses her feelings in vivid but incoherent images. She runs through the forest in fear and confusion. In Section 2, Philomel seeks answers about her predicament from a thrush, a hawk, an owl, and a gull. In the third section, she sings a strophic lament, joined in refrains by her taped voice.

The taped voice often answers the soloist by distorting her line or, speaking, comments like a Greek chorus. Every detail in the vocal sections was worked out in serial terms. The vocal sections alternate with unnotated synthesized and tape interludes that are more freely composed.

The vocal melody is extremely disjunct, with leaps of major sevenths, ninths, and even elevenths. Some of the notes are sung in Sprechstimme, marked by an X instead of a notehead, and expressive glissandos punctuate some phrases. The pitch-class E, the first note sung by the taped voice, is central to the construction of the opening passage. The twelve-tone row is stated, then transposed, in such a way that E becomes successively the first, second, third, fourth, and fifth pitch-class in the row. With each unfolding of the row, the taped voice claims more of the row's pitch-classes up to E—in the second measure two, in the third three, and so on. The accompaniment each time claims the remainder of the row or aggregate (the twelve pitch-classes of the chromatic scale). The first sonority, as the taped soprano screams "Eeeeeee" on E, contains all twelve pitch-classes and covers a seven-octave span. Subsequent simultaneities are less populated, with increasingly arpeggiated and pointillistic unfoldings of the row. The high E is heard as a steady pedal note through the first eight measures. When Philomel's natural voice enters, it begins on F, and E is now the last member of the row, appearing as the highest note in the accompaniment in measure 9.

Like Schoenberg in *Pierrot lunaire* (NAWM 172), Babbitt tore some leaves from the book of the sixteenth-century madrigalists. The pitch E for the scream is a madrigalian conceit, as are the synthesized trills on the word "trilled." But he went beyond the madrigalists in the second section of the poem, where, instead of bird imitations, he introduced recorded birdsong.

This work is extraordinarily difficult to perform. The score and tape can be rented from the publisher; since the tape uses Bethany Beardslee's voice, most sopranos try to match her sound, though some have made their own tape. The piece requires a singer with perfect pitch, outstanding command of rhythm, and total control of dynamic contrasts. It exemplifies the trend among some composers in the 1960s to write music only for the very best performers and to challenge their abilities to the utmost. The performance on the accompanying recording features Beardslee herself.

208

Krzysztof Penderecki (b. 1933)

Threnody for the Victims of Hiroshima

Tone poem for string orchestra

1960

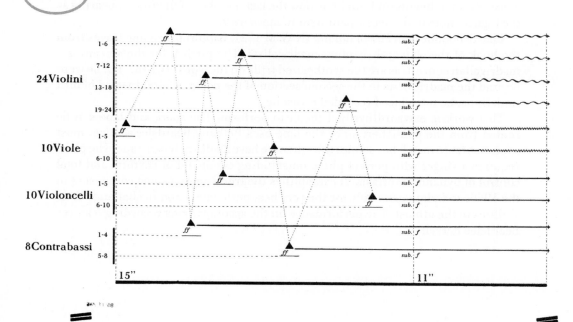

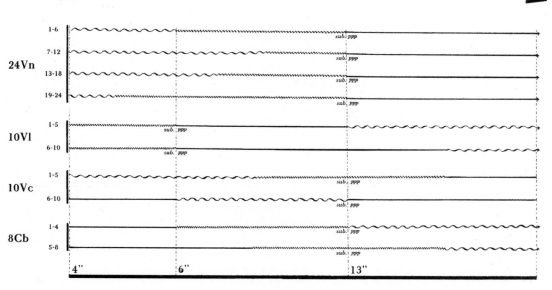

From Krzysztof Penderecki, *Ofiarom Hiroszimy: Tren na 52 Instrumenty Smyczkowe* (Warsaw: Polskie Wydawnictwo Muzyczne, 1961). © 1961 (renewed) EMI Deshon Music, Inc. All rights controlled and administered by EMI Deshon Music, Inc. (publishing) and Alfred Publishing Company, Inc. (print). All rights reserved. Used by permission. For a guide to the notation, see page 726.

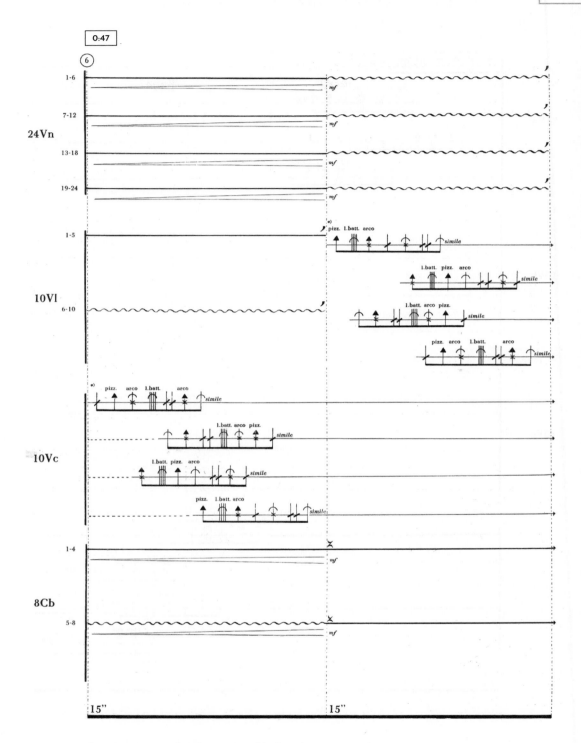

*) Each instrumentalist chooses one of the four given groups and
executes it (within a fixed space of time) as rapidly as possible.

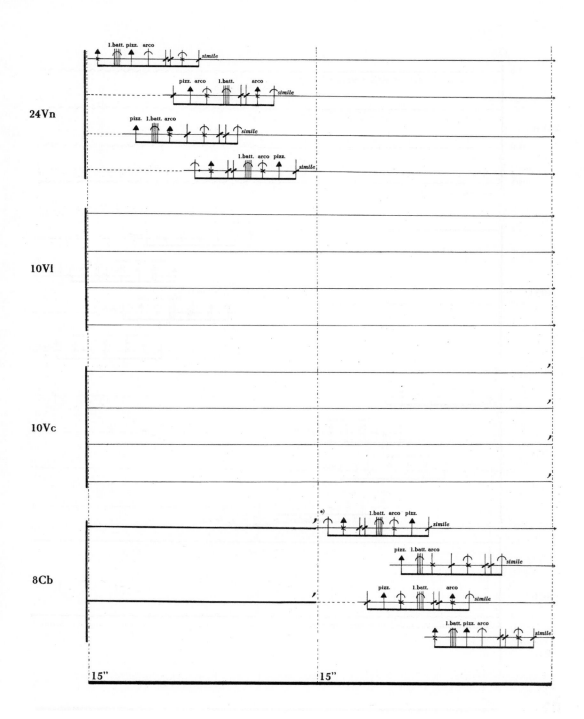

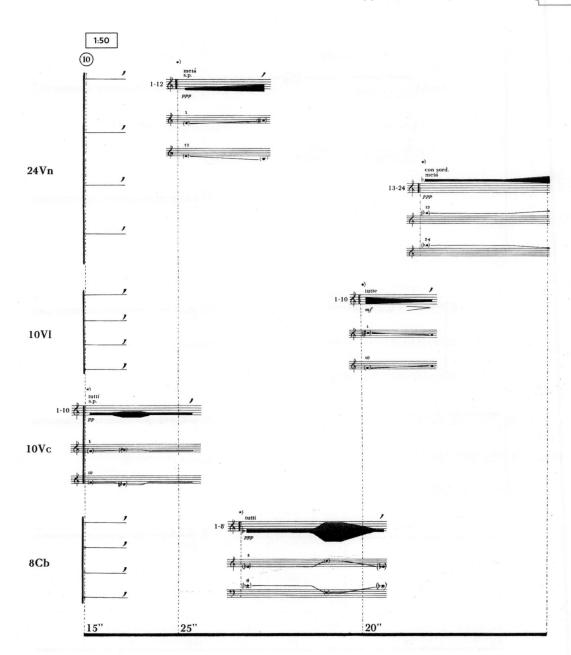

*) Exact notation is given in the parts.

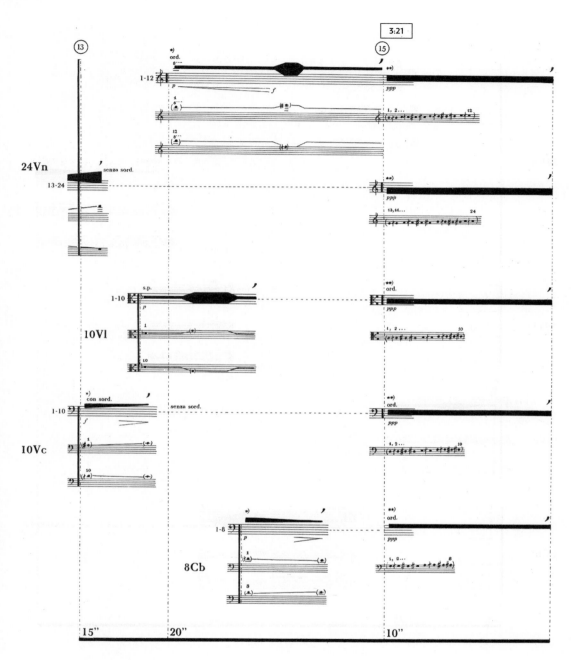

*) See previous note.

**) Each instrumentalist plays the tone allocated to his instrument, so that the whole
   quarter-tone scale between the indicated lowest and highest tones sounds simultaneously.

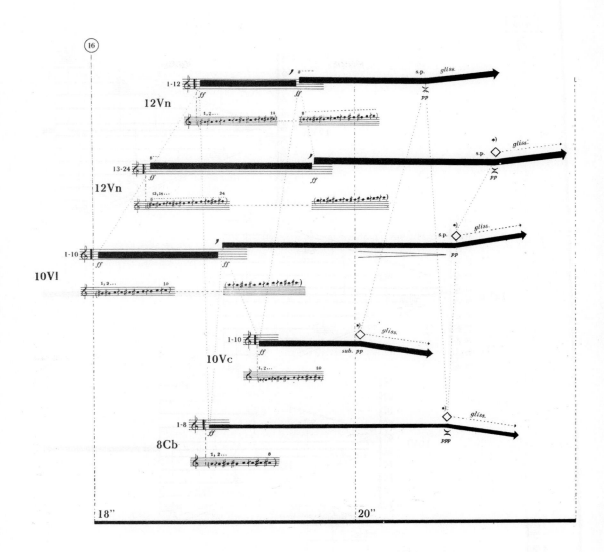

*) Harmonics

716

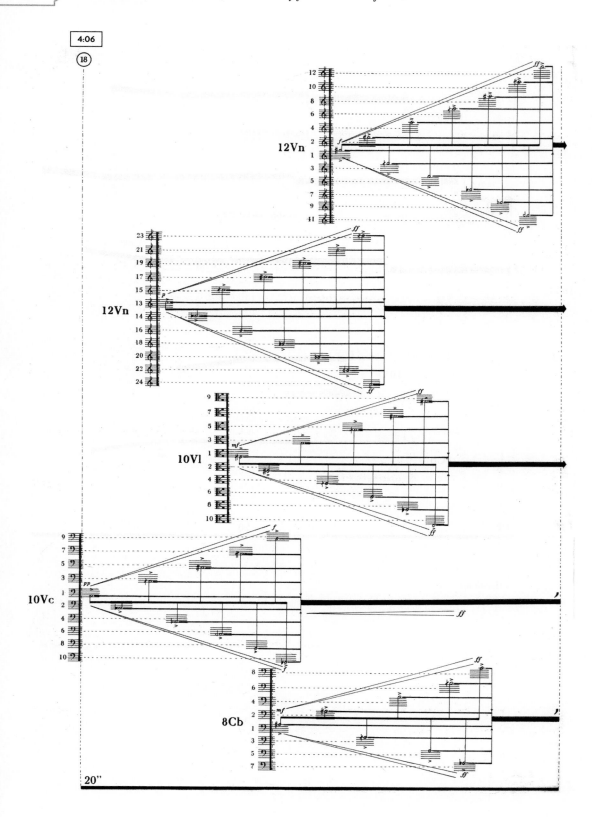

4:06

18

12Vn

12Vn

10Vl

10Vc

8Cb

20"

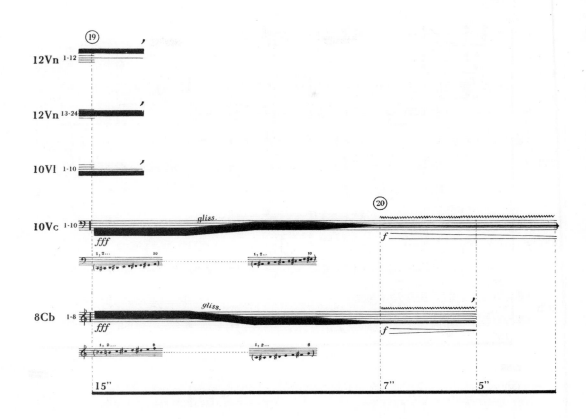

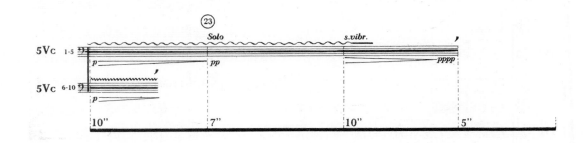

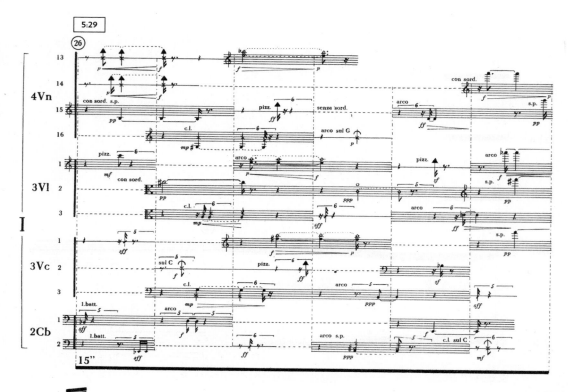

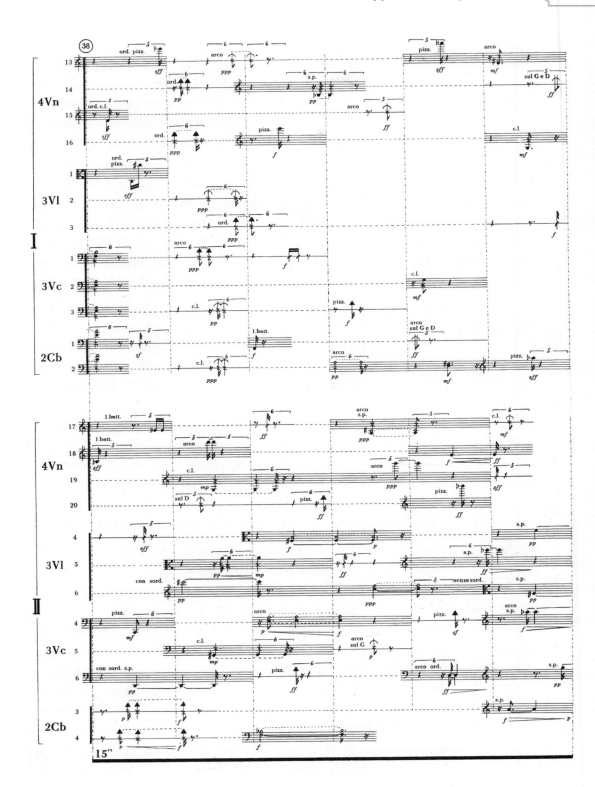

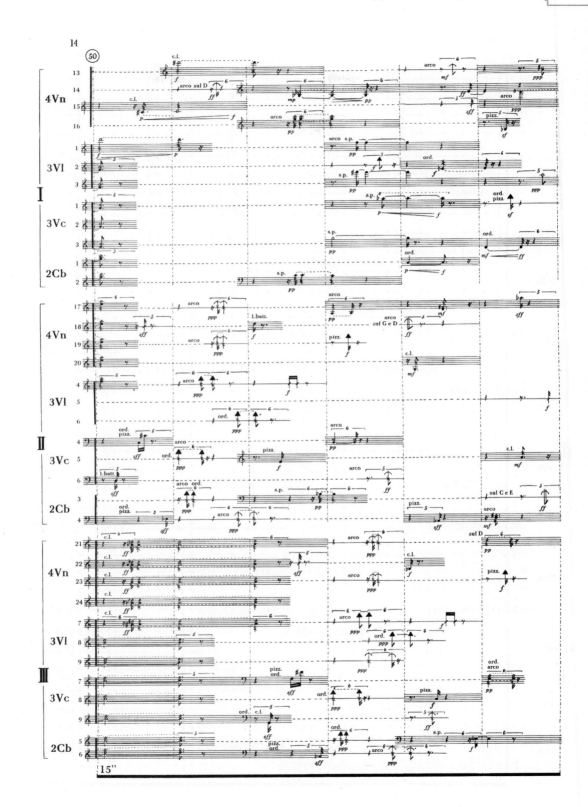

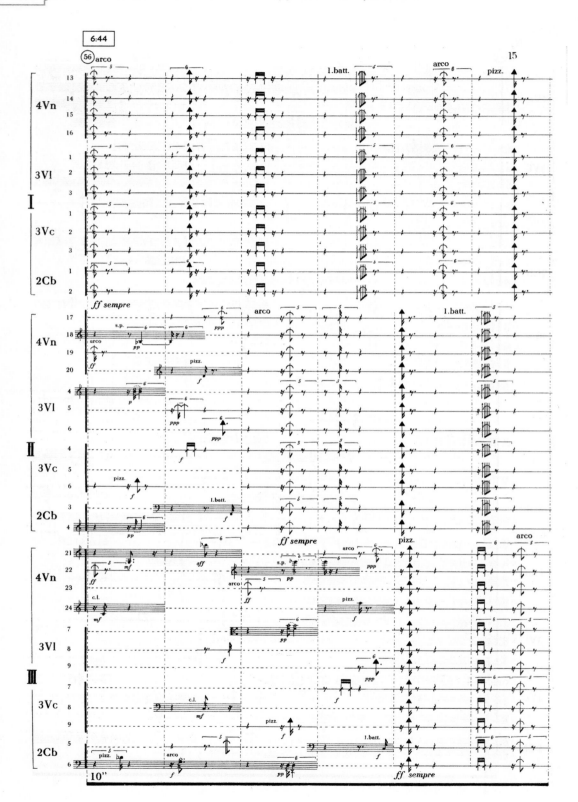

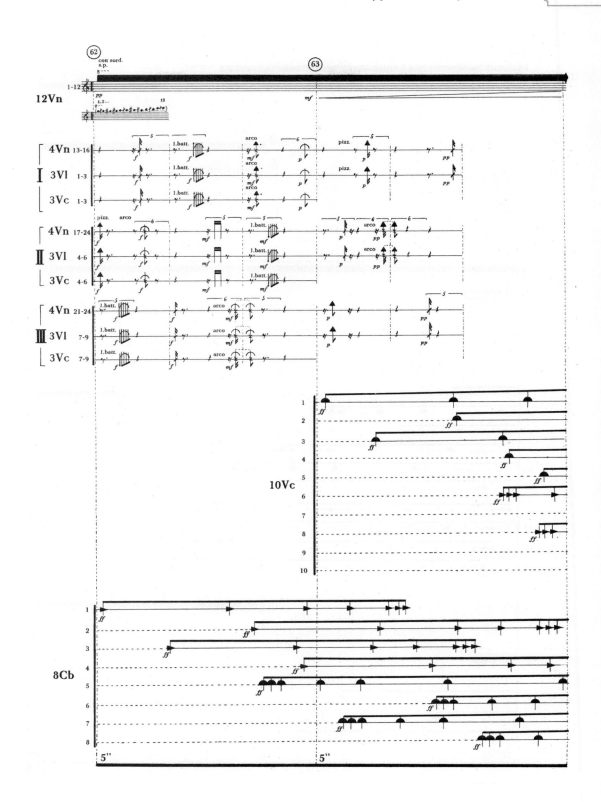

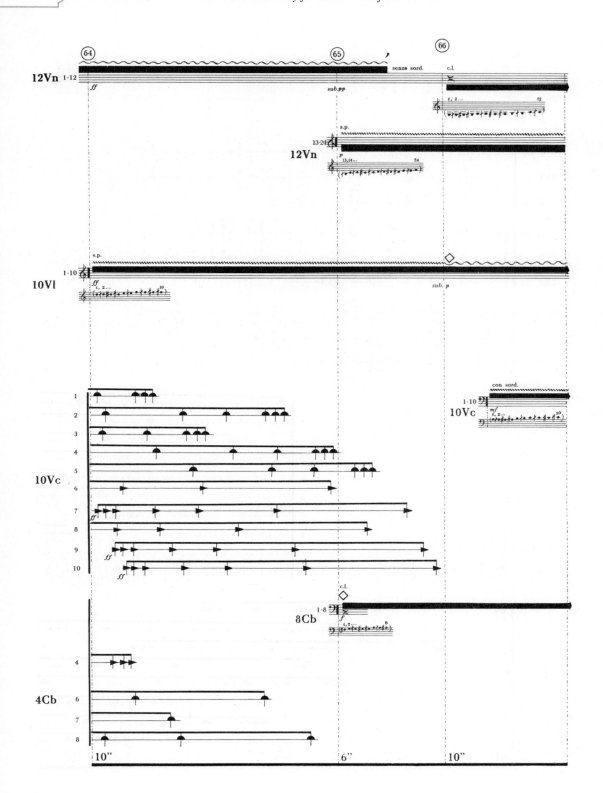

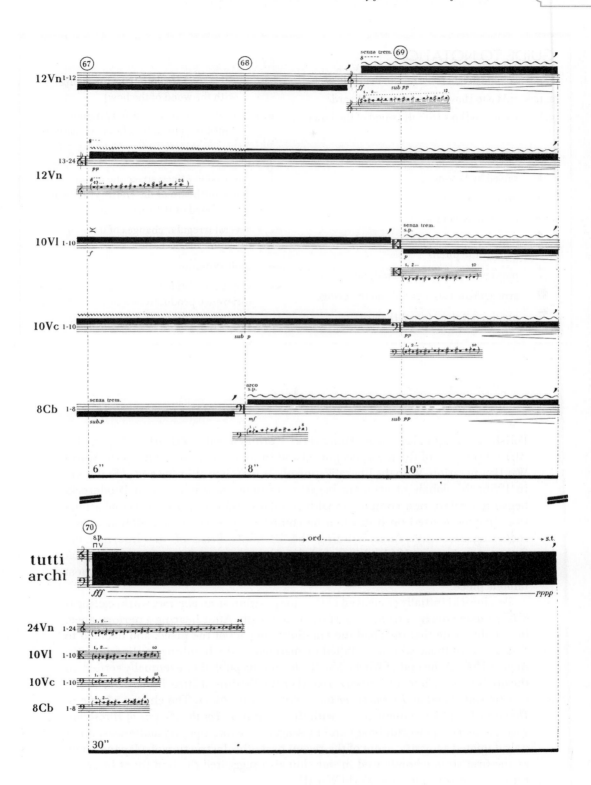

GUIDE TO NOTATION

s. p. = sul ponticello [bow on the bridge]

s. t. = sul tasto [bow above the fingerboard]

c. l. = col legno [bow with the wood of the bow]

† = raised by ¼ tone

‡ = raised by ¾ tone

♭ = lowered by ¼ tone

⌐ = lowered by ¾ tone

↟ = highest note of the instrument (indefinite pitch)

↑ = play between bridge and tailpiece

⩜ = arpeggio on 4 strings behind the bridge

┬ = play on tailpiece (arco) [bowed]

l. batt. = col legno battuto [strike the string with the wood of the bow]

ord. = ordinario [in an ordinary manner, canceling any of the above indications]

┳ = play on bridge

ƒ = percussion effect: strike the upper sounding board of the violin with the nut [of the bow] or the finger-tips

⊓∨ = several irregular changes of bow direction in succession

‿‿ = molto vibrato

⌇ = very slow vibrato with a ¼ tone frequency difference produced by sliding the finger

✕ = very rapid non-rhythmical tremolo

Polish composer Krzysztof Penderecki (pronounced KZHISH-toff pen-de-RETS-ki) is one of the most recognized and influential figures of the post–World War II generation. With the liberalization of communism after the end of Stalinism in 1956, the Polish government began to promote new music, and Penderecki began to explore new compositional techniques and styles. International attention quickly focused on him when he composed a series of sensational works, including *Threnody*. After winning the UNESCO Prize of the International Composers Jury in 1961, this work, for string orchestra, premiered to great acclaim later that year at the Warsaw Autumn Festival, and it remains his most famous piece.

Penderecki initially conceived of the composition as an abstract work, calling it *8'37"*, a name derived from its performance length. After hearing a performance, he sought a title that matched the emotional impact of the piece, and decided to dedicate it to those who were killed or maimed in the bombing of Hiroshima in August 1945 at the end of World War II. He and his publisher eventually settled on the double title *Ofiarom Hiroszimy: Tren* (For the Victims of Hiroshima: Threnody), usually translated as *Threnody for the Victims of Hiroshima*. The change of title to *Threnody* (a song of lamentation) with the dedication *For the Victims of Hiroshima* gave the piece a powerful image and message. For contemporary audiences, it not only depicted a horrific event of the recent past—the destruction of a Japanese city by the first atomic bomb used in war—but also suggested the imminent future in the aftermath of a possible World War III.

For this work, Penderecki employed an effective notation (shown on page 726) that communicates complex effects in relatively simple terms. He incorporated features of traditional notation to denote specific pitches and rhythms when needed. The standard symbol for glissandos, a diagonal line, is the basis for notating shifting tone clusters, which is readily understood by string players. To indicate specific quarter-tone pitches, Penderecki used variants of the symbols for sharps and flats, and for vibrato he simply added a wavy line. For some of the unusual performance techniques, such as playing behind the bridge, Penderecki developed images that can easily be linked to those effects. For example, a small arch suggests the bridge, and four lines represent the four strings. Professional performers would have little difficulty memorizing these symbols.

Traditional concepts of melody, harmony, and meter are absent in this work. Instead, Penderecki creates a sense of form by moving through several sections of diverse sounds. *Threnody* is written for 52 strings: 24 violins, 10 violas, 10 cellos, and 8 double basses. Each performer is given a unique part, often requiring the use of unusual performance techniques and notation (explained in the chart on the previous page). These distinctive timbres help to delineate five large sections, some of which overlap:

Section	Measure	Sounds
1	1	high pitched dissonant clusters
2	6	varied texture of multiple sound effects in rapid succession
3	10	sustained tones and quarter-tone clusters linked with glissandos
4	26	isolated pitches and various sound effects, in canon
5	56	unison sound effects and clusters that lead to the final climactic chord

The sound effects and sustained tone clusters in section 5 recall the sounds of sections 2 and 3, a relationship that is reinforced by parallel climaxes in measures 19 and 70. Based on this sense of return, it is possible to view the entire work as a modified ABA' structure, with the first three sections as the initial A.

Section 1 immediately establishes the mood of the work. Ten groups of four to six instruments enter in quick succession, alternating relatively high and low instruments. Each performer is instructed to play the highest note possible on the instrument; since the highest note differs from player to player, the result is intense high-pitch clusters that suggest screaming. Beginning in measure 2, the sound is varied through dynamic changes and the addition of two kinds of vibrato (variations in pitch)—one rapid, the other wide and slow.

Several unusual effects are featured in section 2. Penderecki requires seven different sounds, including striking the soundboard of the instrument with the hand or bow and bowing on the strings between the bridge and tailpiece (which produces very high but indeterminate notes on these short lengths of string). These sounds are arranged in four patterns, and the performers are instructed to choose one pattern and play it repeatedly as fast as possible, entering in imitative fashion by section (first cellos, then violas, violins, and contrabasses). The resultant effect has been likened to the sound of static from a shortwave radio.

In section 3, Penderecki divides the strings into the five groups of a traditional string orchestra. For the first time, sustained pitches are heard in the middle to lower registers, as the various groups swell with glissando effects between unisons and quarter-tone clusters. The score is written in a graphic notation that conveys the effect of a thickening and narrowing band of sound; the individual parts are shown in standard notation (with glissandos and the signs for quarter-tones). Two further variants of the clusters occur in this section. At measure 15, clusters in each group crescendo before dissolving with upward or downward glissandos. At measure 18, the clusters are formed as each successive instrument in a group enters on a note a quarter-tone higher or lower than is already sounding, and the sound crescendos into a climax at measure 19, before resolving to a solo cello in measure 23.

Section 4 presents the most complex passage of the composition. Penderecki divides the ensemble into three orchestras and initiates what can be analyzed as a three-part canon. Each orchestra has twelve independent parts playing a variety of sounds, pitches, and even rhythmic gestures with traditional notation. The entrance of Orchestra II at measure 38 is at the same pitch level as Orchestra I, but the registers are inverted. Orchestra I begins with a B♭ followed by two E♭s in the double-basses; at the entrance of Orchestra II, these pitches appear in the violins, with the other material similarly reversed. Orchestra III, which enters at measure 44, omits the first four measures of the material and transposes the remaining pitches either up a fourth or down a fifth. The material of all three orchestras begins to appear in retrograde with reverse registers after their seventeenth measure.

The final section begins at measure 56, as each of the three orchestras in succession turns to playing the sound effects from section 2, but now all at the same time. At measure 62, the first 12 violins, absent for section 4, return with a sustained quarter-tone cluster, supported by the lower strings bowing over their tailpieces and bridges. Gradually returning to the five-part division of the strings, Penderecki soon has all groups playing sustained quarter-tone clusters with vibrato. At measure 70, the instruments converge, and each performer sounds a different pitch in a stunning pitch cluster of 52 quarter tones, played *fortississimo*. This remarkable chord is sustained for thirty seconds, gradually diminishing in volume as the players move from playing *sul ponticello* (over the bridge, producing a metallic sound) to *ordinario* (normal playing) to *sul tasto* (over the fingerboard for a rich, somewhat hollow sound). The chord then fades to nothing, bringing the piece to a silent and somber close.

Since measure lengths in this work are defined in seconds rather than beats (except in section 4), the primary roles of the conductor are to keep time and give cues. Some conductors use a stopwatch in order to be as precise as possible, but others treat time more freely. The recording accompanying this anthology maintains a fairly strict time, but many performances are longer than the indicated eight minutes and twenty-six seconds. Indeed, one of the recordings with Penderecki himself conducting extends to nine minutes and forty-five seconds.

Bright Sheng (b. 1955)

Seven Tunes Heard in China: No. 1, *Seasons*

For solo cello

1995

209

Seasons, from Bright Sheng, *Seven Tunes Heard in China*, ed. Yo-Yo Ma (New York: G. Schirmer, 2001), 1.

Bright Sheng was born in Shanghai, China, and worked in the Qinghai province near Tibet for seven years during the Cultural Revolution (1966–76), China's repressive mass mobilization, when young intellectuals were exiled to rural areas to work beside and be "reeducated" by the peasants. When the universities finally reopened in 1978, Sheng was one of the first music students accepted at the Shanghai Conservatory, and four years later he came to the United States. Conversant in both Chinese traditional music and Western classical music, he has synthesized the two traditions in many works. His *Seven Tunes Heard in China* for solo cello was commissioned by the Pacific Symphony on behalf of a patron, George Cheng, and was dedicated to his wife, Arlene Cheng. Sheng wrote the piece for cellist Yo-Yo Ma, who premiered it at Cheng Hall at the University of California, Irvine, in 1995.

In this suite, Sheng combines features of the Bach cello suites, including dancelike rhythms, double stops, motivic repetition, sequences, and simulated polyphony, with the character and style of Chinese music. Each of the seven movements presents a melody Sheng heard in a different province in China, and the ornamentation, glissandos, and free treatment of meter suggest a Chinese performance style. During the course of the suite, the cello imitates the sounds of several Chinese string, wind, and percussion instruments, including the two-stringed bowed *erhu* and the plucked *qin*.

The first movement, *Seasons*, freely treats a melody from the Qinghai province. The tune contains several short melodic ideas that are highly rhythmic, suggesting the playful nature of the song text:

> Spring is coming,
> Narcissi are blooming,
> The maiden is out from her boudoir seeking,
> My love boy, lend me a hand, please.

The opening three measures establish A as the initial pitch center and present two of the recurring motives—the rising fourths followed by descending motion in measure 1 and the repeated pentatonic idea in measures 2–3. The next three measures complete the principal theme, rising to a high vibrato note followed by two mostly pentatonic phrases, and closing with a scalar descent. The remainder of the movement develops these motives.

Numerous characteristics of Chinese music appear in the melody, including quick ornamental turns, slides between pitches, and long held notes that crescendo with an intense vibrato (measures 4 and 16). Yet Sheng also develops motivic ideas in a traditional Western manner. In measures 7–11, the repeated motive with its alternating registers and double stops suggests two-part imitative counterpoint in the manner of J. S. Bach, culminating in a cadence on A in measure 12 that confirms the A-minor tonality suggested in the first measure. The pitch center starts to wander with a move to E♭ in measure 13, and simulated imitation in measures 14–15 suggests polytonality, as motivic statements alternate centers on B♭ and E (measures 14–15). A varied statement of the second phrase of the theme, transposed up a fifth (beginning in the last beat of measure 15), leads to more quasi-polytonal alternations that highlight tritone transpositions between E and B♭ (measures 17–20 and 23–26) and A and E♭ (measures 21–22). The movement comes to a quiet close on an E♭, a tritone away from the pitch center at the beginning.

A performance of this work requires experience with both Western and Asian music. Yo-Yo Ma, heard on the accompanying recording, is ideally suited to these needs, combining mastery of the Bach cello suites with an understanding of Chinese instruments and performance manners. He also edited the published score of the work. Indications of fingerings are not abundant, but his suggestion that the first measure should be played primarily with one finger establishes a technique that can be applied to the entire movement.

210

Steve Reich (b. 1936)

Tehillim: Part IV

For four solo voices and ensemble or chamber orchestra

1981

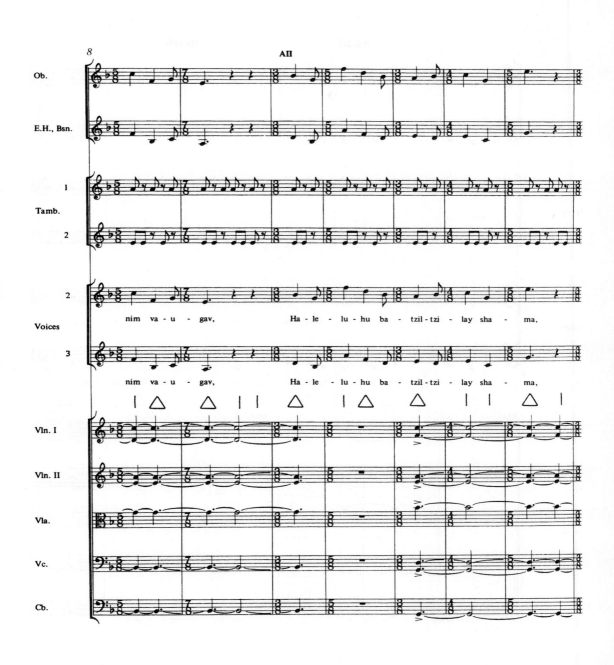

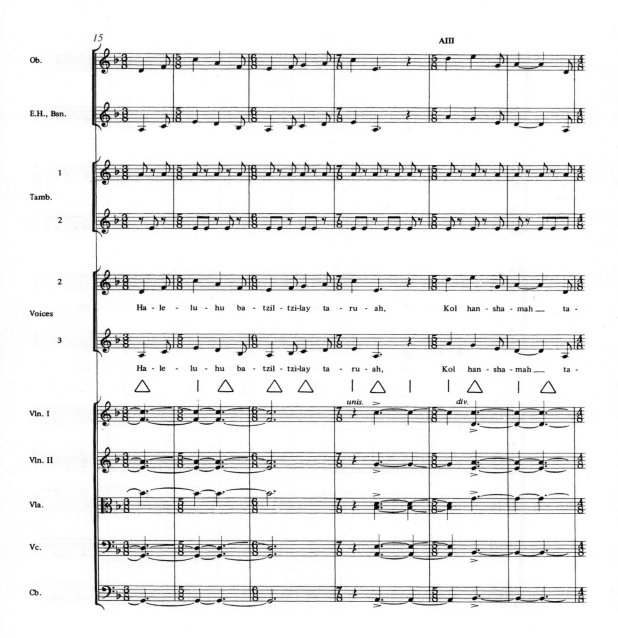

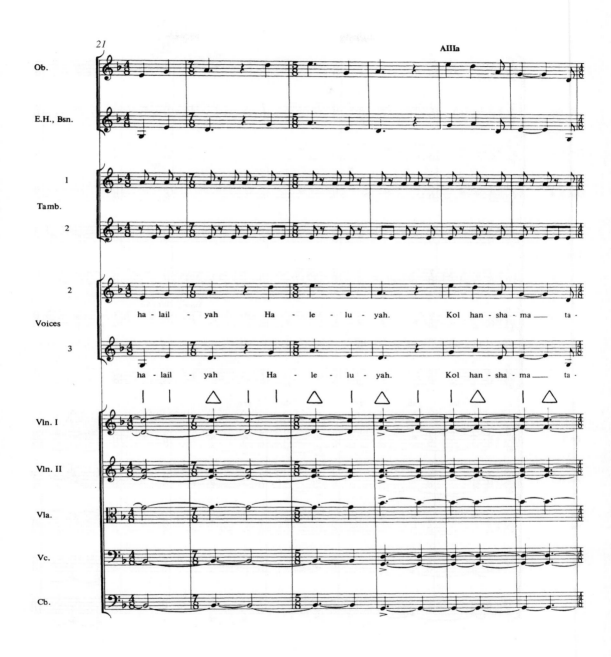

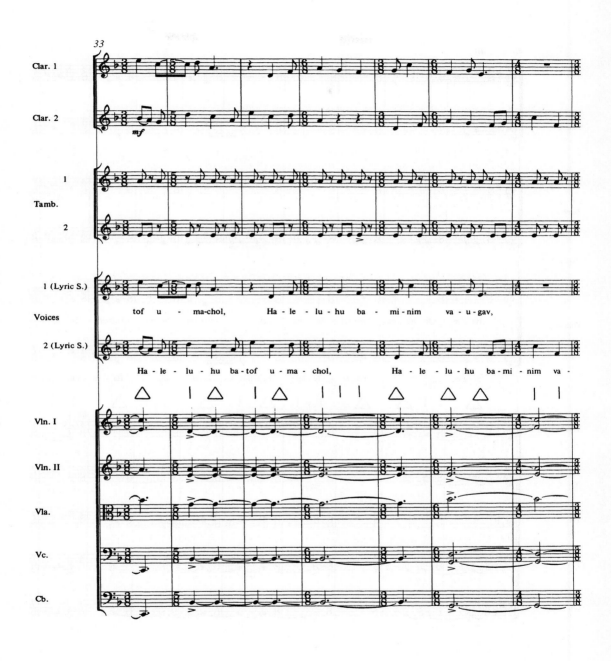

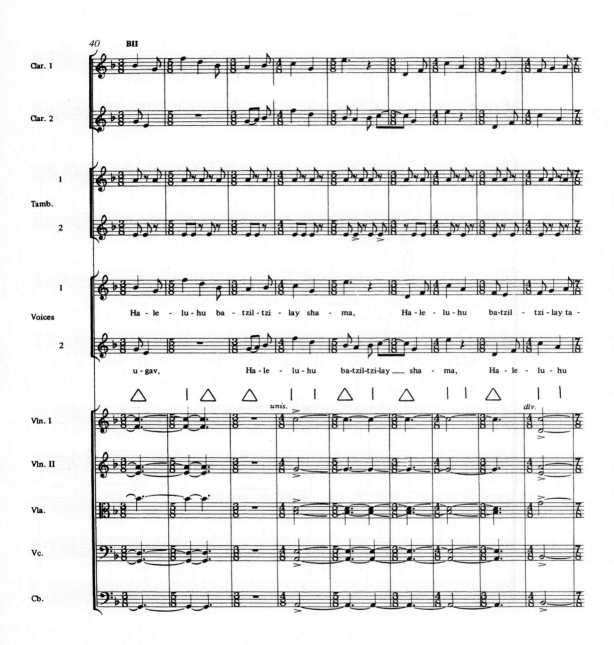

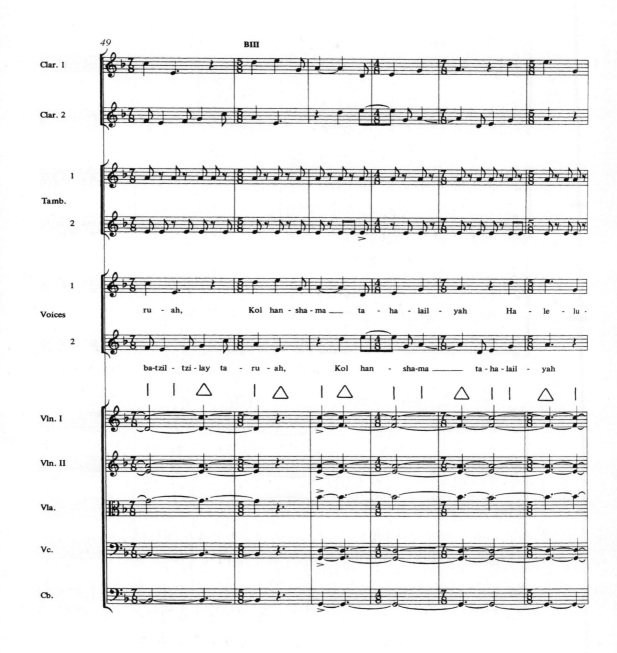

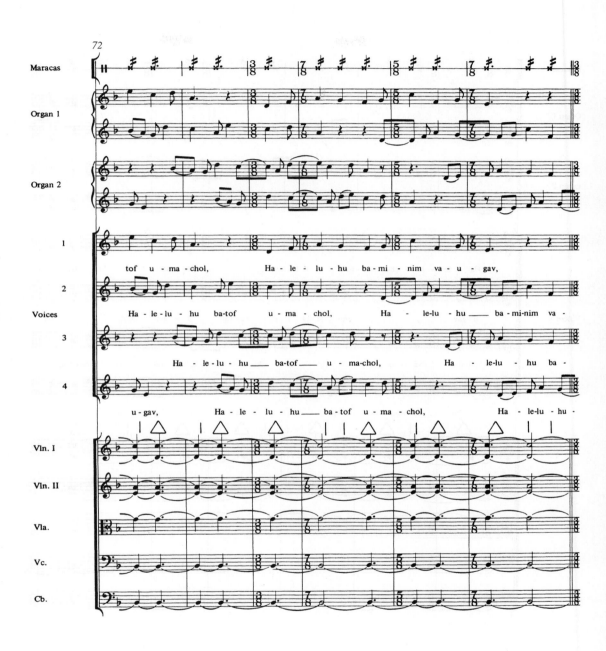

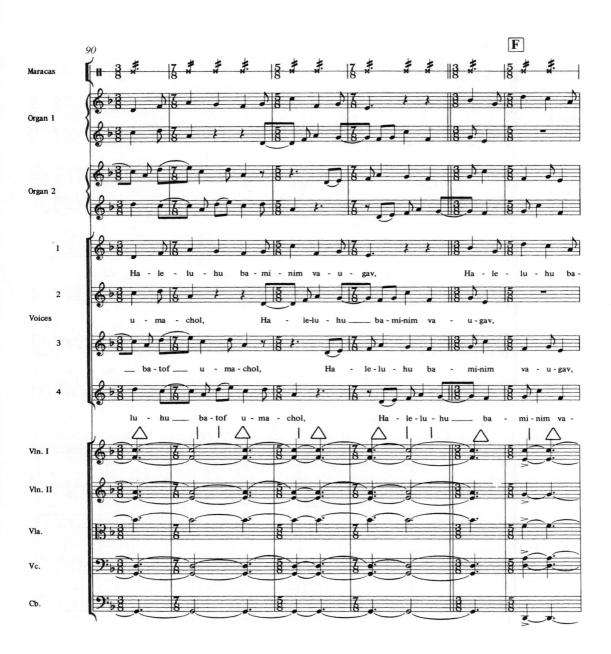

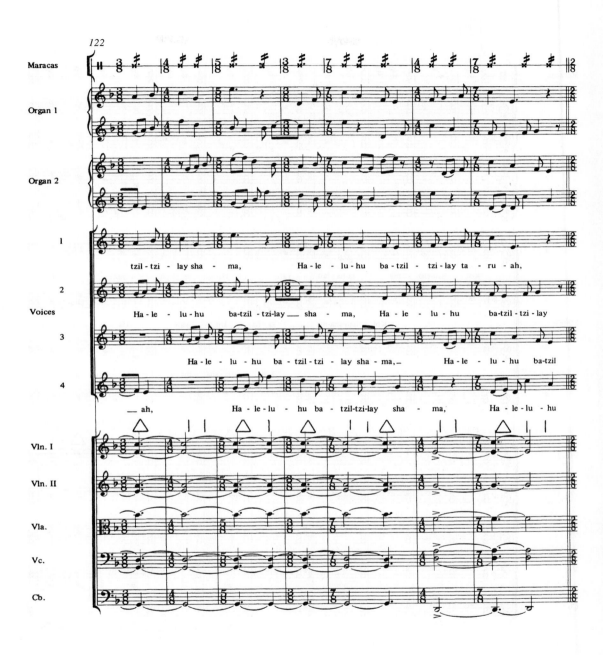

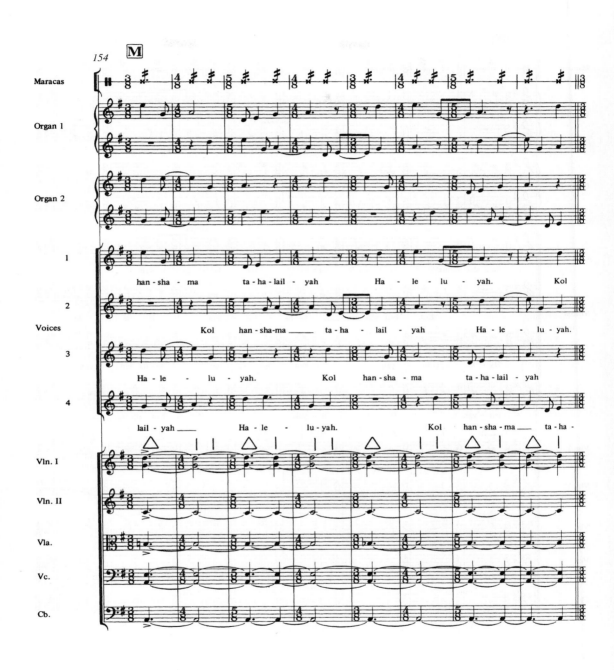

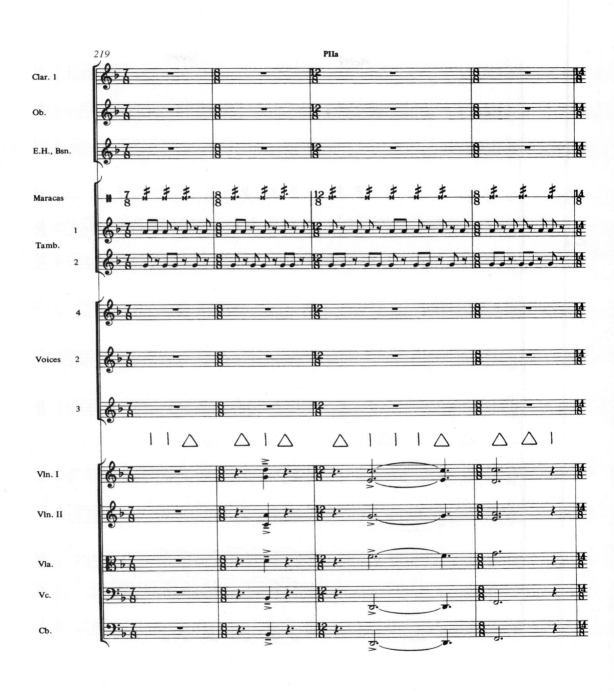

*This movement contains no letter Q.

*sounds an octave higher
**damp vibraphone note on every rest with hand not holding mallet.

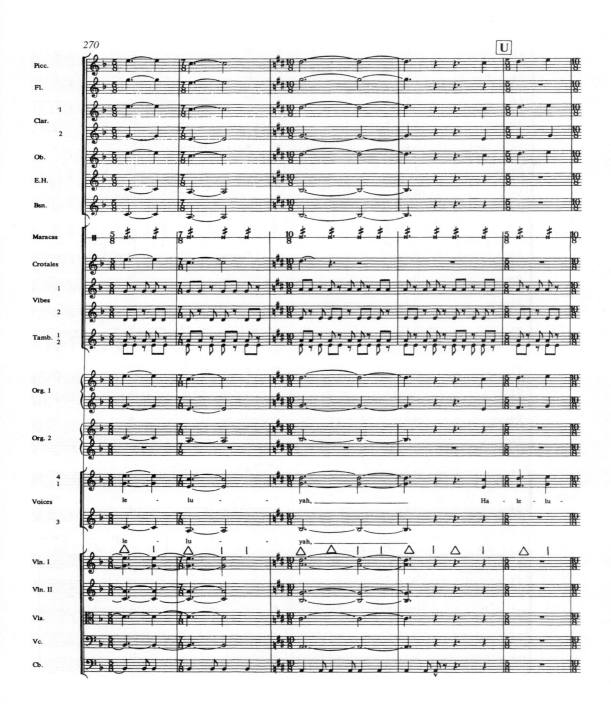

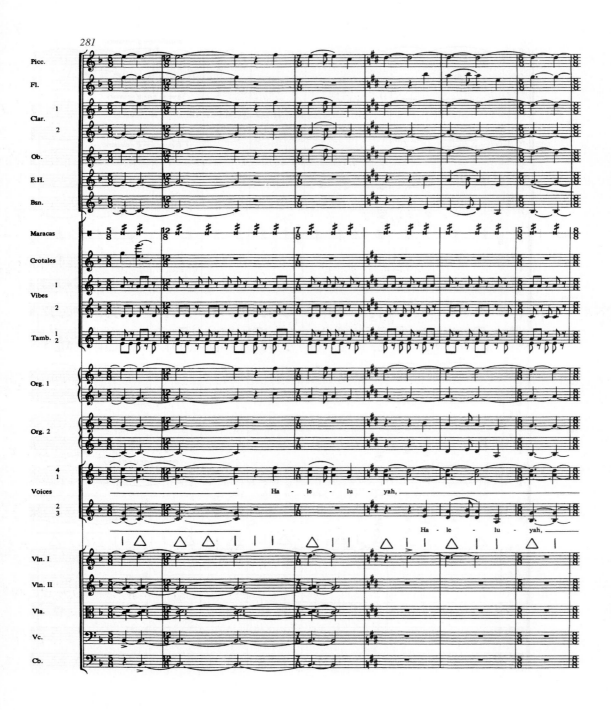

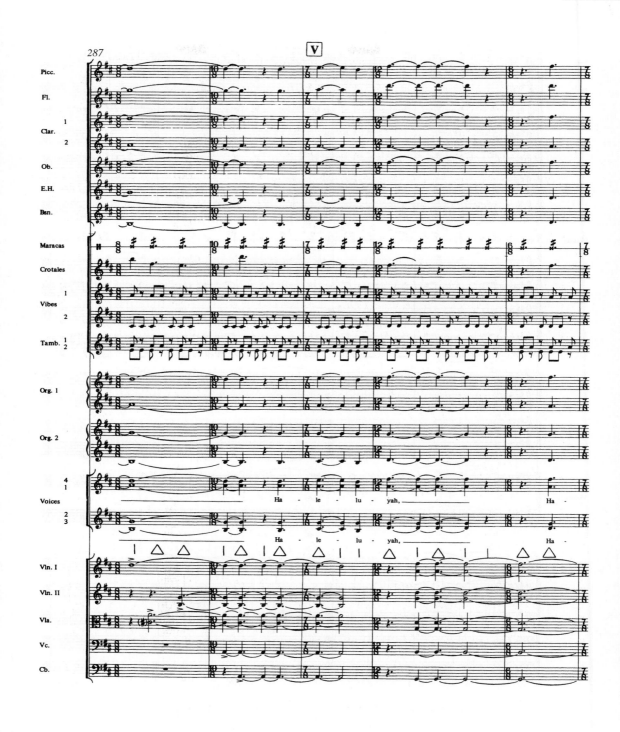

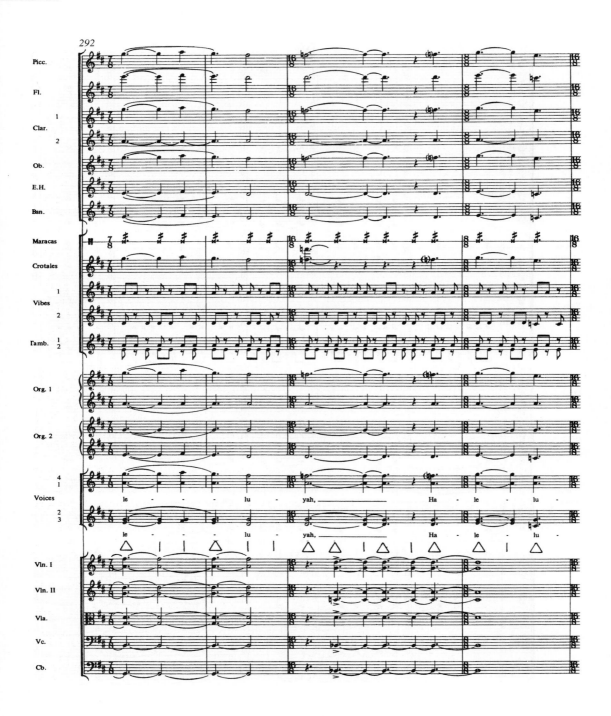

Hal-le-lú-hu ba-tóf u-ma-chól,	Praise him with drum and dance,
Hal-le-lú-hu ba-mi-ním va-u-gáv.	praise him with strings and winds.
Hal-le-lú-hu ba-tzil-tz-láy sha-máh,	Praise him with sounding cymbals,
Hal-le-lú-hu ba-tzil-tz-láy ta-ru-áh.	praise him with clanging cymbals.
Kol han-sha-má ta-ha-láil Yah,	Let all that breathes praise the Eternal,
Ha-le-lu-yáh.	Hallelujah.

— PSALM 150:4–6

Steve Reich made his reputation in the 1960s and 1970s composing pieces in minimalist style, based on obsessive repetition of melodic or rhythmic figures over a steady pulse, with a focus on slow processes of musical change and on the material itself rather than on communicating a feeling or meaning. *Tehillim* marked a departure, continuing many elements of his earlier style while broadening it to embrace longer melodies, chordal harmonies, canons, constantly changing irregular meters, and expressive setting of words. This is Reich's first work to engage his own Jewish heritage and the first in many years to use a text, which accounts for the change in style. The title means "psalms" in Hebrew, and the text, excerpts from four Psalms in Hebrew, is at the center of the piece, both conceptually and musically. As Reich commented in notes to the original recording, he felt a need to set the psalm verses to melodies that reflected the rhythm and meaning of the words, and the other elements of the piece flowed from that decision. The tuned tambourines without jingles and the small pitched cymbals were meant to evoke ancient instruments mentioned in the psalms, and the four vocal soloists are asked to sing without vibrato in the manner of early music (music before 1750). The work was commissioned by West German Radio in Cologne, South German Radio in Stuttgart, and the Rothko Chapel in Houston, and was premiered in September 1981 by Reich's ensemble, Steve Reich and Musicians, on West German Radio. Reich later scored an alternate version with chamber orchestra, which is used on the accompanying recording.

Tehillim is in four parts, each using a different psalm excerpt and setting it in a different way in the four solo voices. Part I begins with a complete melodic setting of the text, then treats phrases of the melody in a series of canons. Part II sets the text syllabically in two-voice and then in three-voice homophony, then sets it again with longer melismas. Part III presents the text in short phrases in a dialogue between voices or pairs of voices, with the final syllable sustained at greater length as the text repeats several times. Part IV, shown here, combines aspects of all three procedures. The main melody appears at the outset with the complete text (including a repetition of the last of the three psalm verses), followed by four variations and a final section on "Haleluyah":

Measure	Section	Musical Description
1	1	Main melody in two-voice homophony
31	2	Main melody in two-voice canon
62 102 129	3	First phrase in four-voice canon, stated five times Second phrase in four-voice canon, stated three times Third phrase in four-voice canon, stated five times
170	4	Main melody varied, in lengthened durations with some altered pitches and brief melismas, alternating two-voice and three-voice homophony
207 225	5	Instrumental interlude (string chords for following vocal passage) Main melody varied in top voice, transposed up a perfect fifth and elaborated with melismas and altered notes, in three-voice homophony
253	6	"Haleluyah" in short phrases in dialogue between paired voices, and later in four-voice homophony

The procedures from the preceding movements appear in order: sections 1 through 3 use procedures from Part I; sections 1, 4, and 5 use procedures from Part II; and section 6 uses those from Part III. In the canons, the following voices often decorate the opening of a phrase by adding a passing tone or other melodic variants, as at measures 33, 42, and 62–65. Reich uses rehearsal letters combined with roman numerals and lower-case letters to delineate sections and subsections; for example, the first section is marked with rehearsal letter A, the three psalm verses are designated AI, AII, and AIII, and the varied repetition of the third verse is marked AIIIa (see measures 1, 10, 19, and 25).

The main melody has more skips and leaps than steps, giving it an active, joyous character appropriate to the text. Both the melody and its counterpoints are diatonic, mostly in the D minor (or F major) scale, then moving back and forth between the F, G, and D major scales from measure 243 to the end. The contrasts of scale collection increase the intensity and sense of elation near the end of the piece, and they exploit a particular quality of the melody: its second half (measures 19–30) uses only the notes D, E, G, and A, which are shared as common tones among all three scales. The main melody appears to be modal, with each phrase ending on either A or E, but the accompanying lines and the chords in the orchestra do not clearly reinforce either as a modal center. The final sonority, combining notes of the A-major and G-major triads with A as the highest and lowest notes, emphasizes A, although Reich's own note on the piece says it ends in D major.

The singers are doubled by wind instruments and organs, and the strings play sustained diatonic but dissonant chords of five to seven notes. Up through measure 128, the strings play a repertoire of only five chords. The strings shift to the G-major scale collection for the third canon in section 3 (measure 129), then return to the original D minor with a much more varied palette of chords. At measure 207, the strings are featured in an interlude, then at measure 225 those same chords accompany the voices. From measure 243 to the end, the strings change diatonic collections frequently, along with the singers. Nowhere is there a clear sense of harmonic progression, or resolution to a pitch center; rather, the chords project the scale collection within which the voices move.

The meter is constantly changing in response to the natural speech rhythms of the text. The barlines follow the rhythm of the voices at the beginning, and usually of the top voice when the rhythmic patterns conflict, as they do during the canons in sections 2 and 3. Because of the fast pace, the eighth notes go by too quickly for the performers to count or for the conductor to beat. The rhythm is best conceived in terms of long beats (three eighth notes long) and short beats (two eighth notes long), as in Bulgarian dance meters (see discussion in NAWM 179). These groups of three and two are indicated in the score to aid the conductor, the threes by triangles (which have three sides) and the twos by vertical lines (which have two), representing a stylization of the patterns conductors use to beat triple and duple time.

The percussion rhythms derive from those of the voices, articulating every vocal note but also reflecting the groups of three and two. In section 1, for example, the first tambourine plays on the first and last eighth note of each group of three, and on the first eighth note of each group of two, resting on the second eighth notes. The second tambourine reinforces the downbeat of almost every measure and otherwise plays when the first tambourine rests, except that both rest together to mark the end of each line of text (as in measure 4) or the words "Halleluhu" ("praise him," as in measure 6), "Kol hanshamah" (measures 19–20, perhaps illustrating the text, "let all that breathes"), and "Haleluyah." When the first canon begins in section 2, the procedure is similar, but tambourine 1 is paired with voice 1 and tambourine 2 with voice 2.

At the beginning of section 3, the tambourines fade out and the maracas enter, continuing to play without a break until the end. The maracas player moves at twice the pace of the others, moving up and down in unbroken sixteenth notes. In order to avoid tiring out, the player alternates hands, playing for a while with one hand, then starting to move the empty hand together with the first, then holding the instrument with both hands, and gradually passing it off to the second hand so the first can rest. In the final section, the vibraphones reinforce the tambourines, and the crotales (tuned cymbals) add echoes of the vocal Haleluyahs (measure 256).

John Adams (b. 1947)

Short Ride in a Fast Machine

Orchestral fanfare

1986

* Clarinets 3 & 4 are optional.
** Synthesizer: the sound should be similar to an "analog brass" voice with a moderately fast attack, for example the "Anna Brass" preset on the Yamaha SY77. The speakers should be placed directly behind the players. The sound should never be mixed into the auditorium PA system. The level should be adjusted to mix with the rest of the orchestra and not predominate. The synthesizer parts are optional.

Short Ride in a Fast Machine, from John Adams, *Two Fanfares for Orchestra* (New York: Hendon Music, Boosey & Hawkes, 1992), 23–66. © 1986 Hendon Music, Inc., a Boosey & Hawkes company. Reprinted by permission.

211 JOHN ADAMS · *Short Ride in a Fast Machine*

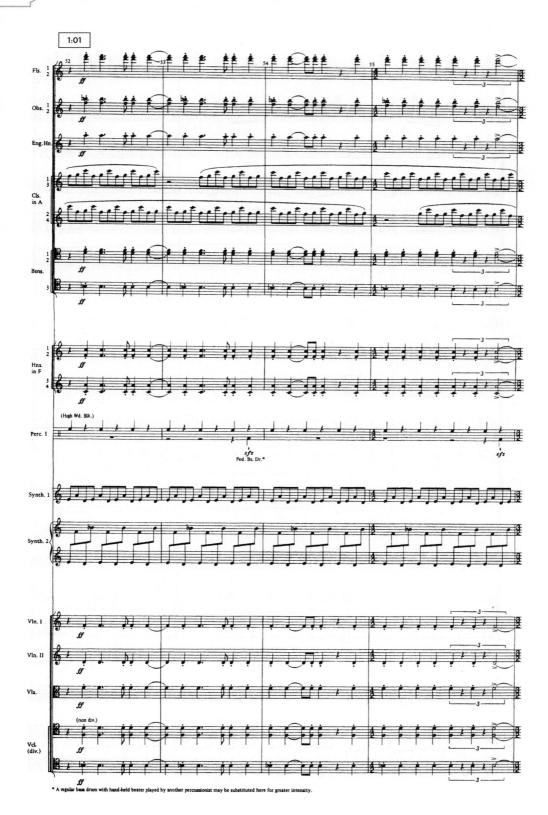

* A regular bass drum with hand-held beater played by another percussionist may be substituted here for greater intensity.

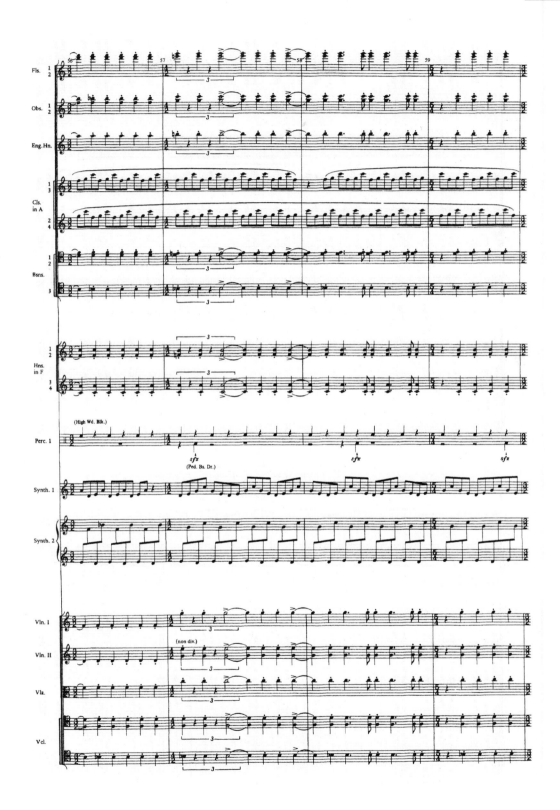

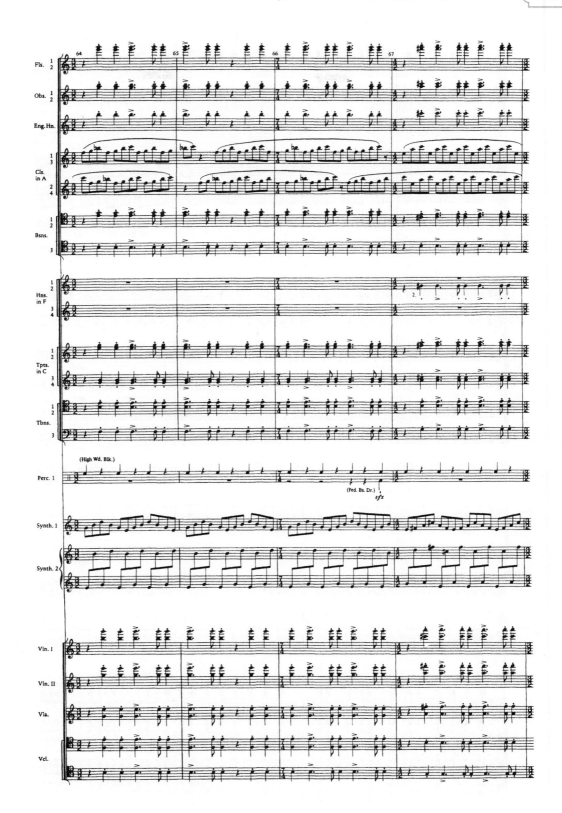

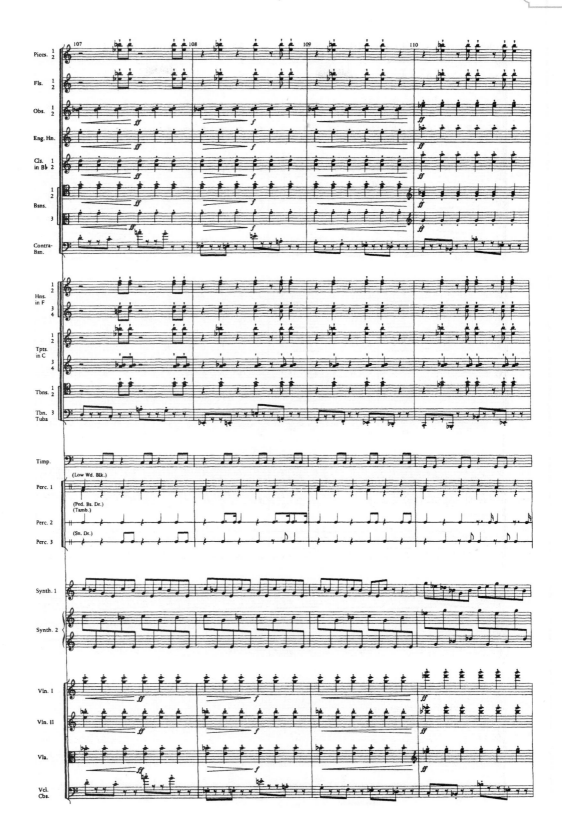

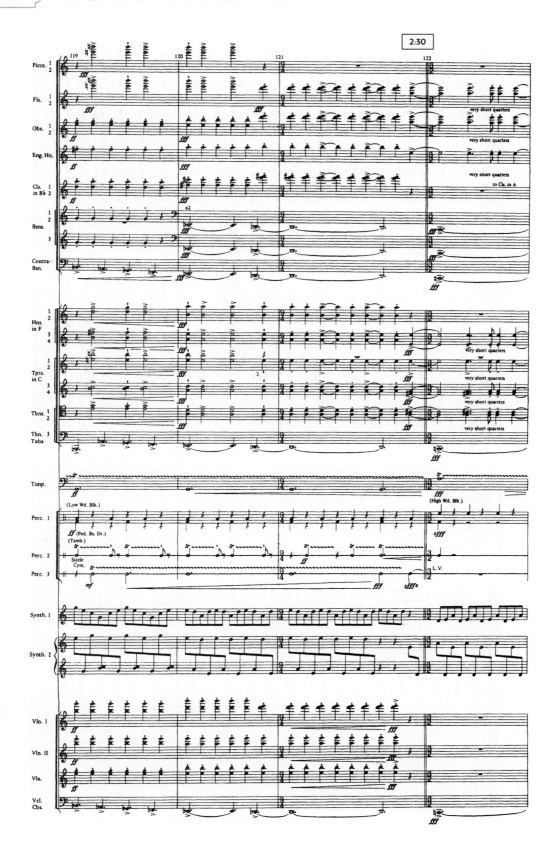

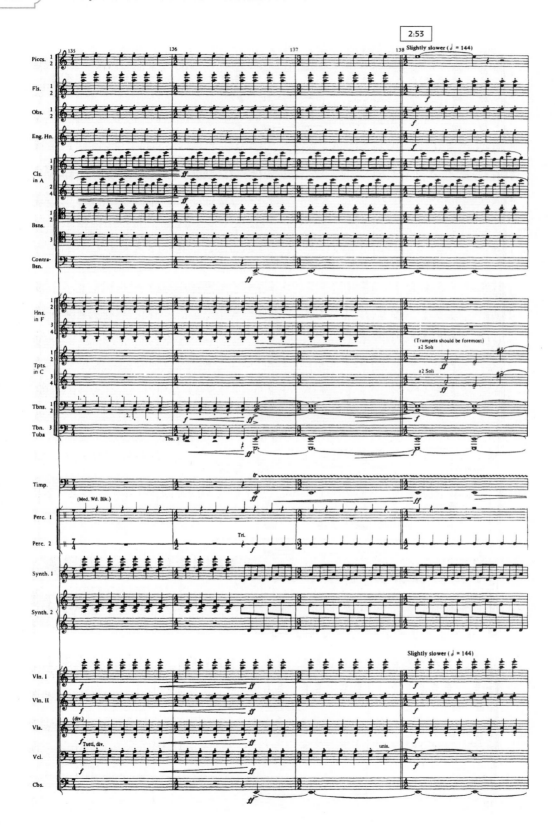

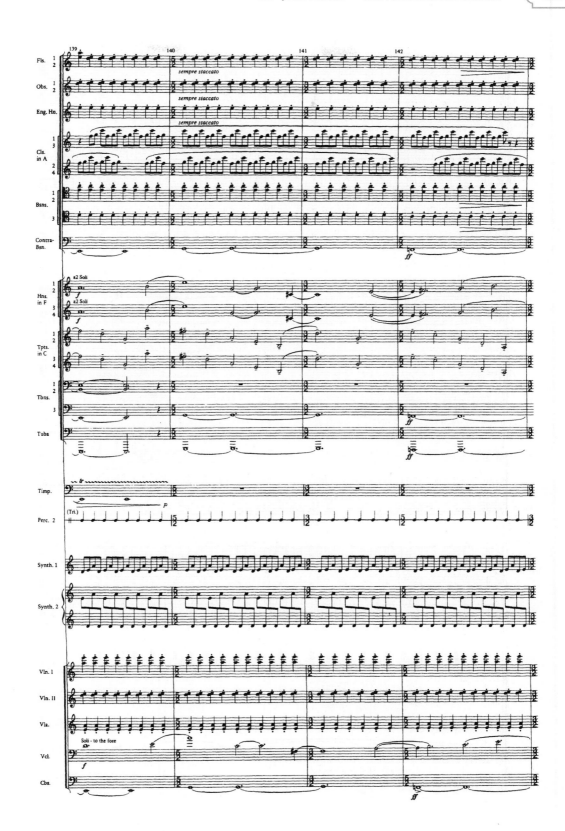

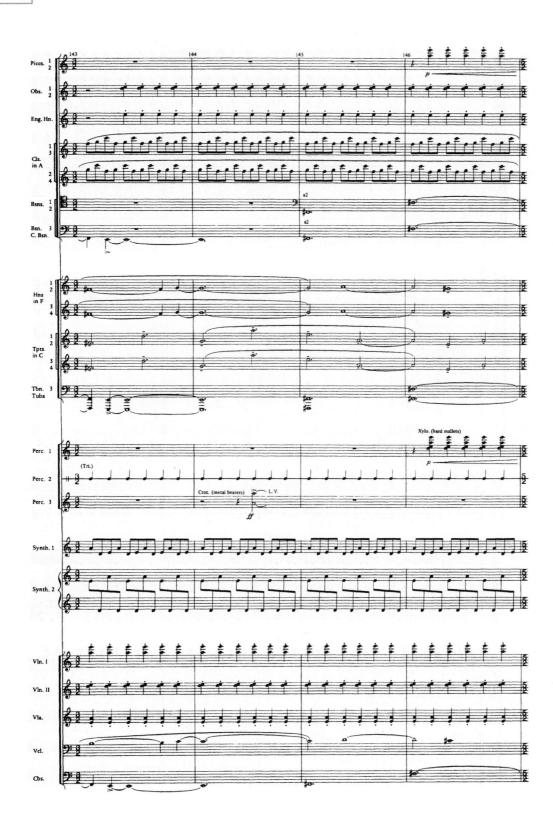

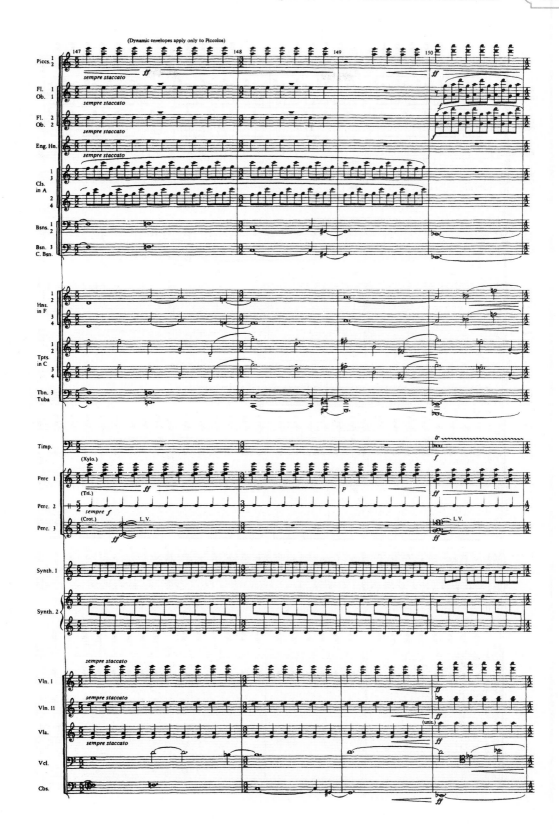

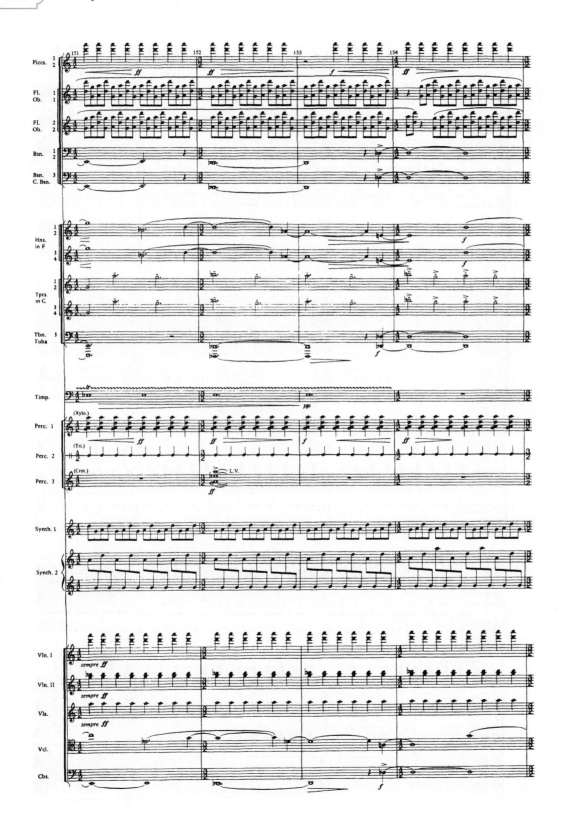

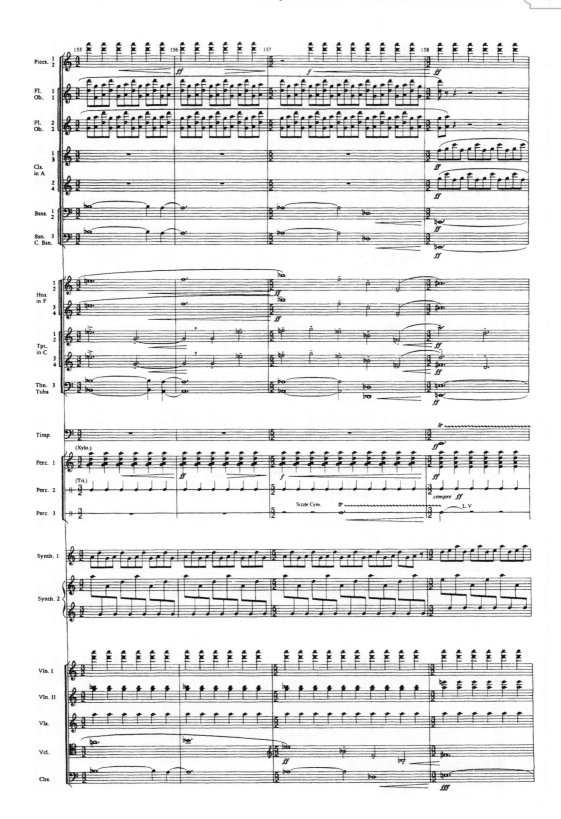

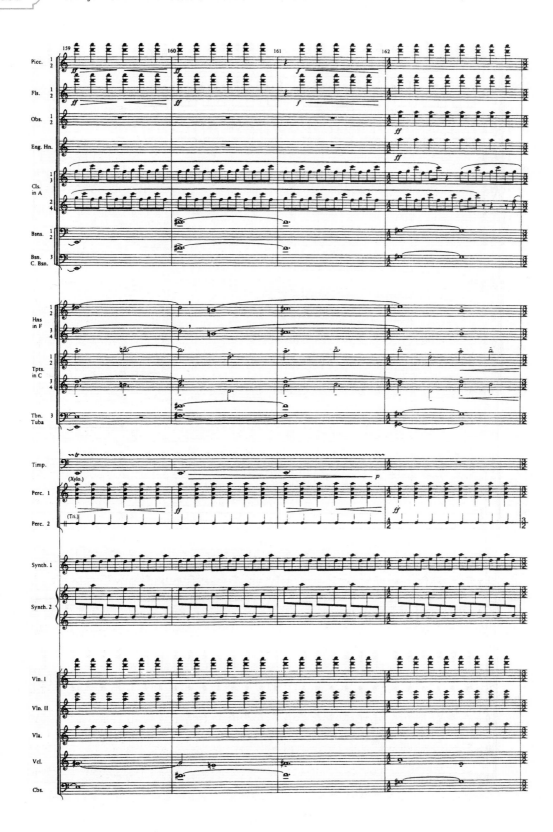

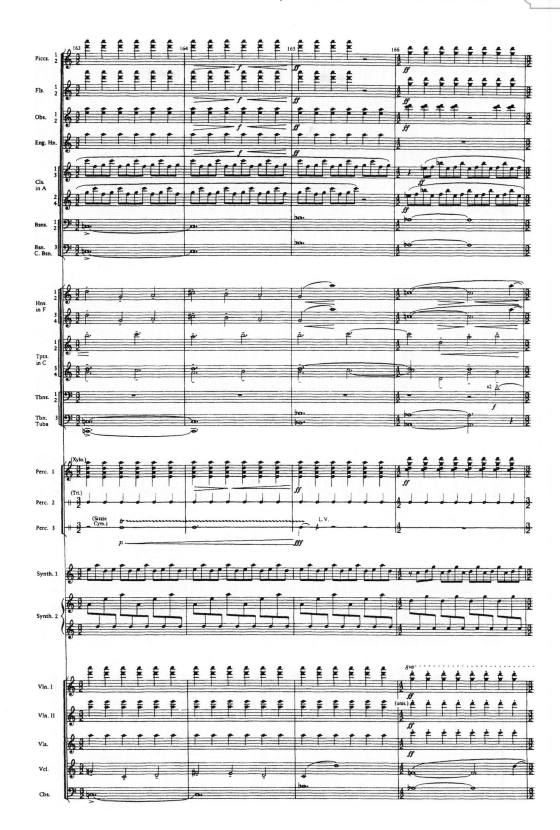

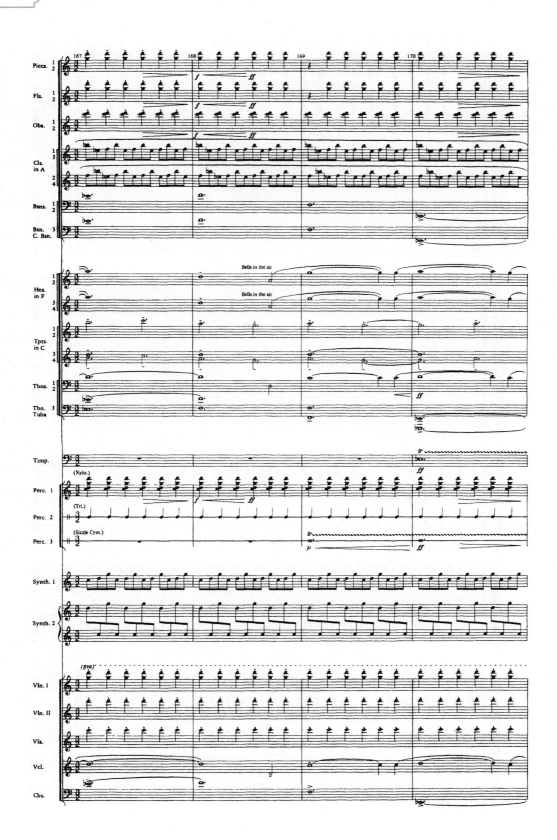

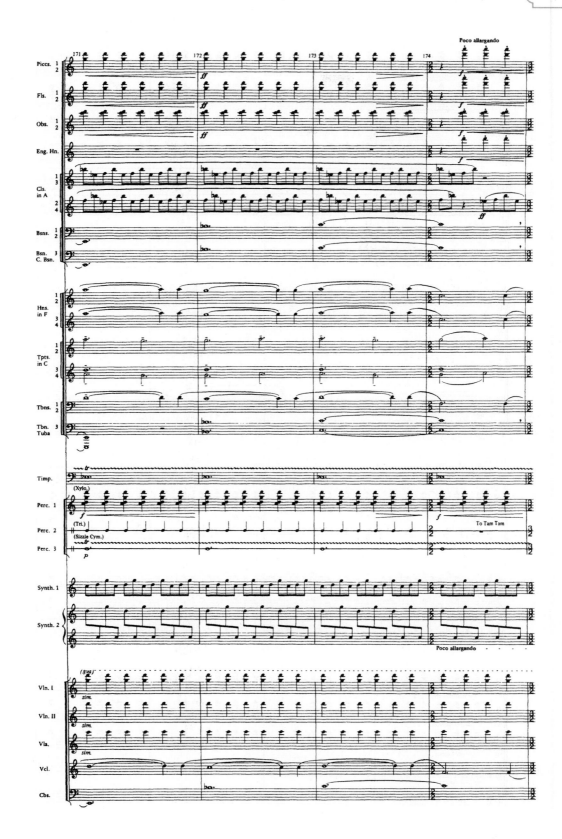

John Adams's *Short Ride in a Fast Machine* was commissioned by the Great Woods Festival in Massachusetts and premiered in 1986 by the Pittsburgh Symphony Orchestra, conducted by Michael Tilson Thomas. Adams called it a "fanfare for orchestra," and it has some of the spirit of a fanfare, featuring the brass and building to a rousing climax. The title refers to the rapid, motoric rhythm of the piece, whose exhilarating effect and audience appeal have made it one of Adams's most frequently programmed compositions.

Like several of his other works of the 1980s, such as the symphonic suite *Harmonielehre* and the opera *Nixon in China*, this piece uses minimalist techniques to create a complex musical fabric that hardly deserves the word "minimalist." Building on a minimalist foundation of constant pulsation and repetition of simple rhythmic and melodic material, Adams enriched his music with more rapid changes, greater harmonic variety, and emotional surges. Most of the ideas are simple, but by varying and layering them in unpredictable ways, he creates ever-changing textures. A woodblock establishes a steady pulse, and the other instruments play off it, some moving in lockstep with it while others feature contrasting meters, syncopations, or irregular accents. Very common throughout are groupings of three at different metric levels; for instance, in measures 7–13, the woodblock and synthesizer 2 articulate half-notes in $\frac{3}{2}$ meter, the brass chords repeat in groupings of three quarter notes, and the clarinet and synthesizer 1 ostinatos move in groups of three eighth notes, so that $\frac{3}{8}$, $\frac{3}{4}$, and $\frac{3}{2}$ meters all sound at once.

The piece begins and ends on a pitch center of D, but the harmony is not tonal. Rather, a sense of harmonic motion is suggested by changing the pitch collection, the set of notes in circulation at any moment. Sometimes several notes in the collection will change at once. Adams calls these points of change "gates," a term borrowed from electronic music, referring to the switches that regulate the flow of electrical current. At other times, single notes will be added, dropped, or altered chromatically, creating a sense of gradual movement Adams calls "landscape," as if one is moving through a landscape that gradually changes character. As in music by Debussy and Stravinsky, changes of pitch collection are often coordinated with changes of figuration and timbre, especially at section breaks.

In the first section, the woodblock sets the pace, joined by rapid ostinatos in clarinets and optional synthesizers that create a twittery background and establish the initial pitch collection of D, E, and A (the clarinets are in A, sounding a minor third lower than written). Over this the trumpets enter, playing repeated chords with the same notes, at first with the woodblock pulse and then in a hemiola against it. Other brass join in on the chords, adding new notes to the collection in the manner of Adams's landscape (F♯ in measure 10, C in measure 13, G in measure 14) as the rhythms grow more complex. Flutes and oboes add quick filigree figures in the upper register, and other percussion instruments join in as well. At measure 39, the pitch collection changes (D, E, F♯ and A continue to sound, but G and C move to G♯ and B), marked by a change in figuration in the upper winds, but the other parts keep rolling along.

A new section begins at measure 52 with the entrance of the strings and bassoons. Brass, winds, and strings now all move in rhythmic unison, playing repeated chords against the background of woodblock, clarinets, synthesizers, and percussion. The new section is set off by a gate: while the D–E–A ostinato continues, the rest of the pitch collection changes from an E-major triad in the preceding measures to a B♭-major triad at measure 52. Now the ostinatos and the repeated chords both change the harmony every few measures; a C-major triad is added at measure 57, and then other combinations appear, adding E-minor, F♯-minor, and E♭-major triads to the mix, which grows more dissonant as the section builds to a climax.

The machine changes gears in the middle of measure 79, introducing the contrasting middle section. The steady pulse continues, but on a lower woodblock; after 254 hits on the high woodblock, the new sound is a very audible change. The pitch content is stripped down to E♭ and B♭—the last two notes to be added in the previous section. Then, through the rest of the middle section, the collection of pitches in the pulsing chords and ostinatos changes every two to four measures. Over this a new idea appears (measure 82): a staccato line in the bass instruments, marching in a meter of four beats per measure against the prevailing $\frac{3}{2}$ meter. The staccato bass line starts with alternating thirds but gradually expands its range and repertoire of intervals, eventually including all but the major seventh. As it becomes increasingly unpredictable, it moves through all twelve notes of the chromatic scale by measure 101 (the D♭ on the downbeat is the twelfth). At this point new layers are added to the texture, most prominently *sforzando* brass and wind chords, snare drum, and timpani. The chord progression of measures 80–100 repeats with variations and omissions, and the staccato bass line continues to expand its range, going through a second round of all twelve notes. The end of the section (measures 117–21) is marked by a crescendo, rolls in drums and cymbal, a descending bass line, and a gradual return to ostinatos and harmonies on D, E, and A, preparing the varied return of the opening section.

The return at measure 122 is marked by the high woodblock, the synthesizer ostinatos, and the rhythms in the brass and wind chords (compare the brass rhythms in measures 37–45 of the first section). A new element is the bass line, which leaps an octave and a sixth back and forth between C and A. After a brief halt at measure 133, the opening D–E–A chord and the clarinet ostinatos return as well.

The final section begins at measure 138 as the ostinatos and pulsating chords continue, the woodblock drops out, and three-part counterpoint begins among three wide-ranging lines: a quickly moving melody in trumpets, a slower mid-range line in horns and cellos, and a still slower bass line in trombones, tuba, contrabassoon, and contrabass. The pulsing chords and ostinatos change pitch collection more slowly now and remain exclusively diatonic, setting off the chromatic melodies in all three contrapuntal lines. From being the main event at the beginning of the piece, the ostinatos and repeating chords have now become the background accompaniment, the typical role such textures play in traditional tonal music. Once more the music swells to a climax, and after a brief fanfare-like coda, the piece concludes on a D major triad.

Music like this can be very hard to play, demanding pinpoint rhythm, rapid playing in the winds, and attention to small changes. It can be difficult to keep track of one's place when repeating a figure as the measures are flying by, but each performer has to be prepared for the next change in an ostinato or rhythm, such as the few spots where the woodblock varies its otherwise incessant beat (measures 59, 63, 121, and 132–35). After the continuously repeating chords, the emergence of a moving bass line in the middle section and then of intertwining, arching melodies in the brass, low strings, and bassoons seems like an emotional release, as satisfying to the players as it is for the listeners.

György Ligeti (1923–2006)

Étude No. 9, *Vertige*

Étude

1990

212

*) So fast that the individual notes—even without pedal—almost melt into continuous lines.

**) The piece has no rhythmic metre—it consists of a continuous flow—therefore the bar lines only serve as a guideline.

***) The first four "bars" serve as a model indicating the compositional structure of the whole piece. After this point consistent notation has been dispensed with in order not to complicate the appearance of the music unnecessarily. The whole piece, however, should be interpreted as shown in the first four "bars": the chromatic runs break over each other like waves from different directions, and the interference pattern is irregular i.e. the time intervals between the entry points of the runs vary constantly. In addition, legato slurs have been omitted with one exception: everything should be played legato according to the example of "bars" one to four.

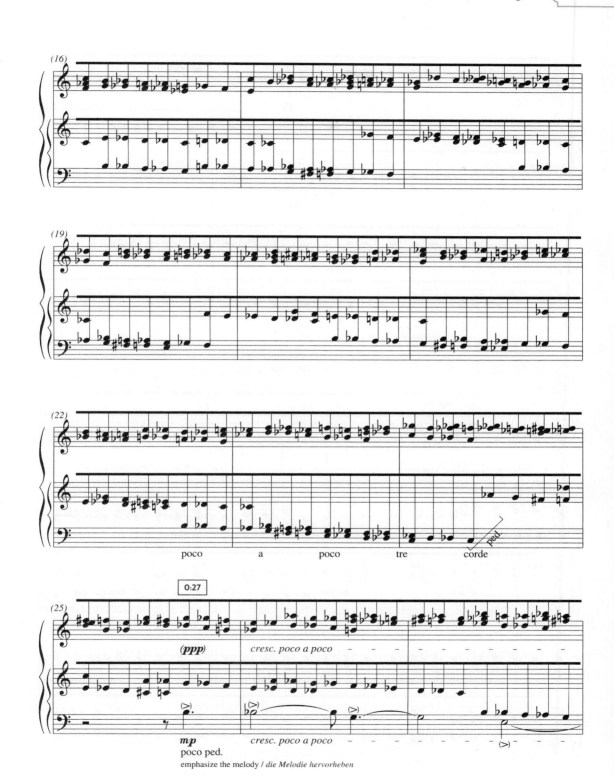

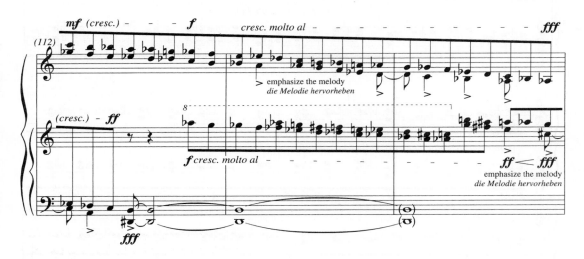

Durata ca. 3'03"

György Ligeti made his international reputation in the 1950s and 1960s with pieces for orchestra, voices, or other ensembles that focused on texture and processes of change rather than themes, melody, or harmony. One of his basic tools was what he called *micropolyphony*, in which a large number of instruments or voices had independent contrapuntal lines (sometimes canonic or nearly so) that could not be heard separately but that combined to create a gradual process of movement, such as a gradually rising cluster of sound. In his eighteen études for solo piano, composed between 1985 and 2001, Ligeti blended many of his earlier concerns with the nineteenth-century tradition of the étude for a virtuoso pianist, in the spirit of his fellow Hungarian Franz Liszt (see NAWM 136). *Vertige* (Vertigo), his ninth étude, was commissioned by the city of Gütersloh in northwest Germany for a concert in May 1990 in honor of composer Mauricio Kagel, to whom the piece is dedicated. It was published in 1998 as part of Ligeti's second book of études.

The whole piece is based on overlapping, rapidly descending chromatic scales of various lengths, which create the sense of vertigo (suggested by the title) through a novel application of micropolyphony. As Ligeti explains in performance notes, there is no meter (the barlines are there for ease of reading), and the notes should move so fast and be played so legato that they blur into continuous lines. This is the étude part of the piece, and it takes enormous skill to play. The emotional effect comes from what those lines do.

At the outset, each descending line begins on *b'* (sometimes notated *c♭"*) and ends on *a♭*, beginning in the right hand and moving seamlessly into the left. (The motion of each line from one hand to the other is made clear by the beams in the opening measures, but it would be cumbersome to continue this notation throughout the piece.) The descending lines enter at irregular intervals between eight and two eighth-notes apart, so that the number of simultaneous lines varies from two to four. These overlapping lines are like waves, all moving within the same range and thereby creating a sense of constant falling without actually getting any lower. This is a paradoxical auditory illusion known as the Shepard effect, invented by computer scientist Roger Shepard and developed further by computer music composer Jean-Claude Risset. Here Ligeti transfers the effect to an acoustic instrument.

From this very regular start, the music moves toward increasing variety over the course of the piece. No definable form emerges, only a series of events marked by constant variation (see the chart on the next page).

In measure 14, the range begins to expand outward in both directions. The beginning note rises chromatically, and the lowest note gradually drops from *g* to *c*. But now not all lines descend through the entire range (the first not to do so begins in measure 16), so the texture grows more varied.

A melody in longer notes and at a higher dynamic level emerges in the left hand in measure 25, comprising a half step, a series of thirds, and a descending fifth, followed by a chord. This melody begins on B (like the opening scales) and ends on a B-minor triad, hinting at a tonal center amid all the chromatics. The descending lines continue, crescendoing along with the melody, and for the first time near

Measure	Events
1	Multiple descending chromatic lines, overlapping (continues throughout, except in measures 83–90)
14	Range expands outward
25	Falling melody in bass
30	Range rises
34	Falling melody in treble, range expands downward
45	Falling melody in bass, followed by rising figures and chords
64	Range rises into highest octave
83	Contrasting texture: parallel descending chromatic lines six octaves apart
90	Return to original texture of overlapping descending chromatic lines, in extreme ranges, gradually converging in high range
110	Falling melody varied twice, followed by rising figures varied
126	Range expands downward
130	Chords, falling melody, and rising figures varied, disappear in extreme ranges

the end of the melody there are brief rising chromatic segments (measures 28–29, both hands).

The descending lines rise into the upper register—another paradox, achieved by making the lines enter more quickly one after another, and making each one shorter so that the bottom of the range gradually drops away. The melody appears again at measure 34, now at the top of the texture, loud against the soft background of the scales. Meanwhile, the scales slowly expand lower again, with each new low note emphasized by being accented and sustained (measures 31–45). The melody emerges a third time at measure 45 and expands into a much longer series of notes and chords, now marked more by rising gestures than falling ones, as if resisting the constantly falling motion of the scales.

Both the scales and the other ideas gradually crescendo. After a climax in measures 54–61, the rising gestures fade, and the falling scales continue softly, moving into the upper reaches of the piano and gradually thinning in texture as each scale grows shorter. Suddenly at measure 83 a new texture begins, with the two hands playing in parallel, six octaves apart, accenting the beginning of each descending scale. The scales begin every seven eighth-notes, then every six, increasing the pace as the music gradually crescendos. Just as suddenly, the texture returns to that of multiple descending lines in measure 90. As the intensity continues to build, the right hand slowly descends from its stratosphere and the left hand works its way upward until the two meet and the left hand returns to playing the continuation of scales that originated in the right hand (measure 100).

After a sudden *pianissimo* (measure 107), the melodic idea returns in new variations. Triads on F♯ minor, F major, and B major (measures 121 and 130–31) again suggest tonal sounds within the chromaticism, but nothing is confirmed. After a final climax on the B-major triad, the music fades to nothingness.

Besides maintaining the constant flow of descending scales, the pianist must also distinguish between a wide range of dynamic levels, including simultaneous contrasting ones. There are many changes of pedaling as well, often changing gradually, such as the shift from *una corda* (one string) at the beginning to *tre corde* (three strings, the normal piano sound) on the second page.

Sofia Gubaidulina (b. 1931)

Rejoice! Sonata for Violin and Violoncello: Fifth movement,
Listen to the still small voice within

Sonata
1981

213 SOFIA GUBAIDULINA · *Rejoice!* Sonata for Violin and Violoncello: Fifth movement

Sofia Gubaidulina's sensitivity to sound is reflected in *Rejoice!*, a duo sonata for violin and cello that is a study in chromaticism, glissandos, tremolos, and harmonics. The piece also reflects her interest in spirituality, which put her at odds with the authorities in the Soviet Union, where she was born and trained. Like many of her works, this sonata was first performed outside the Soviet Union; it was premiered in Kuhmo, Finland, in 1988, seven years after she composed it. The quotations heading the movements are from the spiritual lessons of the Ukrainian philosopher Grigory Skovoroda (1722–1794).

In the fifth movement, *Listen to the still small voice within*, Gubaidulina introduces a sequence of gestures, then offers three variations on the same series of ideas. There are four principal motives in the violin: a leaping and pulsing figure, A (measures 1–5); a neighbor-note figure, B (measures 5–10); a tremolo glissando, C (measures 10–13); and a pizzicato jumping figure, D (measures 29–33). All of them suggest a tonal center on the note D, which is often the lowest or most frequently repeated note in the phrase. The cello, playing with intense vibrato throughout, traces a slowly moving, mostly chromatic line that gradually winds down two octaves from *d'* to D over the course of the piece, confirming D as the pitch center.

Figure A remains essentially the same at each appearance, serving to introduce each main section (at measures 1, 33, 70, and 122). Figure D undergoes extension but is also otherwise unchanged, closing off each section but the last. But figures B and C are constantly changing. In the first section, B appears in three variants—in the upper octave (measures 5–10), in the lower octave (measures 13–16), and climbing into the stratosphere (measures 20–28)—and C in two, either falling (measures 10–13) or rising (measures 16–20). Neither ever returns in exactly the same form. In the second section, B is lengthened at each occurrence, and in later sections it ranges widely, adding large leaps alongside its original stepwise motion (see at measures 93–104 and 151–74). C is transformed even more radically, as the glissandos morph into diatonic scales (measures 80–93), arpeggios (measures 104–7, 134–38, and 142–46), and rising and falling waves of glissandos (175–81).

Near the end, soon after the cello descends to *D♯*, its lowest note so far, the violin soars up to *c♯''''*, where it becomes transfixed (measure 194). The cello finally finds its voice, moving around chromatically and then rising repeatedly in a glissando from low *E♭* to a natural harmonic on the C string. Gubaidulina commented about this sonata that the transition from normal sound to harmonics was a metaphor for transfiguration, a "transition to another plane of existence," representing both the "voice within" of the movement's title and the emerging joy suggested by the title of the entire sonata. After the cello touches its low D *col legno* (with the wood of the bow), the piece ends with high natural harmonics in both instruments, sounding an inverted F♯-major triad.

Most of the notation is traditional, but at the end several new signs are used. The notation for the violin in measure 198—featuring stems without noteheads and beams that are not parallel, but gradually merge together—is used to indicate that the player repeats the same note while gradually slowing down from sixteenth notes to eighths (and even slower, as signaled by the widening distance between the stems). The wavy beams in measures 206 and 219 indicate wide vibrato, a fast rocking of the finger against the fingerboard that changes the pitch slightly. Measure 219 calls for each player to repeat a pattern, without coordinating it with the other player, for about ten seconds, until both performers stop at the same time.

Alfred Schnittke (1934–1998)

Concerto Grosso No. 1: Second movement, Toccata

Concerto

1976

214

214 ALFRED SCHNITTKE · Concerto Grosso No. 1: Second movement, Toccata

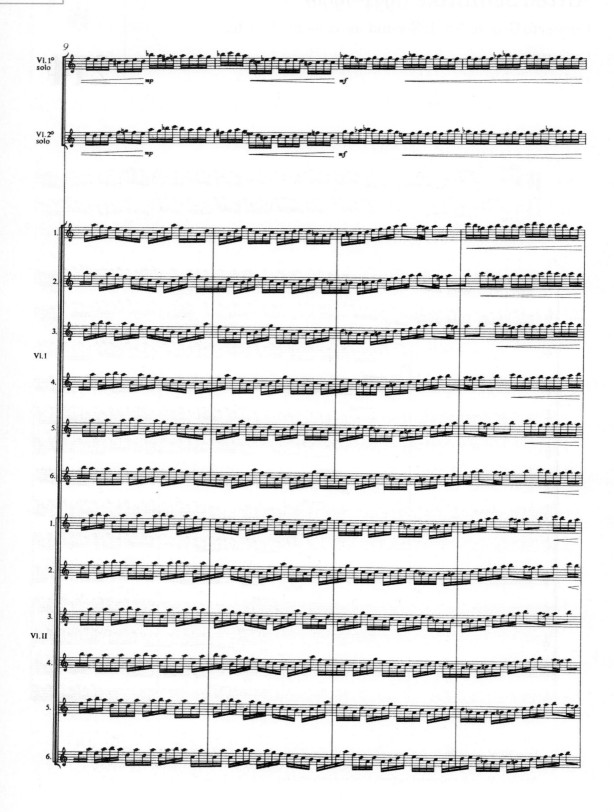

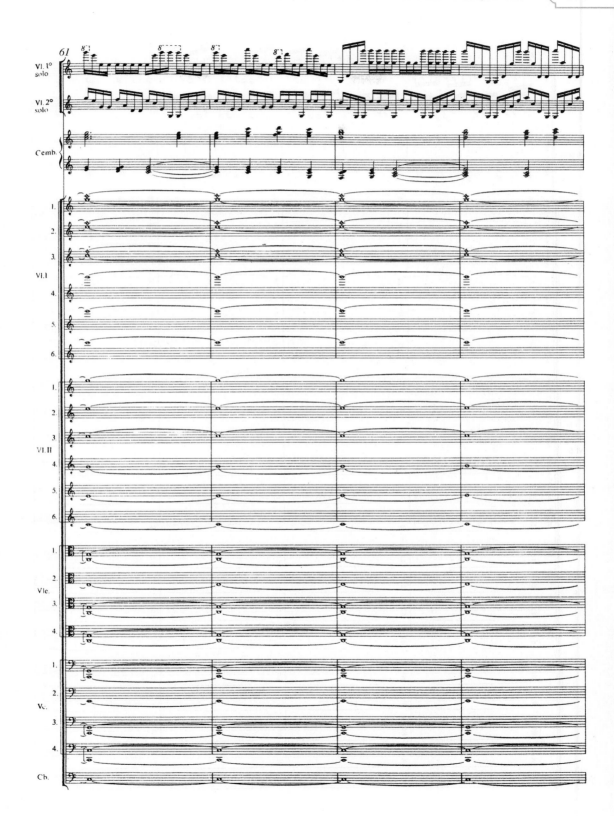

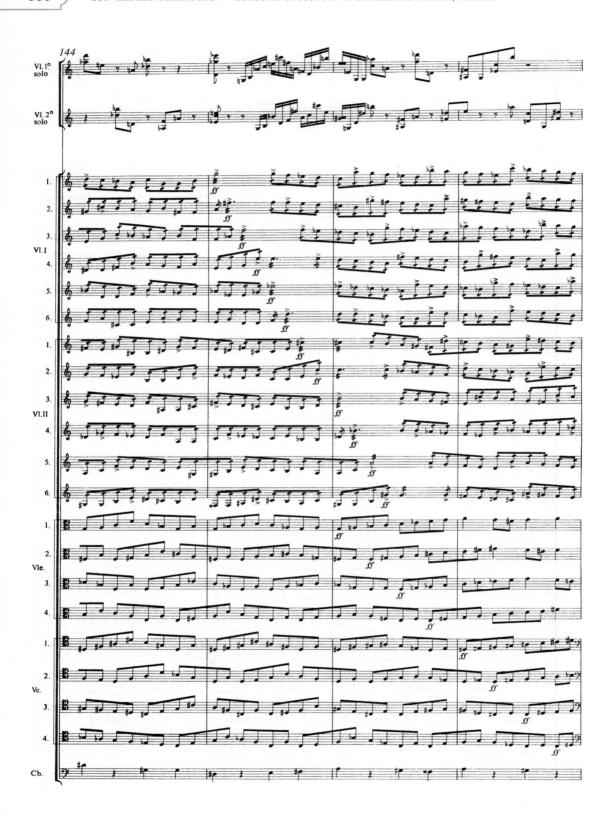

attacca

Alfred Schnittke's Concerto Grosso for two violins, harpsichord (doubling on piano), and string orchestra was commissioned by violinists Gidon Kremer and Tatiana Grindenko and premiered with them as soloists in March 1977 in Leningrad. Kremer, one of the leading young Soviet violinists, and his wife Grindenko played the concerto in several Soviet cities that year and took it on tour through West Germany and Austria, helping to establish Schnittke's reputation in the West.

The concerto is in six movements: Preludio, Toccata, Recitativo, Cadenza, Rondo, and Postludio. The titles of the work and its movements invoke Baroque models. The alternation of soloists and orchestra resembles that of a Vivaldi concerto (see NAWM 96), although the fast movements do not use Vivaldi's ritornello form. Some of the musical material, such as the figure that opens the Toccata, is close to Vivaldi's style. And the harpsichord is identified with Baroque music.

But not all is Baroque. Schnittke was interested in contrasting elements of diverse styles with each other, an approach he called *polystylism*. In this concerto, he plays off three stylistic categories: eighteenth-century styles, modern atonality, and what he called "banal popular music," represented here by a hymnlike tune presented at the beginning of the Preludio. This juxtaposition of very different styles gives new meaning to the word and genre *concerto*, which originally meant a work that combined diverse performing forces to work in concert. Schnittke took some of the material in this work from film scores he had composed, and this adds another level of juxtaposition, between the popular medium of film music and the classical genre of the concerto.

The Toccata alternates sections with contrasting thematic material and stylistic allusions (see chart on the following page). Part of the point of combining styles from the past and present, and from the classical and popular traditions, is that all these types of music coexist in the modern world. The same is true in the piece. Each style is evoked through melodic material and procedures associated with that style, but no style appears in its pure form. Rather, the traits of each style are mixed with modernist procedures, bringing that style into the modern era, and in the final section all the thematic material appears simultaneously, representing a coming together of all these contrasting types of music.

In the A section (measures 1–30), Schnittke uses Baroque ideas and material to generate modern textures. The main theme (measures 1–8) is a motoric melody in A minor marked by sequences, scales, arpeggiations, and other Vivaldi-like figuration. It is introduced by solo violin 2, joined in canon a beat later by solo violin 1. The initial entrance of the soloists sounds neoclassical, almost Baroque. What could be more Baroque than a canon? But when the orchestra comes in, Schnittke uses canon to create a very un-Baroque texture. A twelve-part canon in the violins on the main theme, imitated at the unison and at the time interval of one eighth note, has an effect similar to Ligeti's micropolyphony (see NAWM 212), creating a mostly diatonic wash of sound. Over this the soloists modulate around the circle of fifths from A minor to F minor (measures 8–11). This adds polytonality to the

Measure	Section/ Theme	Style invoked	Traditional devices	Modern procedures
1	A	Baroque/Vivaldi	Canon at unison, circle-of-fifth progressions	Micropolyphony, diatonic dissonance, canon at semitone, chromatic saturation, polytonality
31	B	Galant/Haydn	Melody-accompaniment texture, tonal harmony, canon at octave	Micropolyphony, canon at semitone, polytonality, chromatic saturation, clusters
52	A'	Baroque/Vivaldi	Canon at unison, canon in augmentation	Micropolyphony, canon at semitone, polytonality, chromatic saturation
60	C	Popular/ hymnlike	Tonal harmony, homophonic harmonization, canon in inversion	Diatonic dissonance, polytonality, canon at semitone, chromatic saturation
78	D	Twelve-tone plus Stavinskian blocks	Twelve-tone techniques, canon in inversion, juxtaposed blocks	Micropolyphony, polytonality
109	B' + C'		Canon	Clusters, polytonality
129	All		Twelve-tone techniques, canon in inversion, augmentation	Canon at semitone, polytonality, micropolyphony

mix, plus chromatic saturation—because, through the modulations, the soloists touch upon all the chromatic notes that were missing from the theme. Although the basic ideas—the Vivaldi-like theme, canon, sequence, and motion down the circle of fifths—are all typical of Baroque concertos, Schnittke uses them to create a very modern effect.

At measure 14, the violins stop and the violas and cellos begin their own canon, based on the middle segment of the A theme. The first viola plays this segment in F♯ minor, and each of the other five instruments descends from one to five semitones and then begins to play the same segment in canon with the others, until the six minor keys from F♯ down to C♯ are all sounding at once. This texture recurs in the violins at measure 19 with all twelve minor keys in order from B minor on down, and again at measures 23 and 27 in the entire orchestra, starting on E minor and A minor respectively. The beginning keys in these four canons create another circle-of-fifths motion, F♯–B–E–A. These passages expand on the micropolyphony, polytonality, and chromatic saturation already evident in the opening section.

In between these canonic passages in the orchestra, the soloists play their own canons over descending-third patterns in the harpsichord. Each successive canon is at a closer interval in time, shrinking from three sixteenth notes to one. Each canon rapidly moves through a circle of fifths. Throughout measures 14–27, the alternation of soloists and orchestra, the motoric theme, the canons and sequences, and the circle-of-fifth motions are all right out of Vivaldi's playbook, but the sound is nothing Vivaldi would have ever imagined.

The canons end on a total chromatic cluster in measure 29, and the B section begins (measures 30–51). Here the style changes to something like the galant style of the mid-to-late eighteenth century. If we extract from the texture just the harpsichord and solo violin 2, the two sound like a passage from a Classical-era sonata: the keyboard plays a simple accompaniment, the violin a Classical-phrased melody, and both follow a tonal harmonic progression in C♯ minor. But again Schnittke uses canon to create a more complex texture. Solo violin 1 echoes the melody, first a measure later, then half a measure (measure 35), and finally just a beat later (measure 39). Meanwhile, the orchestral strings treat the melody in canon at the semitone, creating chromatic clusters. In measures 44–51, the soloists play dissonant double stops that fill in notes necessary for chromatic saturation.

At measure 52 the A theme returns, now in a complex 21-part canon in the five chromatic keys from C♯ minor (in the contrabass, in augmentation) down to A minor (in the first violins)—the keys of the B and A sections, respectively.

Section C begins at measure 60 with a more dramatic contrast of style. The orchestral lines converge on an expansive C-major triad. The harpsichord plays the hymnlike tune introduced at the beginning of the concerto's first movement, harmonized homophonically, and echoed in inverted canon in the harpsichord's left hand. Over this the soloists play widely spaced arpeggiations and double stops, drawing notes from the chords in the harpsichord. At measure 68 the soloists begin a new, chromatic figuration of trills and arpeggios. Simultaneously, the orchestra instruments begin another canon, based on an undulating ostinato in the upper three instruments that repeats in six-beat cycles; it is imitated by successively lower trios of instruments, each entering a major seventh lower and five beats later.

So far, Schnittke has used techniques of tonal styles to generate unusual modernist textures. In the D section (measures 78–108), he evokes two modern styles: twelve-tone music (see NAWM 173 and 175) and the pulsating style of Stravinsky's *Rite of Spring* (NAWM 176). The twelve-tone melody starts with B–A–C–H (B♭–A–C–B♮) in measure 78, an allusion both to Bach and to Schoenberg, whose row for his Piano Suite also includes BACH (see NAWM 173). The pulsating dissonances also build from B♭ and A (measure 85) to B♭, A, and C (measure 93) and finally to all four notes of BACH (measure 101). After being juxtaposed as alternating blocks several times—a Stravinskian technique—the twelve-tone and pulsating styles combine at measure 102. Meanwhile, hints of the A theme have appeared periodically in inverted canon (measures 82, 90, and 98) and canon at the semitone (measures 106–7, hidden in the pulsating texture).

The rest of the movement mixes the elements already presented. In the next section (measures 109–128), material from section B returns (in reverse order) in the solo violins, joined by the C theme at measure 113 in the harpsichord (with the melody in F♯ minor and accompaniment in C minor). The orchestra enters at measure 121 with the first part of the B theme (altered to use the intervals of the BACH motive) in canon at the semitone. The final section (measures 129–51) combines all the themes at once: the soloists play twelve-tone canons derived from the D theme; the orchestral violins play the B theme (again altered to begin with BACH) in canon in all minor keys from G down to G♯; the violas and cellos play the A theme in augmentation in all minor keys from G down to C; and the contrabass plays the C theme in augmentation in C♯ minor. The movement ends with repeating dissonant figures in the solo instruments and a closing twelve-note chord in the orchestra. In this final section, the stylistic contrasts in the movement are resolved paradoxically, with all the themes coexisting, but in a modernist world of maximal density and complexity.

Arvo Pärt (b. 1935)

Seven Magnificat Antiphons: Excerpts

Choral antiphons

1988, REVISED 1991

215

(a) No. 1: *O Weisheit*

O Weisheit, hervorgegangen aus dem
  Munde des Höchsten,
die Welt umspannst du von einem Ende
  zum andern,
in Kraft und Milde ordnest du alles:

o komm und offenbare uns den Weg der
  Weisheit und der Einsicht.

O Wisdom, sprung forth from the mouth
  of the most high,
you embrace the world from one end to
  the other,
in strength and mildness you put
  everything in order;
O come and reveal to us the way of
  wisdom and understanding.

(b) No. 6: *O König aller Völker*

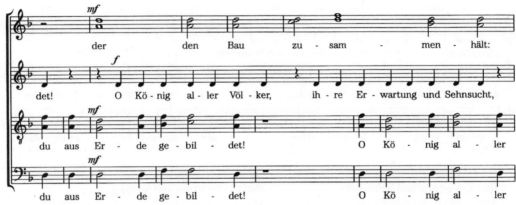

O König aller Völker,
ihre Erwartung und Sehnsucht,
Schlußstein, der den Bau zusammenhält:
o komm und errette den Menschen, den
    du aus Erde gebildet!

O king of all peoples,
their expectation and longing;
keystone, which holds the building together:
O come and redeem mankind, whom you
    have fashioned out of clay!

Arvo Pärt left his native Estonia (then a constituent republic of the Soviet Union) in 1980 and settled in Berlin, seeking artistic freedom and greater international opportunities. In 1988, he wrote *Seven Magnificat Antiphons*, his first major choral work in German, the language of his adoptive country. The texts are translations of the Latin antiphons that are sung just before and after the Magnificat in Vespers services on the seven evenings immediately preceding Christmas Eve. These seven antiphons, one for each evening's service, are known as the "O Antiphons" because they all begin with the exclamation "O" and conclude with a line beginning "O come," appropriate for the season of Advent. The work is dedicated to the RIAS-Kammerchor, the chamber choir of RIAS (Radio in the American Sector).

The *Magnificat Antiphons* exemplify Pärt's distinctive *tintinnabuli* style (named after the Latin word for ringing bells), which he devised in the mid-1970s after studying Gregorian chant and early polyphony. In this technique, one voice presents a diatonic melody that generally moves by step around a central pitch, and the other voices sound notes of the tonic triad that are determined by a preset system. The two movements included here demonstrate different ways of applying this simple method.

The text of *O Weisheit* is set syllabically and homophonically. Measure lines are used to indicate lengths of individual words but do not suggest a meter. One-syllable words are set with half notes, but longer words are set with a whole note on the syllable that receives the greatest stress. Throughout, the soprano and bass sing every other word, regardless of syllable lengths or declamation, and a three-beat measure of rests follows every comma.

The principal melody appears in the tenor, where it is doubled in parallel thirds. The tenors reiterate a C♯ and E for each half note, and alternate moving up and down a step for whole notes. The entire melodic range remains within the span of a third. The other voices of the ensemble derive their pitches from the A-major triad. The bass and soprano lines are limited to E and A, arranged as a perfect fourth or fifth. The repetition of these open harmonies at irregular intervals suggests the ringing of a bell. The upper and lower alto lines sing the two pitches from the A-major triad that are higher than and closest to the notes of the comparable tenor lines. For the most part, the altos remain on *e'* and *a'*, but when the tenors descend to *b* and *d'*, the altos move down to a *c♯'* and *e'*.

As a result of this simple construction, the movement has only six different harmonies; the tenors and altos sound a first-inversion A-major triad on each half note and alternate two four-note dissonant diatonic sonorities on the whole notes, and each of these three chords may either sound alone or be accompanied by the notes in the bass and soprano. This simplicity, coupled with the sustained quiet dynamics, effectively supports the antiphon's plea for wisdom and understanding. The movement recalls the recitation of prayers in Gregorian chant and the sonorities of early polyphony, thereby suggesting prayerful contemplation and creating an aura of mysticism and a sense of the medieval. The simple pitch structure also foreshadows the principal tonal centers of the work as a whole. The first two chords contain all the pitches that will serve as tonal centers for the seven movements: A–F♯–C♯–A–E–D–A.

O König aller Völker employs tintinnabuli techniques in a different manner. The texture is divided into three distinct parts. The sopranos sing with half notes and whole notes, following a pattern similar to that observed in *O Weisheit*, although some single-syllable words at the beginning of phrases receive whole notes. The tenors and basses sing the same rhythmic values as the sopranos, but in diminution. The third line is provided by the altos, who chant independently on D in quarter notes.

The principal melody is sung by the second tenor and the second soprano in a canon in augmentation. As in *O Weisheit*, the melody moves primarily by step within a limited range. The other voices draw their pitches from the D-minor triad in a predetermined manner. The first soprano always sings the pitch from the D-minor triad that is above and closest to the note of the second soprano. The bass and first tenor are given pitches that are second closest to those of the second tenor, respectively below and above it. In the first measure, for example, the second tenor and second soprano are on A. The closest higher pitch to A in the D-minor triad is D, which is sung by the first soprano. The second closest higher pitch is an F, heard in the first tenor. The second closest pitch below A in the D-minor triad is D, which is given to the bass.

In *O König aller Völker*, because of the shifting relationship between the voices, harmonies are more varied than in *O Weisheit*, dissonances are more prevalent, and there are no rests in all voices at once—a note is always sounding in at least one voice. The recited D in the alto line also builds in intensity. Initially, it echoes the text as presented in the lower voices, but as the dynamics climb, the alto line pushes forward so that it must repeat the line "o komm und errette den Menschen" (O come and redeem mankind) twice before the movement comes to a dramatic fortissimo close.

The utmost simplicity of Pärt's music makes it rewarding and approachable for choirs and audiences alike, conveying a reverent atmosphere through its smooth restraint. Yet the frequent small changes maintain interest. The rhythmic complexities of *O König aller Völker* present some challenges to performers. Traditional beating patterns from the conductor cannot be applied, since there are three different rhythmic notations in the score. The unifying factor in these lines is the beat, indicated as a quarter note.

Kaija Saariaho (b. 1952)

L'amour de loin: Act IV, Scene 3, Tempête (Storm)

Opera

2000

216

concise

Troisième tableau: Tempête

Le jour se lève, mais la mer est de plus en plus agitée. Jaufré est cramponné au bastingage, livide.

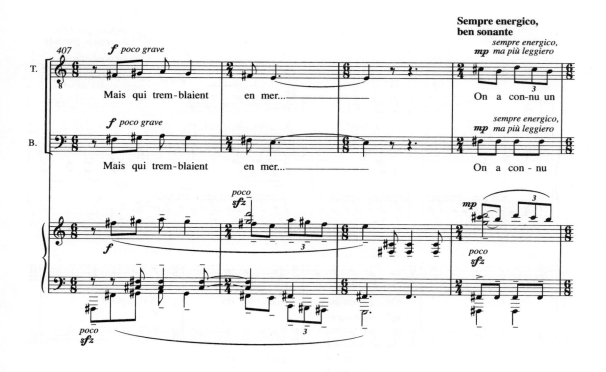

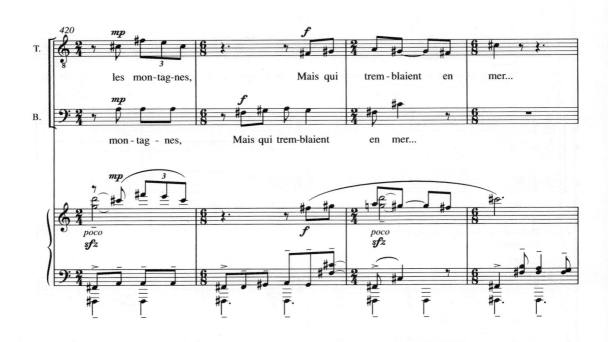

chan-te-raient pas ain-si.   Ce n'est pas la   mer   qui   m'ef-fraie...

S4 **Dolce, ma sempre agitato**

Le Pèlerin hoche la tête et ne dit rien.

Jamais— je n'au-rais dû m'em-bar-quer pour cet-te tra-ver-sée.—

De loin,————— le so-leil—— est

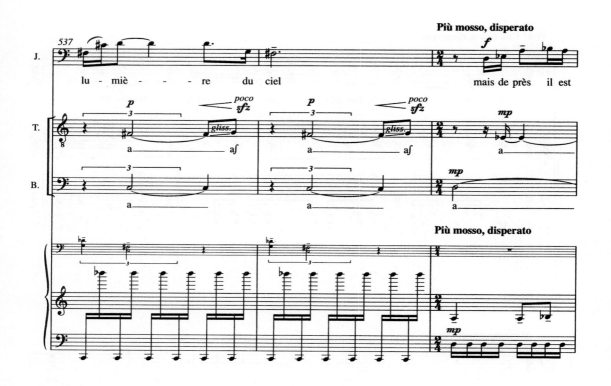

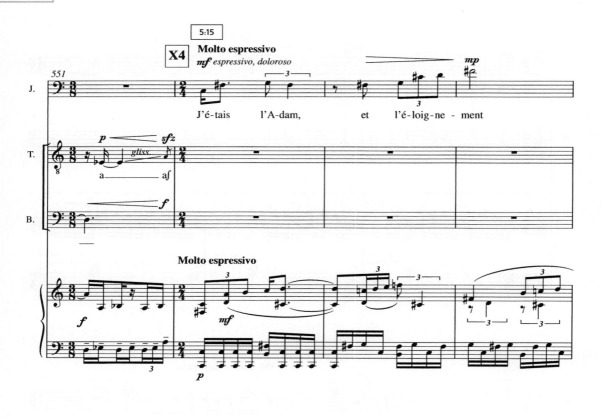

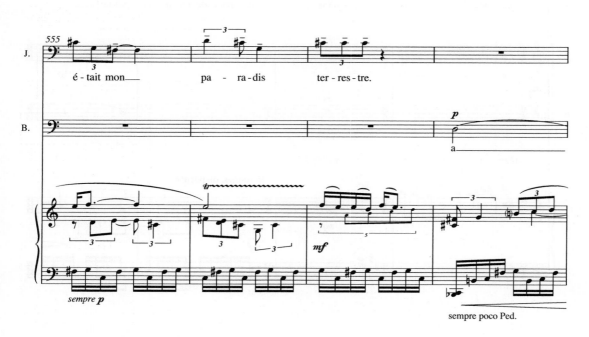

attacca

*(Dawn is breaking, but the sea grows more and more agitated.
Jaufré is holding on tightly to the ship's railing, deathly pale.)*

JAUFRÉ
(to himself)

Je devrais être l'homme le plus heureux au monde,	I should be the happiest man in the world,
Et je suis le plus désespéré . . .	but I am the most despairing . . .

*(A jolt. He loses his balance, and straightens up with great difficulty.
His companions make fun of him.)*

CHORUS OF COMPANIONS

0:47

On a connu des guerriers intrépides	We have known intrepid warriors
Qui se jetaient dans la mêlée et offraient leurs corps	who threw themselves into the fray and offered their bodies
Aux lames de l'ennemi	to the swords of the enemy
Mais qui tremblaient en mer . . .	but who trembled at sea . . .
On a connu un roi puissant	We have known a powerful king
Qui d'un regard faisait frémir comtes et chevaliers,	who with one look made counts and knights quiver,
Qui, à la tête de ses troupes,	Who, at the head of his troops,
Savait franchir les déserts, les montagnes,	could cross deserts and mountains
Mais qui tremblaient en mer.	but who trembled at sea.

JAUFRÉ
(listening to them, not without irritation, then turning toward the Pilgrim)

1:20

Si nos compagnons savaient pourquoi je tremble	If our companions knew why I tremble,
Ils ne chanteraient pas ainsi.	they would not sing that way.
Ce n'est pas la mer qui m'effraie . . .	It is not the sea that frightens me . . .

(The Pilgrim nods his head and says nothing.)

1:43

Crois-tu qu'on lui a dit, Pèlerin?	Do you think anyone told her, Pilgrim?
Crois-tu qu'on lui a dit que je venais à Tripoli?	Do you think they told her that I am coming to Tripoli?
Crois-tu qu'on lui a dit que je m'étais croisé?	Do you think they told her that I was crossing over?

THE PILGRIM

1:57

Ces choses se savent, oui.	These things become known, yes.
J'ignore par quelle bouche, mais elles se savent, oui.	I do not know from whom, but these things get around, yes.
Moi qui parcours les mers et les royaumes	I who travel over many seas and realms,
Chaque fois que j'apporte une nouvelle dans une ville	Each time that I bring a piece of news to a town,
Quelqu'un avant moi l'avait déjà apportée.	someone before me has already brought it.
Certains prétendent que les secrets des hommes	Some people claim that the secrets of men
Sont chuchotés à tout vent par les anges . . .	are whispered on the wind by the angels . . .

(Jaufré barely listens to him.
Having fallen back into melancholy, he again takes up his lament.)

JAUFRÉ

3:14 Je devrais être l'homme le plus heureux au monde,	I should be the happiest man in the world,
Et je suis le plus désespéré . . .	but I am the most despairing . . .
Je devrais avoir hâte d'atteindre sa ville de Tripoli	I should be in haste to reach her city of Tripoli,
Et je me surprends à supplier le Ciel qu'il n'y ait plus dans nos voiles le moindre souffle de vent.	but I surprise myself by beseeching Heaven that there be in our sails not the least breath of wind.
3:42 Si, a cet instant, un génie sortait des flots pour me dire	If, at this moment, a genie came out of the waves to say to me,
"Ordonne, Jaufré, et ton voeu sera exaucé!," je ne saurais quoi souhaiter?	"Command, Jaufré, and your wish will be granted!," I would not know what to wish for.
Ai-je envie de voir devant moi la femme sans tache, et qu'elle me voie devant elle?	Do I want to see before me the spotless woman, and that she see me before her?
Aurai-je envie de chanter l'amour de loin, quand mes yeux la contempleront de près et que je guetterai chacun de ses battements de paupière, chacun de ses plissements de lèvres, chacun de ses soupirs?	Would I want to sing love from afar, when my eyes can contemplate her from nearby and I can watch every flutter of her eyelashes, every crease of her lips, every one of her sighs?
4:30 Jamais je n'aurais dû m'embarquer pour cette traversée.	I should never have embarked on this crossing.
De loin, le soleil est lumière du ciel mais de près il est feu de l'enfer!	From afar, the sun is the light of the sky, but up close it is the fire of hell!
J'aurais dû me laisser bercer longtemps longtemps par sa clarté lointaine au lieu de venir me brûler!	I should have let myself be lulled for a long long time by its light instead of coming to burn myself!
5:15 J'étais l'Adam et l'éloignement était mon paradis terrestre.	I was Adam and the distance was my earthly Paradise.
Pourquoi fallait-il que je marche vers l'arbre?	Why did I have to go toward the tree?
Pourquoi fallait-il que je tende la main vers le fruit?	Why did I have to hold out my hand toward the fruit?
Pourquoi fallait-il que je m'approche de l'étoile incandescente?	Why did I have to come near the radiant star?

(The sea seems more and more agitated. The sky is stormy.
Jaufré staggers. The Pilgrim supports him and helps him lie down.)

—AMIN MALOUF

Finnish composer Kaija Saariaho has made her home in Paris since 1982, when she came to work at Pierre Boulez's IRCAM electronic-music studio. After seeing Olivier Messiaen's opera *Saint Francis of Assisi* as staged by Peter Sellars at the Salzburg Festival in 1992, she was inspired to write a stage work along similar lines, with a historical figure as its centerpiece, organized as a series of self-contained tableaux, and focused less on external drama than on the inner lives of the protagonists. For the subject of her first opera she chose twelfth-century troubadour Jaufré Rudel (fl. 1120–1147), a noble of Blaye in Aquitaine, a region in southwestern France. His best-known poem, *Lanquan li jorn*, describes an idealized "love from afar," or *amor de lonh* in the Occitan language of the troubadours. In 1996 Saariaho set the poem as a miniature monodrama for soprano and electronic instruments under the title *Lonh*. This twenty-minute piece became the germ of *L'amour de loin*, a full-length opera jointly commissioned by the Salzburg Festival and the Théâtre du Châtelet in Paris, and premiered at the Salzburg Festival on August 15, 2000.

At the suggestion of Sellars, who directed the first production, Saariaho worked closely with the librettist Amin Maalouf, a Lebanese-French author and journalist who also lives in Paris (and who in 2011 was elected to the Académie Française, France's highest literary honor). A refugee of the civil war between Christians and Muslims that engulfed Lebanon between 1975 and 1990, Maalouf often explores in his work the theme of communication and conflict across cultural and religious divides. *L'amour de loin* is based on the probably apocryphal account in Jaufré's *vida* (biographical narrative) of his love for the Countess of Tripoli, a city in present-day Lebanon. A third character, the Pilgrim, serves as an emissary between the western and eastern realms. The action of the opera, such as it is, consists largely of the lovers' reflections as the Pilgrim shuttles back and forth between them. In Act IV, Jaufré sets sail for Tripoli but encounters a storm at sea—a metaphor for his turbulent emotions—and falls gravely ill as the ship approaches the coast. Carried to the Countess's citadel on a stretcher, he declares his love before dying in her arms in the fifth and final act.

Jaufré's impassioned lament in the third tableau of Act IV (measures 485–573), expressing his growing grief and despair at his decision to meet his distant love rather than worship her from afar, harks back to the medieval genre of the *complainte*, as well as to the genre of lament in early Baroque opera, cantata, and oratorio (see NAWM 74c, 77, 80, and 89b). The half-step motion in Saariaho's vocal lines, while modernist in sound, evokes the chromatic semitones in the Baroque laments. Occasional references to modal melody and harmony, as in the comments of Jaufré's companions (measures 397–426), suggest the style of troubadour song (see NAWM 8 and 9).

But the strongest reference to medieval song is in the form of Jaufré's lament, which uses varied repetition in ways similar to troubadour melodies. The lament uses variants of three melodic cells, based on three different pitch arrays:

A, mm. 485–90

Je de-vrais ê - tre l'homme le plus heu - reux au mon - de,

Et je suis le plus dé - ses - pé - ré . . .

B, mm. 505–7

Si, à cet in-stant, un gé - nie sor-tait des flots pour me dire

C, mm. 539–40

mais de près il est feu de l'en - fer!

Melodic phrases derived from these cells appear in alternation, woven together in a long and intricate chain to create the following form for the lament:

Cell	A	B	C	B	A	B	C	A	C	A	C	A	C
Measure	485	505	508	511	518	522	531	535	539	542	549	552	561

While much more complex, this form is similar in concept to the types of repetition found in troubadour songs, such as the ABABCDB form in Comtessa de Dia's *A chantar* (NAWM 9). These same melodic cells are used throughout the dialogue between Jaufré and the Pilgrim that precedes the lament, and more distant variants of similar material pervade the orchestral figuration.

As shown in the example below, the pitch structures of these melodic ideas are very similar, based on arrays of semitones and tritones that create interlocked fifths and fourths:

Such prominent fifths and fourths are reminiscent of medieval melodies, which move in modal spaces bounded by fifths and fourths. At the same time, the whole melody is extremely chromatic—these three arrays of pitches include all the chromatic notes except E and F—a trait that is modernist rather than medieval.

Near the end, as he asks why he gave up the paradise of a distant love for the burning torment of love in person, Jaufré twice exceeds the range of these cells, touching a high *f#'* (measures 554 and 571), expressing his rising grief and despair in a dramatic, quintessentially operatic gesture. The result is a highly expressive arioso that combines medieval and modern characteristics on several levels.

The undulating, repetitive figurations in the orchestra, unobtrusively enhanced by electronics, in some respects resemble figurations in minimalist works by John Adams (see NAWM 211 and 219). Unlike Adams, however, Saariaho avoids tonality in favor of shimmering sonorities and billowing masses of sound associated with the late-twentieth-century movement known as spectralism, with which Saariaho became entranced during her early years in France. She once remarked that her music "is all about color and light," a perspective that is consistent with the spectralists' emphasis on timbre over pitch as a large-scale structure feature, including electronically produced or altered timbres and harmonies abstracted from computer analysis of timbres and scored for acoustic instruments. Certain passages in this scene are organized around central pitches; for example, Jaufré's first words are anchored on C (measures 391–96), while his companions' choral response is rooted on F♯ (measures 397–426). But such passing tonal referents are overshadowed by Saariaho's vivid timbral effects, from the roiling orchestra clusters depicting the fury of the tempest to the wordless vocalizing of the chorus.

When *L'amour de loin* premiered in Salzburg in 2000, the stage in Act IV was flooded with real water on which sparkles of light danced restlessly, visually reinforcing Saariaho's musical imagery. Her word setting is sensitive to the subtle stresses of the French language, as expressed in Maalouf's highly singable and richly poetic libretto, which in places incorporates Jaufré's own poetry.

217

Osvaldo Golijov (b. 1960)

La Pasión según San Marcos: Nos. 24–26

Passion

2000

(a) No. 24: *Escarnio y Negación* [Scorn and Denial]

* Don't start together, build up entering "at random" within the 3 repeats
(**Caja 2** and **Quinto** enter last).

From Osvaldo Golijov, *La Pasión según San Marcos* (N.p.: Ytalianna Music Publishing, 2000), 204–20.
Translation adapted from ibid., xx–xxi. Copyright © 2000 by Hendon Music, Inc., a Boosey & Hawkes company.
International copyright secured. All rights reserved. Reprinted by permission.

* 2 or 3 men imitate rooster's crow

(b) No. 25: *Desgarro de la Túnica* [Tearing of the Garment]

25. Desgarro de la Túnica

*Repetir tantas veces como sea necesario para que la soprano y las cuerdas de **Lúa Descolorida** esté preparadas para empezar.*

*Repeat as many times as necessary so that the soprano and the strings of **Lúa Descolorida** are prepared to begin.*

attacca **Lúa Descolorida**

(c) No. 26: *Lúa descolorida (Aria de las lágrimas de Pedro)*
[Colorless Moon (Aria of Peter's Tears)]

26. Lúa Descolorida

cor de ou - ro pá - li - do,___ ves - me ves - - - eu non qui-

xe - ra me___ vi - ses de tan al - to.___   Ó es -

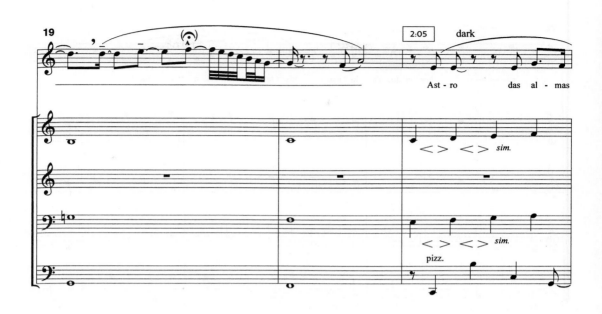

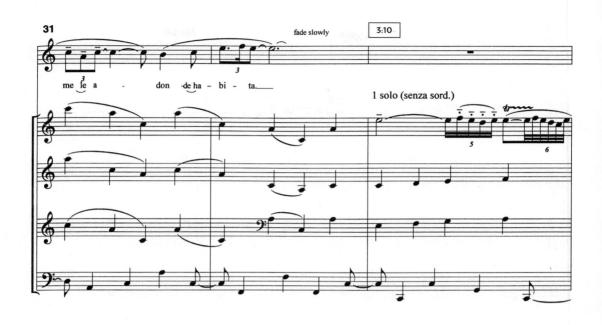

me le a - don -de ha – bi – ta.___

dissolving gradually

quietly radiant

ossia:

xun - ta—men - te   me le ve a don - de   non   re - cor - den   nun - ca,

nin _____ no mun - do en que es tóu   nin _____ en _____ las al - tu - ras. ____

24. *Escarnio y Negación* [Scorn and Denial]

[Texts in brackets are passages from the Passion narrative not set to music.]

ALL

Oh! Él es culpable!   Oh! He is guilty!
A morir!   To the death!

[Y le taparon los ojos: lo escupieron y le   [And some began to spit on him, and to
  pegaron:]   cover his eyes, and to strike him, and to
                                               say to him:]

Jesu Cristo!   Jesus Christ!
Ya no puedes ver!   Now you can no longer see!
Profetizador!   Prophesy!
Adivinanos   Tell us
pues quien te pegó.   if you can who struck you.

[Pedro estaba en el patio y llegó una de las   [And as Peter was beneath in the palace,
  críadas del jefe de los sacerdotes: lo vio y   there came one of the maids of the high
  le dijo:]   priests: And when she saw Peter warming
                                               himself, she looked upon him, and said:]

MAID (WOMEN)

Y tú tambien   And you also
vas con el   were with him
de Nazareth.   from Nazareth.

[Y saliendo fuera del patio cantó el gallo.]   [And he went out into the porch, and the
                                               cock crowed.]

PETER (MEN)

No, yo no.   No, not I.

MAID (WOMEN)

Tú tambien . . .   You also . . .

PETER (MEN)

Yo no, yo no . . .   Not I, not I . . .

[Y el gallo cantó por segunda vez   [And the cock crowed for a second time.
y Pedro se acordó   And Peter called to mind
de lo que le dijo Jesús   the word that Jesus said to him.
y lloró.]   And when he thought of it, he wept.]

—Adapted from Mark 14:64–72

25. *Desgarro de la Túnica* [Tearing of the Garment]

CHORUS

Oh, Jesús!   Oh, Jesus!

[Entonces el sacerdote se rasgó las   [Then the high priest rent his clothes, and
  vestiduras: said,
"Basta ya   "What need we

Que no haya mas testigos.	any further witnesses?
Ya la blasfemia ustedes han oído:	You have heard the blasphemy:
Entonces qué les parece."]	what think you?"]

—Adapted from Mark 14:63–64

26. *Lúa descolorida (Aria de las lágrimas de Pedro)* [Colorless Moon (Aria of Peter's Tears)]

Peter (Solo)

0:00

Lúa descolorida	Moon, colorless
como cor de ouro pálido,	like the color of pale gold:
vesme i eu non quixera	You see me here and I wouldn't like you
me vises de tan alto.	to see me from the heights above.
Ó espaso que recorres,	Take me, silently, in your ray
lévame, caladiña, nun teu raio.	to the space of your journey.

2:05

Astro das almas orfas,	Star of the orphan souls,
lúa descolorida,	Moon, colorless:
eu ben sei que n'alumas	I know that you do not shed light on
tristeza cal a miña.	sadness as sad as mine.
Vai contalo ó teu dono,	Go and tell it to your master
e dille que me leve adonde habita.	and tell him to take me to his place.

3:49

Mais non lle contes nada,	But don't tell him anything,
descolorida lúa,	Moon, colorless,
pois nin neste nin noutros	because my fate won't change
mundos teréis fertuna.	here or in other worlds.

4:20

Se sabe onde a morte	If you know where Death
ten a morada escura,	has its dark mansion,
dille que corpo e alma xuntamente	tell her to take my body and soul together
me leve adonde non recorden nunca,	to a place where I won't be remembered,
nin no mundo en que estóu nin nas alturas.	not in this world, not in the heights above.

—Rosalía de Castro   —Trans. Osvaldo Golijov

Passions—musical settings of the events leading up to the Crucifixion of Jesus as recounted in one of the four Gospels—have a prominent place in the history of music, thanks in large part to the two great Passions of Johann Sebastian Bach, his *St. Matthew Passion* (excerpt in NAWM 104) and *St. John Passion*, which are among his best-known works. To commemorate the 250th anniversary of Bach's death, the International Bach Academy in Stuttgart commissioned four composers from different parts of the globe to create new settings of the four Gospel accounts in their own idioms: Chinese-American Tan Dun (Matthew), Argentine composer Osvaldo Golijov (Mark), Wolfgang Rihm from Germany (Luke), and Sofia

Gubaidulina of Russia (John). The four passions were premiered in September 2000 at the European Music Festival in Stuttgart.

Golijov's contribution, *La Pasión según San Marcos* (The Passion according to St. Mark), incorporates elements of Latin American popular music into the Baroque genre of the Passion. Descended from Eastern European Jews, Golijov emigrated to the United States by way of Israel in the 1980s. His style is a distinctive fusion of Latino, klezmer, African, Arab, and Western classical idioms. He has written movingly about growing up as a Jew in predominantly Catholic Argentina during a brutal military dictatorship when opponents of the regime would simply disappear, presumably killed. That experience, set against the often violent history of Christianity in Latin America, provides the backdrop for Golijov's work.

Scored for chorus, soloists, drummer, small orchestra (including guitar and accordion), and dancers, *La Pasión según San Marcos* is part sacred drama and part theatrical extravaganza, with roots in the religious street processions of Latin America and the Caribbean. Golijov's score includes detailed instructions for the placement of the performers on stage. The principal characters—Jesus and three of his disciples, Peter, Mark, and Judas—are variously portrayed by singers and dancers, both male and female, solo and chorus. Like Bach's Passions, Golijov's is structured as a series of discrete vocal solos, choruses, and instrumental numbers. However, his desire to present Jesus as an indigenous person of color, rather than "a pale European" as he was traditionally painted in Europe, led him to tell the biblical story the way it might have been told in traditional African, Cuban, and Brazilian societies: through voices and movement. Brazilian samba, Cuban salsa, Spanish flamenco, and Argentine tango are among the dance-based styles evoked in the score, which calls for a kaleidoscopic array of percussion instruments. The polyglot musical vocabulary is reflected in the texts Golijov assembled from an equally wide range of sources, which are sung in Spanish, Aramaic, Latin, and Galician. The overall effect is at once popular, even primitive, and sophisticatedly cosmopolitan.

The three numbers included here parallel the excerpt in NAWM 104 from Bach's *St. Matthew Passion*, depicting the judgment of Jesus' guilt and Peter's denial that he knows Jesus, followed by Peter's anguished repentance. This entire passage illustrates Golijov's use of folk and folklike idioms, contrasts, and repetition to highlight the internal and external drama of the story.

In *Scorn and Denial*, a double chorus (modeled on the double chorus at the same spot in the *St. Matthew Passion*, nos. 36b and 36d in NAWM 104a) spits out the crowd's malevolent jibes at Jesus in a hypnotic samba rhythm in quick duple meter. Then the women and men alternate, playing the roles of the maid and Peter as she says he was with Jesus and he denies it; twice they are interrupted by the crowing of a rooster, reminding Peter of Jesus' comment that Peter would deny him three times before the cock crowed. Throughout this scene, Golijov omits the narration that in Bach's version is rendered in recitative by the Evangelist, so that the events are reduced to the words and raw emotions of the participants. As in Latin American music, the percussion undergirding the singers includes a wide variety of instruments, each with a distinctive timbre and rhythmic pattern, that enter at different times and interlock to create a rich tapestry of sound.

Tearing of the Garment depicts the high priest rending his clothing as he asks for judgment against Jesus. Here even the priest's words are omitted from the musical setting, which focuses on the chorus, supported by trumpets and trombones, sustaining dissonant chords on "Oh, Jesus" against an arpeggiated riff for guitar and piano, repeated ad libitum. This expressive outburst also serves as a transition, as the chorus changes location and other performers take up their positions for the next number.

Like Bach in the *St. Matthew Passion*, Golijov captures Peter's remorse in an aria for female voice that is an emotional and musical high point of the entire work. For this moment Golijov chose a poem in Galician, a Spanish dialect, by the nineteenth-century poet Rosalía de Castro, *Lúa descolorida* (Colorless Moon). At times the melody has the simple, haunting character of a folk song, and at other times the vocal flourishes and improvisatory freedom of flamenco singing, all over the steadily rocking beat of the muted string accompaniment. Both singer and instrumentalists are directed to cultivate a light "early music" sound, in contrast to the earthier style that Golijov calls for elsewhere in the Passion and appropriate to the poetic imagery of a pale, still, ethereal moon. The tripartite form of the aria (AA'B) mirrors that of Castro's poem. The second stanza (measures 17–32) is a musical variant of the first. In the third section (measures 33–60), after a lyrical violin interlude, the soprano first rises, then gradually descends to a monotone *c'* to meditate on the reunion of body and soul, before climbing ecstatically to *c'''* on the words "nin no mundo en que estóu nin nas alturas" (not in this world, not in the heights above). According to the composer, the tension between text and music is deliberate: the words express Peter's grief and despair, while the music reflects "the luminosity of his spirit" as the founder of the Christian church.

Elliott Carter (1908–2012)

Caténaires

Piano piece

2006

NOTE: Very little pedal should be used.

All accidentals are maintained throughout the measure unless cancelled.

The distribution of the notes between the hands can be modified to suit the performer.

New York, September 23, 2006

In a career that spanned eight decades, American composer Elliott Carter produced a large, varied, and highly individual body of work that stretched the boundaries of music in the realms of pitch, texture, harmony, structure, and especially rhythm. His use of complex polyrhythms has been quite influential, and he became known especially for the related technique of metric modulation, in which changes of meter and tempo occur in precise proportion through shared short durational units. Carter remained productive to the end of his long life, composing about twenty substantial works after his hundredth birthday in 2008.

He was ninety-seven when he wrote *Caténaires* in 2006. It was commissioned by the French pianist Pierre-Laurent Aimard, who premiered it at New York's Carnegie Hall on December 12 that year (the day after Carter's ninety-eighth birthday). Three years later Carter published it along with *Intermittences* (2005) as *Two Thoughts About the Piano*. Carter described the genesis of the work in a note to the score:

> When Pierre-Laurent Aimard, who performs so eloquently, asked me to write a piece for him, I became obsessed with the idea of a fast one line piece with no chords. It became a continuous chain of notes using different spacings, accents, and colorings, to produce a wide variety of expression.

Although passages of single-line melody appear in keyboard music going back to the toccatas and preludes of Buxtehude and J. S. Bach (see the opening measures of NAWM 95 and 100a), keyboard pieces that feature a single melody throughout are rare. The most famous example is the finale of Chopin's Piano Sonata in B♭ Minor, Op. 35, a scintillating Presto featuring a continuous melody in rapid unbroken triplets, played by the two hands in octaves, with a startling *fortissimo* chord at the end. Given how unusual this texture was for Carter, it seems likely that he meant to invoke Chopin as a predecessor.

Despite the metronomic regularity of its rhythm, *Caténaires* packs more than its share of surprises within its highly compressed four-minute span. The music's extraordinary expressive range derives from Carter's masterly manipulation of contours, dynamics, registers, accents, and the harmonies implicit in the rapid-fire torrent of sixteenth notes. The score is appropriately marked "jaillissant," French for "gushing forth." (Although he lived most of his life in New York, Carter grew up in Europe and spoke French as his first language.) The piece's title suggests the U-shaped catenary curve produced by suspending a cable between two fixed points, rather like the garlands of notes that spill across the pages of the printed score. In French, *caténaires* refers more specifically to the overhead wires used to power electric trains, conveying an image of uninterrupted energy and streamlined sleekness. Either way, *Caténaires* presents a formidable challenge for the pianist in terms of speed, accuracy, touch, and stamina.

As usual with Carter, there is more to this engaging little piece than meets the ear on first hearing. Although he never identified himself as a twelve-tone composer, Carter was deeply interested in the possibilities of organized pitch collections. He was particularly drawn to "all-interval" twelve-tone chords, where every note of the chromatic scale appears once and every possible interval from semitone to major seventh is represented within adjacent notes of the chord. *Caténaires* is based on just such a chord, shown as A in this example:

From this chord, Carter derives other twelve-note chords and six-note subsets, using transposition, inversion, and other ways of manipulating twelve-tone rows. Chord B in this example is an inversion of A around the two middle notes in the chord, *d♯'* and *e'*. In between chords A and B is a six-note chord that consists of the pitches these two twelve-note chords have in common. A great variety of chords throughout the piece are derived in similar ways.

Instead of presenting any of these chords as a simultaneous sonority, Carter treats them as background sonorities from which his linear melody is drawn, animating each chord through melodic figuration and arpeggiation of all or part of the chord. He then moves from chord to chord in a kind of harmonic progression, linking each chord to the next through common tones. In this way he creates a sense of harmonic motion, while technically fulfilling his intention of writing a piece "with no chords." For example, the passage from the second half of measure 8 through the first half of measure 12 arpeggiates chord A; from the last three notes of measure 14 through the first two notes of measure 18 arpeggiates chord B; and in between them is a transition that uses only the six notes the two chords share (plus a stray *b'* on the downbeat of measure 13), effecting a change of harmonies that is like a common-tone modulation in tonal music. Through these changes of chord, and the common pitches that link them to one another, Carter gives *Caténaires* its underlying sense of continuity, coherence, and variety.

John Adams (b. 1947)

Doctor Atomic: Act I, conclusion, *Batter my heart*

Opera

2005

*Upbeat to m.831 – downbeat of m.838: for fuller sonority on piano, L.H. may play one octave lower.

*Mm.907 – 915: for greater sonority on piano, L.H. may play one octave lower.
†Mm.917 – 928: W.W. actually play one octave higher.

End of Act One

Batter my heart, three-person'd God; for you
As yet but knock, breathe, shine, and seek to mend;
That I may rise and stand, o'erthrow me, and bend
Your force to break, blow, burn and make me new.
I, like an usurp'd town, to another due,
Labour to admit you, but Oh, to no end;
Reason, your viceroy in me, me should defend,
But is captiv'd, and proves weak or untrue.
Yet dearly I love you and would be lov'd fain,
But am betroth'd unto your enemy:
Divorce me, untie or break that knot again,
Take me to you, imprison me, for I,
Except you enthrall me, never shall be free,
Nor ever chaste, except you ravish me.

— JOHN DONNE

The title character of John Adams's *Doctor Atomic*, the physicist J. Robert Oppenheimer, led America's crash effort to develop an atomic bomb as director of the Manhattan Project during World War II. For the libretto, Peter Sellars drew on a variety of sources, including declassified government documents, interviews with project personnel, Native American songs, the Hindu *Bhagavad Gita*, and poetry by John Donne, Charles Baudelaire, and Muriel Rukeyser. Sellars, best known for his anachronistic productions of operas—such as Mozart's *Don Giovanni* set in Harlem and Handel's *Orlando* set on an international space station—also directed Adams's first two operas, *Nixon in China* (1987) and *The Death of Klinghoffer* (1991). *Doctor Atomic* was their first collaboration in which Sellars also served as librettist. Adams completed the opera in 2005 on a commission from the San Francisco Opera, where it premiered on October 1 that year, directed by Sellars and conducted by Donald Runnicles.

Most of the opera takes place in the hours just before the prototype bomb was tested in July 1945. In the closing scene of Act I, Oppenheimer and his colleagues debate whether to abort the test because of a violent electrical storm that is threatening the Alamogordo, New Mexico test site. Pressure from Washington, hysterical scientists who have to be sedated, and conflicting weather reports contribute to an atmosphere of mounting panic. The project's commanding officer, General Leslie Groves, tells the men to go to bed and says they will reevaluate the situation in the morning. Left alone, Oppenheimer sings the soul-searching baritone aria *Batter my heart*. Set to the fourteenth of Donne's Holy Sonnets, the aria invokes the "three person'd God"—the Trinity of the Father, the Son, and the Holy Spirit. Sellars incorporated this poem into the libretto because Oppenheimer, who was deeply conflicted about unleashing the atom's awesome power of destruction, had dubbed the test site "Trinity" with this seventeenth-century sonnet in mind. Later he quoted a line from the *Bhagavad Gita* to describe his feelings upon witnessing the blast: "Now I am become Death, the destroyer of worlds."

Like much of Adams's minimalist and postminimalist instrumental music (see NAWM 211), the orchestral introduction to *Batter my heart* is characterized by rapid, continuous motion, ostinatos, gradual accretion of dissonance, and subtle changes of texture. Adams creates an agitated effect, suggesting Oppenheimer's anguished apprehension about the impending test, with irregular syncopations embedded in layers of hemiola (eighth notes and triplet eighth notes in measures 768–86, with triplet quarter notes added in measure 787).

The orchestra's restless activity ceases abruptly in measure 802 in preparation for the entrance of the voice, conveying a sense that time has stopped. Oppenheimer's lyrical, pleading melody is in D harmonic minor, and beneath it the orchestra sustains slowly shifting sonorities drawn from the same scale, which sometimes suggest tonal progressions. Adams repeats some words or lines of the poem for emphasis (compare the original sonnet on page 974), and sometimes marks the rhymes with a high note (on "mend," "bend," and "new") or short melisma (on "you"). The repeated "snap" rhythms (short-long, with the short note on the beat) in the vocal line articulate a chain of appoggiatura-like dissonances that underline the textual repetitions (as at measures 808–10) and alliteration (at measures 821–23 on "break, blow, break, blow, break, blow, burn"). In its tunefulness and emotional intensity, Oppenheimer's aria echoes the operatic style of nineteenth-century composers such as Giuseppe Verdi (see NAWM 150), who, like Adams, sought to express the inner conflicts and psychological nuances of the characters in their music.

After the orchestra plays a compressed version of the introduction (measures 826–35), Oppenheimer repeats the first four lines of Donne's sonnet (measures 836–60), then segues directly into the last ten lines, creating an overall tripartite form of AAB. In this section (beginning at measure 861), Oppenheimer's words are accompanied softly by eighth-note-triplet string ostinatos from the orchestral introduction, coupled with syncopated triads in the low brass. These subliminal echoes of the aria's opening passage remind both the listener and Oppenheimer that the fateful moment is imminent. In the last six lines of the poem (beginning at measure 879), over the relatively quiet orchestra, Oppenheimer repeatedly surges to a high G, exclaiming to God—or perhaps to the bomb itself?—that "Except you enthrall me, [I] never shall be free, Nor ever chaste, except you ravish me." After the close of the aria, the loud layers of ostinato return in measure 903, but Adams avoids hemiola in the closing instrumental passage; instead of conflicting triplet figures, the string ostinato is punctuated with regular eighth and sixteenth notes in the winds. Panic has given way to a restored sense of scientific precision and predictability.

Canadian baritone Gerard Finley portrays Oppenheimer in the Metropolitan Opera performance of this aria on the accompanying video. A respected interpreter of modern vocal music as well as a champion of new operatic repertoire, Finley created the role of Oppenheimer at the San Francisco Opera in 2005. A second scene on the video is from late in Act II, shortly before the bomb is to be detonated, as the chorus sings a text from the *Bhagavad Gita* expressing fear at the sight of the Hindu god Vishnu. Dressed in 1945 clothing, with the spirits of native peoples of the western United States above them, the members of the chorus look stunned at what is about to happen.

▶ Opera video available

Jennifer Higdon (b. 1962)

blue cathedral: Opening excerpt

Orchestral work

2000

220

From Jennifer Higdon, *blue cathedral* (Philadelphia: Lawdon Press, 1999), 1–15. © Jennifer Higdon. Used with permission from Lawdon Press.

220 JENNIFER HIGDON · *blue cathedral*: Opening excerpt

Commissioned by the Curtis Institute of Music in honor of its 75th anniversary, Jennifer Higdon's *blue cathedral* was premiered by Robert Spano and the Curtis Symphony Orchestra on May 1, 2000. In a program note, Higdon describes her colorfully orchestrated work as a "journey through a glass cathedral in the sky." She invites listeners to imagine themselves floating down the aisle to the strains of "heavenly music" sung by stained-glass figures magically sprung to life. Slowly at first, then faster and faster, the traveler rises through the open ceiling into the firmament, moving from "contemplation and quiet peace" to a "feeling of celebration and ecstatic expansion of the soul." For Higdon, the cathedral is both a spiritual portal, "a symbolic doorway into and out of this world," and, like the Curtis Institute (where she is on the faculty), a place of learning. The color blue evokes images of the sky, of limitless potential, of journeys through space and time. Most poignantly, it recalls the composer's brother, Andrew Blue Higdon, in whose memory *blue cathedral* was written shortly after he died of cancer in 1998.

   The musical journey opens quietly with bell-like percussion and strings playing parallel triads, reminiscent of Debussy (see NAWM 167). At measure 7 the strings divide and expand in dissonant diatonic harmonies, providing a rich tonal backdrop for the luminous flute solo. A solo clarinet responds, and the two woodwinds continue in dialogue over harmonies that slowly shift pitch collections—another Debussy trait—from the major-mode diatonic collection on C to those on E♭, D, A, F, and A♭ (at measures 12, 16, 18, 20, and 22 respectively). Through such simple means, Higdon establishes a sense of forward motion and of rising waves of sound. The notes of the soloists are taken from the accompanying major scale collections, but the melodic lines avoid suggesting a tonality or pitch center by lingering on notes that are dissonant against the orchestra and by highlighting tritones and sevenths. Alternating sustained tones with unpredictable rhythms and melodic motions, the soloists trace elegant arabesques high in their range. The effect is ethereal. A solo violin joins the conversation in measure 24, and the harmonic shifts now come every measure, reinforced by soft triads in the brass; here the Debussy techniques of parallel triads and changing pitch collections join forces.

As the interweaving solo lines spiral upward, the music builds to *fortissimo* at measure 39, marked by a brief return to the C-major region. Here the horns enter with a much more rhythmically active figure in parallel triads, joined in dialogue by the upper strings, piano, and flutes, then by trombones (measure 43) and low winds and basses (measure 47), each group a series of chords in rhythmic unison, like a harmonically enriched contrapuntal line in a counterpoint of groups. The melody in the upper strings and flutes reaches a zenith in measures 49–50, creating an aural image of the listener's ascent toward the immense glass dome of the cathedral. Then, suddenly, the melody falls back on itself, the sumptuous texture of the music thins, and the tension relaxes.

Over open fifths and parallel fifths, the parallel triads of the opening briefly return (measures 52–55). Then the English horn picks up the solo line in measure 56, answered by a succession of instruments in short solos, often in dialogue with other members of the orchestra (measures 62–69); Higdon likens this interplay to a person touching the lives of others. At measure 70, a change in tempo and texture ushers in the active middle section of *blue cathedral* (not included in the excerpt in this anthology). The flute and clarinet solos return in the final section, this time accompanied by the unearthly sounds of Chinese health bells (also known as Chinese reflex balls) and musical glasses. A prepared piano adds its voice to the ringing texture, bringing the work to an ethereal conclusion.

Several elements in *blue cathedral* have a biographical or autobiographical significance. According to Higdon, because she plays the flute and is the older sibling, the flute solo comes first; the clarinet, her brother's instrument, enters later and has the last word, its final ascending solo symbolizing the "upward progressing journey" of Andrew's soul. The composer does not identify the two other prominent solo instruments with specific people or personas, leaving the interpretation up to the listener. In the last seven measures, the prepared piano chimes thirty-three times, signifying Andrew's thirty-three years of life.

The emotional directness of Higdon's musical language, and its firm grounding in tonality, have given *blue cathedral* wide appeal with audiences. Since its premiere, the thirteen-minute work has received hundreds of performances around the world, and it has ranked at or near the top of the League of American Orchestras's annual list of the most frequently performed works written in the last twenty-five years.

INSTRUMENT NAMES AND ABBREVIATIONS

The following tables set forth the English, Italian, German, and French names used for the various musical instruments in these scores, and their respective abbreviations.

WOODWINDS

English	Italian	German	French
Piccolo (Picc.)	Flauto piccolo (Fl. Picc.); Ottavino (Ott.)	Kleine Flöte (kl. Fl.)	Petite flûte
Flute (Fl.)	Flauto (Fl.), pl. Flauti; Flauto grande (Fl. gr.)	Flöte (Fl.), pl. Flöten; Große Flöte (gr. Fl.)	Flûte (Fl.)
Alto flute	Flauto alto (Fl. alto); Flauto contralto (fl.c-alto)	Altflöte	Flûte en sol
Oboe (Ob.)	Oboe (Ob.), pl. Oboi	Hoboe (Hb., Hob.), pl. Hoboen; Oboe (Ob.), pl. Oboen	Hautbois (Hb., Hautb.)
English horn (E.H.)	Corno inglese (C. ing., C. ingl., Cor. ingl., C.i.)	Englisches Horn, Englisch Horn (engl. Horn, Egl. H., Englh.)	Cor anglais (C.A., Cor ang.)
Heckelphone		Heckelphon	
Sopranino clarinet	Clarinetto piccolo (clar. picc.)		
Clarinet (C., Cl., Clt., Clar.)	Clarinetto (Cl., Clar.), pl. Clarinetti (Cltti.)	Klarinette (Kl., Klar.), pl. Klarinetten; Clarinette (Cl., Clar.)	Clarinette (Cl.)
Alto clarinet (A. Cl.)			

WOODWINDS (continued)

English	Italian	German	French
Bass clarinet (B. Cl.)	Clarinetto basso (Cl. b., Cl. bas., Cl. basso, Clar. basso); Clarone (Clne.)	Bass Klarinette, Bassklarinette (Bkl., B.-Kl., Basskl.), Bassclarinette (Basscl., B.-Cl.)	Clarinette basse (Cl. bs.)
Contrabass clarinet (Cb. Cl.)			
Saxophone (Sax.) [soprano, alto (A. Sax.), tenor (T. Sax.), baritone (Bari. Sax.), bass]	Sassofone	Saxophon [Sopransaxophon (Ssax.), Altsaxophon (Asax.), Tenor-saxophon (Tsax.)]	Saxophone
Bassoon (Bn., Bsn., Bssn.)	Fagotto (Fag., Fg.), pl. Fagotti	Fagott (Fag., Fg.), pl. Fagotte	Basson (Bn., Bssn., Bon.)
Contrabassoon (C. Bn., C. Bsn.); Double bassoon (D. Bsn.)	Contrafagotto (Cfg., C. Fag., Cont. F.)	Kontrafagott (K.-Fag., Kfg.); Contrafagott (Contrafag.)	Contrebasson (C. bssn.)
Cornett	Cornetto	Zink	Cornet-à-bouquin

BRASS

English	Italian	German	French
Horn, French horn (Hr., Hn.)	Corno (Cor., C., Cr.), pl. Corni	Horn (Hr.), pl. Hörner (Hörn., Hrn.)	Cor; Cor à pistons
Trumpet (Tpt., Trpt., Trp., Tr.)	Tromba (Tr., Trb.), pl. Trombe (Trbe., Tbe.); Clarino, pl. Clarini	Trompete (Tr., Trp., Trpt., Tromp.), pl. Trompeten	Trompette (Tr., Trp.)
Piccolo trumpet	Tromba piccola (Tr. picc.)		
Bass trumpet	Tromba bassa (Tr. bas.)		
Cornet	Cornetta, pl. Cornetti	Kornett	Cornet à pistons (C. à p., Pist.)

BRASS (continued)

English	Italian	German	French
Trombone (Tr., Tbe., Tbn., Trb., Trm., Trbe.) [alto, tenor]	Trombone (Trbn., Tromb.), pl. Tromboni (Tbni., Trbni., Trni.) [alto, tenore]	Posaune (Ps., Pos.), pl. Posaunen [alt, tenor]	Trombone (Tr., Trb.)
Bass trombone (B. Tbn.)	Trombone basso (Trne. B.)	Bass Posaune	
Contrabass trombone	Cimbasso (Cimb.)		
Baritone horn (Baritone, Bar.)			
Euphonium (Euph.)			
Tenor tuba		Tenortuba	
Tuba (Tb., Tba.)	Tuba (Tb., Tba.), pl. Tube	Tuba (Tb.); Basstuba (Btb.)	Tuba (Tb.)
Ophicleide	Oficleide	Ophikleide	Ophicléide

STRINGS

English	Italian	German	French
Violin (V., Vl., Vn., Vln., Vi.)	Violino (V., Vl., Vn., Vln., Viol.), pl. Violini (Vni.); Viola da braccio	Violine (V., Vl., Vln., Viol.), pl. Violinen; Geige (Gg.), pl. Geigen	Violon (V., Vl., Vln., Vn., Von.)
Viola (Va., Vl., pl. Vas.)	Viola (Va., Vla., Vl.), pl. Viole (Vle.)	Bratsche (Br.), pl. Bratschen	Alto (A., Alt.)
Violoncello (Vcl., Vc.); Cello, pl. Celli	Violoncello (Vc., Vcl., Vcll., Vcllo., Vlc.), pl. Violoncelli	Violoncell (Vc., Vcl., Violinc.), pl. Violoncelli (Vcll.); Cell.	Violoncelle (Vc., Velle., Vlle., Vcelle.)
Contrabass (Cb.); Double bass (D. B., D. Bs.); String bass; Bass viol	Contrabasso (Cb., C. B.), Basso, pl. Contrabassi or Bassi (C. Bassi, Bi.); Violon, violone [may also designate or in-clude cello or bass viola da gamba]	Kontrabass (Kb., K.-B.), pl. Kontrabässe; Contrabass (Contrab., C.-B., C. B.); Bass, pl. Bässe	Contrebasse (C. B.)

STRINGS (continued)

English	Italian	German	French
Viola da gamba; Viol; Gamba	Viola da gamba	Gambe	Viole
Bass violin			Basse de violon

PERCUSSION

English	Italian	German	French
Percussion (Perc.)	Percussione	Schlagzeug (Schlag., Szg.)	Batterie (Batt.)
Timpani (Timp.); Kettledrums (K. D.)	Timpani (Timp., Tp.)	Pauken (Pk.)	Timbales (Timb.)
Snare drum (S. D., Sn. Dr.) [soprano, alto, tenor]; Side drum	Tamburo piccolo (Tamb. picc.); Tamburo militare (Tamb. milit.); Tamburo (Tro.)	Kleine Trommel (Kl. Tr.)	Caisse claire (C. cl.); Tambour militaire (Tamb. milit.)
Tenor drum (Ten. Dr., T. D.)	Cassa rullante	Rührtrommel	Caisse roulante
Indian drum			
Tom-tom		Tomtom (Tom.)	
Tumba; Conga drum; Quinto		Tumba	
Bongos			
Caja			
Cuica			
Bass drum (B. drum, Bass dr., Bs. Dr., B. D.)	Gran cassa (Gr. Cassa, Gr. C., G. C.); Cassa (C.); Gran tamburo (Gr. Tamb.)	Große Trommel (Gr. Trommel, Gr. Tr.)	Grosse caisse (Gr. c., G. C.)
Tambourine (Tamb.)	Tamburino (Tamb.)	Schellentrommel, Tamburin	Tambour de Basque (T. de Basq., T. de B., Tamb. de Basque), Tambourin (Tambin., Tin.)
Lion's roar			

PERCUSSION (continued)

English	Italian	German	French
Cymbals (Cym., Cymb.)	Piatti (P., Ptti., Piat.); Cinelli	Becken (Beck.)	Cymbales (Cym., Cymb.)
Traps			
Suspended cymbal (Sus. cym., Susp. cymb.)		Becken-freihängend	
Sizzle cymbal (Sizz. cym.)			
Hi-Hat (HH)			
Tam-Tam (Tam-T.); Gong	Tam-Tam (Tam-T., T-tam)	Tam-Tam, Tamtam	Tam-Tam
Triangle (Trgl., Tri.)	Triangolo (Trgl.)	Triangel (Trgl.)	Triangle (Triang.)
Anvil			
Glockenspiel (Glocken.)	Campanelli (Cmp., Campli.)	Glockenspiel (Glsp.)	Carillon
Bells; Tubular bells (Tub. bells); Chimes	Campane (Cam., Camp., Cmp.); sing. Campana (Cna.)	Glocken	Cloches
Agogó			
Japanese bells	Campanelli giapponesi (Camp. giapp.)		
Cowbells	Cencerro	Kuhglocken	Sonnailles
Sleighbells	Sonagli	Schellen	Grelots
Crotales (Crot.); Antique Cymbals	Crotali; Piatti antichi	Antiken Zimbeln	Cymbales antiques (Cym. ant.)
Xylophone (Xyl., Xylo.)	Xilofono, Silofono	Xylophon (Xyl.)	Xylophone (Xyl.)
Xylorimba			Xylorimba
Vibraphone (Vibr.)			Vibraphone (Vibr.)
Marimba			
Woodblock (Wd. Blk.)	Cassa di legno	Holzblock, Holztrommel (HzTr.)	Bloc de bois

PERCUSSION (continued)

English	Italian	German	French
Chinese blocks			
Slap stick			
Rattle			
Claves			
Raspador			
Gourd			
Maracas; Maraca			Maracas (Mrc.)
Shaker			
Gua gua			
Siren			
Whistle			

OTHER INSTRUMENTS

English	Italian	German	French
Harp (Hp., Hrp.)	Arpa (A., Arp.); Harpa	Harfe (Hfe., Hrf.), pl. Harfen	Harpe (Hp.)
Piano (Pno., Pa.)	Pianoforte (P.-f., Pft., Pfte.); Piano	Klavier (Klav.)	Piano
Celesta (Cel.)	Celesta (Cel.)	Celesta (Cel.)	Céleste
Harpsichord	Cembalo (Cemb.); Clavicembalo	Cembalo	Clavecin
Organ (Org.)	Organo (Org.) [Organo di legno is an organ with wooden pipes]	Orgel	Orgue
Harmonium		Harmonium (Harm.)	
Synthesizer			
Guitar (Gtr.)	Chitarra	Gitarre (Git.)	Guitare (Guit.)
Electric Guitar (Elec. Guit.)			
Lute	Lauto, leuto, liuto	Laute	Luth
Theorbo	Teorba; Chitarrone	Theorb; Chitarron	Téorbe
Archlute	Arcileuto	Erzlaute	Archiluth
Banjo		Banjo (Bjo.)	

Transposing instruments and timpani tunings are indicated using the following pitch names:

English	C	D♭	D	E♭	E	F	G	A♭	A	B♭	B
Italian	Do	Re♭	Re	Mi♭	Mi	Fa	Sol	La♭	La	Si♭	Si
French	Ut	Ré♭	Ré	Mi♭	Mi	Fa	Sol	La♭	La	Si♭	Si
German	C	Des	D	Es	E	F	G	As	A	B	H

For transposing instruments, if the music is written in C major, it will sound in the designated key; thus "in A" means that a notated C will sound as A, and every notated pitch will sound a minor third lower than written. Horns, clarinets in B♭ and A, and trumpets in B♭ sound lower than written; clarinets in D and E♭ and trumpets in D and F sound higher than written. English horns are in F, sounding a fifth lower than written; alto flutes are in G, sounding a fourth lower.

GLOSSARY OF SCORE AND PERFORMANCE INDICATIONS

For a glossary of general music terms, including terms used in the commentaries, see *A History of Western Music*, 9th ed.

a, à The phrases *a 2* (*à 2*), *a 3* (*à 3*, etc.) indicate that the part is to be played in unison by 2, 3 (etc.) players, or that the group is to divide into 2, 3 (etc.) different parts (which meaning holds is usually obvious from the context); when a simple number (1., 2., etc.) is placed over a part, it indicates that only the first (second, etc.) player in that group should play.

A Alto.

à parti du 4me tempo rall. et molto Starting at the fourth tempo in the piece (in Varèse's *Hyperprism*, Lent), growing much slower.

a tempo At the (basic) tempo.

ab Off; *Dämpfer ab*, remove mute.

abdämpfen Damp; stop from vibrating.

aber But.

accelerando (accel.) Growing faster.

accentuato Accentuated.

accompagnato, accompagnata Accompanied.

ad libitum (ad lib.) An indication giving the performer liberty; for example, to vary from strict tempo, to include or omit the part of some voice or instrument, or to include a cadenza of one's own invention.

adagio Slow, leisurely.

affettuoso Tender; with feeling.

agitato, agité Agitated, excited.

agitez l'une contre l'autre Shake or agitate one (cymbal) against the other.

al Until.

alla marcia Like a march; in march tempo.

allargando (allarg.) Growing broader or slower.

alle All; tutti.

alle mit tiefen H All with low C string tuned down to B.

allegramente Cheerfully, gaily.

allegretto A moderately fast tempo, between allegro and andante.

allegro A rapid tempo, between allegretto and presto.

allegro moderato At a moderately fast tempo.

allegro molto Very rapid tempo.

allegro possibile As fast as possible.

also Thus, therefore.

alto, Alt (A); pl. alti The deeper of the two main divisions of women's (or boys') voices; in vocal music in four or more parts, a part above the tenor and below the highest voice.

altri The others; used to designate the other players in an orchestral section when one or more players in the section are given separate parts.

am Griffbrett On a string instrument, bow near, or over, the fingerboard; *sul tasto*.

am Steg On a string instrument, bow over or very near the bridge, producing a thin, metallic sound; *sul ponticello*.

ancora Still, even.

andante A moderately slow tempo, between adagio and allegretto, about walking speed.

animant Growing more animated.

animato, animé Animated.

archi Strings, the string section of the orchestra.

arco Played with the bow; used to mark a return to bowing after a pizzicato passage.

ardente Ardent, passionate.

arpège Arpeggio, arpeggiation.

arpeggiando, arpeggiato (arpeg., arpegg., arp.) Arpeggiated; played in harp style, sounding the notes of the chord in quick succession rather than simultaneously.

arrêt moyen Pause of medium duration.

assai Very.

assez lent Quite slow.

at the frog Play with the part of the bow nearest the player's hand (the *frog* of the bow).

attacca, attacca subito Begin the next movement or section without pause.

attacca *pp* Very soft attack.

auf On; *Dämpfer auf*, put mute in place.

auf der Bühne (a.d. Bühne) On stage.

Ausdruck Expression.

ausdruckslos Expressionless.

avec With

avec une émotion naissante With new feeling.

avec une joie de plus en plus tumultueuse With a joy growing more and more tumultuous.

avec une joie voilée With veiled joy.

B Bass.

bacchetta (bacch.) Drumstick.

bacchetta di legno (bacch. di legno) Wooden drumstick.

bacchetta di triangolo (bacch. di Triang.) Metal stick used to play the triangle.

baguettes, baguettes tambour Drumsticks.

bass, basso, Baß (B); pl. bassi, Bässe A low male voice, or the lowest part in a vocal or instrumental work.

bedeutet Means, indicates.

begleitend Accompanying; indicates that another part has the leading voice in the texture.

beide Both.

beide Spieler Both players at a music stand are to play, after one had a solo; see *Pult*.

bell in the air Sign for horn players to lift the bell of the instrument (where the sound comes out) to direct the sound forward.

ben Very, well.

ben sonante Well sounding, very resonant.

bewegt, bewegte Agitated.

bewegter More agitated.

bien Very, well.

bis Until.

bis auf Except for.

bocca chiusa With mouth closed.

bois Wood; play with wooden drumstick.

bouché Stopped.

bravura Skill, virtuosity.

breit Broad, broadly.

bridge On a string instrument, the arched piece of wood that holds the strings away from, and transmits vibrations to, the body of the instrument. Bowing strings over or near the bridge (*sul ponticello*) produces a thin, metallic sound, and playing behind the bridge (on the short part of the string) produces a very high pitch.

brillante Brilliant, showy.

brushes Play with wire brushes rather than drumsticks.

Bühne Stage.

bzw. Or.

ca. Circa.

cadenza A short or extended passage for solo instrument or voice in free, improvisatory style, usually at or just before or after a cadence.

calando Diminishing in volume and speed.

calmato a tempo Calming to return to the previous tempo.

calme, calmo Calm.

caloroso Warm, warmly.

cambiare l'arco ad lib. Change bow direction as necessary; used to indicate that on a sustained tone the entire section should not bow simultaneously.

cantabile (cant., cantab.) In a singing style.

cantando Singing; in a singing manner.

cédez Hold back.

chaud Warm.

chiaro Clear, clearly.

Chorauszug Transcription of the chorus parts, used for rehearsal or for cues during performance.

chorus (1) Group of singers, normally several on each part. (2) In a popular song, the refrain.

circa (ca.) About.

c.l. Col legno.

col, colla, coll' With the.

colla parte With the part; indicates that the player is to follow or coordinate with another part in tempo and expression.

col legno (c.l.) With the wood of the bow.

col legno battuto (col legno batt., c. l. batt., l.batt.) Striking the strings with the wood of the bow.

come prima As at first.

come sopra As above, as previously.

comme Like, as.

comme une fanfare Like a fanfare.

comme un oiseau Like a birdcall.

comodo Comfortable, easy.

con With.

con agilità Nimbly, with agility.

con fuoco With fire; very fast.

con sordino (con sord.) (1) With mute. (2) In piano music, press the *una corda* pedal.

coro Chorus.

court Short, brief.

crescendo (cresc.) Increasing in volume.

cuivré, cuivrez On a brass instrument, play with a loud, brassy tone.

cup mute Mute for trumpet or trombone, like a straight mute but with a cup on the wide end that covers the bell of the instrument.

da capo (D.C.) Repeat from the beginning, through the first section of the movement.

daher Therefore, hence.

damp, dampen Muffle, silence; stop from vibrating.

damped Of a cymbal, muffled as soon as it is struck.

damper pedal Sustaining pedal.

Dämpfer (Dpf., Dpfr.); pl. Dämpfern Mute.

dann Then.

dans In; during.

dans en sentiment sourd. et tumultueux With a muffled and tumultuous feeling.

dans le < comme le > la 1ère trompette legèrement dominante In crescendos and diminuendos trumpet 1 should be slightly dominant.

de blancas On the white notes of the piano (for a glissando).

de plus en plus More and more, gradually.

decrescendo (decresc., decres.) Decreasing in volume.

delirando Raving, delirious.

der neue ganze Takt = letztes ♩ The whole measure in the new tempo equals in duration a quarter note in the previous tempo.

descendez le "la" un demiton plus bas Tune the A string a semitone lower.

détaché Detached; with a broad, vigorous bow stroke, each note bowed singly.

deutlich Distinctly.

di Of.

die The.

die neuen Viertel (in Pianino und Gesang der Margret) sind gleich den Vierteln der vorigen Triole The quarter note in the new tempo (in the onstage piano and Margret's song) is like the quarter notes in the previous quarter-note triplets.

die Saiten ans Holz anschlagen Snapping the strings against the wood of the fingerboard (with a pizzicato).

diese, dieser This, these.

diese Couronne so lange, daß alle Instrumente Gelegenheit haben, allmählich (ohne plötzliches cresc.) ihre höchste Kraft zu entfalten This fermata should last long enough that all instruments have the opportunity, gradually (without a sudden crescendo), to reach their highest possible dynamic level.

diminuendo (dim., dimin.) Decreasing in volume.

disperato Despairing.

distinto Distinctly.

divisi, divise (div.) Divided; indicates that the group should be divided into two or more parts to perform the passage in question.

dolce Gentle, soft.

dolcissimo (dolciss.) Very gentle.

doloroso Sad, sorrowful.

dominante Dominant, dominating.

Doppelgriff Double stop; on string instruments, playing two strings at once.

doppelt so langsam Twice as slow.

doppio movimento Twice as fast.

Dpf., Dpfr. *Dämpfer*; mute.

dreifach Divided into three parts.

Dur Major; *C–Dur* is C Major.

e And.

ebenso Likewise; continue in a similar manner.

echo tone, Echoton Like an echo.

éclatant Sparkling, brilliant.

ein, eine One; a.

en In.

en dehors Emphasized, prominent.

en poudroiement harmonieux In a harmonious ray of sunlight (literally, airborne dust made visible by the sun's rays).

enchaînez Play the next movement without a break.

encore Still, yet (as in *encore plus lent*, still more slowly).

energico Energetic.

enveloppé de pedale Veiled or enveloped by the sustaining pedal, which allows notes on the piano to continue sounding and thus blur the harmony.

environ About.

espressivo (espress., espr.) Expressive, expressively.

et And.

étouffée Damped, muted.

étouffer ces sonorités en jouant ceci avec le plat de la main Dampen these sounds as they are played with the flat of the hand.

etwa *Circa*; about.

etwas Somewhat, rather.

eventuell mit der Altstimme (ev. mit der Altstimme) If necessary, with the choral altos.

eventuell nur eine (event. nur eine) If necessary, only one player.

eventuell ohne das "des" (ev. ohne das "des") If necessary, without the D♭.

expressif (express.) Expressive.

f Forte.

feroce Ferocious.

ff Fortissimo.

fff Fortississimo.

fine End, close.

Flageolet (Flag.) Harmonic.

Flatterzunge Flutter-tongue.

flautando (flaut.) On a string instrument, producing a flute-like tone by bowing lightly and swiftly above the fingerboard.

flüchtig Fleeting, transient.

flutter-tongue, Flatterzunge (fl. t., Flttzg., Fltzg., Flzg.) Very fast tonguing technique for wind and brass intruments, producing a rapid trill-like sound.

fois Time; *la 2e fois* means the second time.

folgt There follows.

forte (*f*) Loud.

forte-piano (*fp*) Loud, then immediately soft on the same note.

fortissimo-piano (*ffp*) Loud, then immediately very soft on the same note.

fortissimo (*ff*) Very loud.

fortississimo (*fff*) Extremely loud; *ffff* indicates a still louder dynamic.

fortsetzend Continuing.

forza Force.

forzando, forzato (*fz*) Play with a strong accent.

fp Forte-piano; loud, then immediately soft.

fpp Forte-pianissimo.

frei Freely; ad libitum.

frog The part of the bow nearest the player's hand, used to tighten the bowhairs.

frottées l'une contre l'autre Rub one (cymbal) against the other.

furioso Furious, furiously.

fz Forzando, forzato.

ganz langsam Very slowly.

gebrochen Broken, arpeggiated.

gedämpft Muted or stopped.

gedehnt Held back; slow and restrained.

gehende Moderate tempo, walking speed; andante.

Generalpause (G.P.) Rest for the complete ensemble.

geschlagen (geschl.) Struck.

gesprochen Spoken.

gestopft Stopped.

gestoßen Detached, not legato.

gestrichen (gestr.) Bowed.

gesungen Sung.

geteilt (get.) Divided, divisi; indicates that the group should be divided into two or more parts to perform the passage in question.

gewöhnlich (gew., gewöhnl.) Usual, customary; used to cancel an indication to play in an unusual manner, such as *am Steg* or *col legno*.

gioviale Jovial.

giusto Moderate.

gleichmässig Equal; even; at a steady pace.

gleichsam versuchend, eine Begleitung für das Lied Wozzecks zu finden As if seeking to devise an accompaniment for Wozzeck's song.

gli altri The others; used to designate the other players in an orchestral section when one or more players in the section are given separate parts.

gli altri contano The others rest (as a soloist plays).

glissando (gliss., gl.) Rapidly gliding over strings or keys, producing a fast scale on a harp or piano or a fast continuous slide on string instruments, timpani, or trombone.

G.P. *Generalpause*; rest in all parts.

grandioso Grandiose; grandly.

grazioso Graceful.

Griffbrett Fingerboard of a string instrument.

gross, groß, große, großene Large, big, great.

Ħ *Hauptstimme* or *Hauptrhythmus*.

haletantes Breathless, panting.

Halt Stop, hold, pause.

hängend mit Paukenschlägen Linked to the timpani roll.

Harmon mute Mute for trumpet or trombone that can be adjusted or covered with the hand to allow different amounts of air through, producing a more or less distant sound.

harmonic, harmonique (harm.) A flute-like sound produced on a string instrument by bowing or plucking while lightly touching the string with the finger instead of pressing down on the string (natural harmonic), or by stopping the string with one finger and lightly touching the string at another point, usually a perfect fourth higher (artificial harmonic). On a harp, a harmonic is produced by plucking the string while touching it precisely in the middle of the string, and sounds an octave higher. On a wind instrument, a harmonic is produced by fingering the note indicated and blowing lightly to produce a note an octave higher.

hastig Hurried.

Hauptrhythmus Principal rhythm; the main rhythmic pattern.

Hauptstimme Principal voice; the most important part in the texture.

hauteur réelle Actual pitch.

heftiger More intense.

hervor Given prominence.

hervortretend Prominent; coming to the fore.

hinter der Scene Offstage.

hörbar Audible.

hurlant Blaring out.

il ritmo sempre molto preciso Play the rhythm always very precisely.

im Tempo, im Takt In tempo.

immer Always, still.

impetuoso Impetuous, violent.

in Used for indicating transposing instruments or changes of pitch. An instrument *in C* sounds as written, but one designated as in another key sounds in that key when its notated part is in C major; thus a clarinet *in A* will sound an A when it plays a C. See the chart of pitch names, p. 999.

in der Art eines Leierkastens In the manner of a barrel organ.

in tempo Resume the previous tempo; used after a ritardando or other variation in tempo.

innig Sincere, tender, fervent.

Instrumente Instruments.

intenso Intense.

jaillissant Gushing forth.

jazz break Solo for drummer, playing freely in jazz style.

jouer ceci Play this.

klagend Lamenting.

klangvoll Sonorous, full-sounding.

klingen lassen Let ring; allow to sound.

klingt wie notiert Sounds as written, meaning that the score shows the sounding pitches for harmonics or for transposing instruments (like horn in F or clarinet in A) as a convenience to the score-reader; for transposing instruments, the normal transpositions appear in the parts from which the instruments play.

kreischend Shrill.

kurz Short.

kurzer Halt Brief pause.

l', la, le, les The.

laissez vibrer, laissez vibrer et s'éteindre, lascia vibrare (lasc. vibr., l.v.) Let vibrate; an indication to the player of a harp, cymbal, etc., that the sound must not be damped but should be allowed to die away.

lang Long.

lang gezogen Long bowstrokes.

langsam Slow, slowly.

langsamer Slower.

largamente Broadly.

largo A very slow tempo.

l.batt. Col legno battuto.

Le trille indique le pouce, l'accent le coup frappé avec le poing In notation for tambourine, the trill indicates rubbing the side of the drumhead with the thumb (to produce jingles), and the accent indicates striking the instrument with the fist.

legatissimo Very legato.

legato Performed without any perceptible interruption between notes; the opposite of staccato.

legèrement Lightly, gently, slightly.

leggerissimo Very light and graceful.

leggéro, leggiero Light and graceful.

leggio (legg.) Music stand; in an orchestral score, *legg. 5.6.* indicates the players at the fifth and sixth stands in the section (normally there are two players at each stand in the string sections).

legno The wood of the bow.

leidenschaftlich Passionate, vehement.

lent Slow, slowly.

lento A slow tempo, between andante and largo.

l.h., L.H. Left hand; play with the left hand.

liberamente Freely.

lip Change pitch using mouth position rather than fingers.

l'istesso Tempo Same tempo.

loco To be played where written; cancels an *octava* sign.

lumineux Luminous, brilliant.

lunga Long; hold for a long time.

l.v. Let vibrate; *laissez vibrer, lascia vibrare*.

m. *Mit*; with.

ma But.

ma non troppo But not too much.

maestoso Majestic; stately.

maggiore (magg.) Major; for a harp, *Do♭ magg.* indicates C♭ major, meaning set all string tunings to flats.

mailloche Mallet, beater.

mais But.

malevolo Malevolent, malicious.

mano destra (m.d.) Play with the right hand.

mano sinistra (m.s.) Play with the left hand.

marcatissimo (marcatiss.) With very marked emphasis.

marcato (marc.) Marked, with emphasis.

marcia March.

marqué Marked, with emphasis.

martellato (mart., martell.) Hammered.

mäßig, mäßige Moderate, andante.

matt Faint, languid.

m.d. *Main droite, mano destra*; play with the right hand.

m.D., m.Dpf. *Mit Dämpfer*; with mute.

m.d. Pianino *Mit dem Pianino*; with the upright piano.

membrane On the drumskin.

meno Less.

meno mosso Less fast.

Menuett Minuet.

metà Half of the indicated group of players.

metronome marking Indicates metronome setting for the correct tempo, in beats per minute.

mezzo forte (*mf*) Moderately loud.

mezzo piano (*mp*) Moderately soft.

mf Mezzo forte.

misterioso Mysteriously.

mit (m.) With; *mit dem*, *mit den*, with the.

mit dem Schlägel schlagen Beat or roll with drumsticks.

mit Erschütterung Trembling with emotion.

mit leidenschaftlichem Ausdruck With passionate expression.

mit verhaltener Stimme Held back, with restraint.

m.o. Modo ordinario.

moderato, modéré At a moderate tempo.

modo ordinario (modo ord. m.o.) In an ordinary fashion; cancels a previous indication to play in an unusual manner, such as *sul ponticello*.

moins Less.

molto Very, much.

morendo Dying away; becoming very soft.

mosso Rapid; with movement.

mp Mezzo piano.

m.s. *Mano sinistra*; play with the left hand.

muta in Change the tuning of the instrument as specified; or change to another instrument as specified.

mysterieux Mysteriously.

N *Nebenstimme.*

nach To.

Nachschlag Auxiliary note at the end of a trill.

naturale (nat.) Natural; used to cancel a previous indication for an unusual technique (such as *coperto* for a drummer), or to indicate a natural harmonic on an open string.

Nebenstimme The second most important voice in the texture; compare *Hauptstimme.*

nehmen, nimmt Take; used to indicate a change of instrument, as from flute to piccolo, or adding a mute.

nerveux, nervoso Nervous.

neue New.

nicht Not.

nicht lauter als die Hörner Not louder than the horns.

niente Nothing; inaudible.

nimmt Takes; used to indicate a change of instrument, as from bass clarinet to clarinet.

noch Still, yet.

noch langsameres Tempo Still slower tempo.

non Not.

non troppo, non tanto Not too much.

Noten Notes.

o. *Ohne*; without.

octava (okt., 8va, 8.) Octave; *8va alto* means an octave higher, *8va basso* an octave lower. If not otherwise qualified, the notes marked should be played an octave higher than written if *8va* is written above the affected notes, or an octave lower if written below them. *15ma* indicates two octaves higher.

o.D. *Ohne Dämpfer*; without mutes.

offen Open; cancels *gedämpft.*

ohne (o.) Without.

open (1) In brass instruments, the opposite of muted or stopped. (2) In string instruments, refers to the unstopped string (i.e., sounding at its full length).

ordinario, ordinairement, ordinère-ment (ord.) In the usual way; cancels an instruction to play in some special manner, such as *sul ponticello.*

ossia Or rather; used to indicate an optional alternate reading of a passage.

ôtez Remove; *ôtez la sourdine*, remove mute.

ouvert Open.

p Piano (the dynamic level); soft.

parlando As if speaking.

passionato Passionate, impassioned.

pause Rest; pause.

pavillon en l'air (pav. en l'air) Bell in the air; sign for horn players to lift their bells to direct the sound forward.

pedal, pedale (ped., P.) In piano music, indicates that the sustaining pedal should be depressed; an asterisk indicates the point of release (brackets below the music are also used to indicate pedalling).

perdendosi Gradually dying away.

pesante (pes.) Heavy.

pesantissimo Very heavy.

peu Little, a little.

Pianino Upright piano.

pianissimo (*pp*) Very soft.

pianississimo (*ppp*) Extremely soft; *pppp* indicates a still softer dynamic.

piano (*p*) Soft.

più More.

più lento Slower.

più mosso Faster.

pizzicato (pizz.) On a string instrument, plucked with the finger instead of played with the bow; compare *arco*.

plötzlich Sudden, suddenly, immediately.

plunger A kind of mute for brass instruments used in jazz to create a wah-wah effect.

plus More.

pochissimo (pochiss.) Very little.

poco, un poco Little, a little.

poco a poco Little by little.

ponticello (pont.) The bridge of a string instrument.

portamento (port.) Fast slide between notes.

pp Pianissimo.

pp possibile (*pp* poss.) As soft as possible.

ppp Pianississimo.

précise (préc.) Precisely.

prenez Take; used to indicate a change of instrument, as from flute to piccolo.

près de la table On the harp, pluck the strings near the soundboard, producing a metallic sound.

prestissimo Very fast; faster than presto.

presto A very quick tempo (faster than allegro).

prima, primo (Imo) First, as in first bassoon part.

Pult Music stand. There are normally two string players per stand in an orchestra; *2 Pult.* means "second stand" (i.e., the third and fourth players in the section).

quasi Almost, as if, like.

quasi Echo Like an echo.

quasi in den Tanz einfallend As if joining in the dance.

quasi niente Almost nothing, i.e., as softly as possible.

quasi recitativo Like a recitative.

rallentando (rall., rallent.), ralentir Growing slower.

rapido, rapide Fast.

rasch Fast.

rascher Faster.

rebord The rim of a drum.

rechtes Pedal Sustaining pedal.

Rezitation Reciting voice.

r.h., R.H. Right hand; play with the right hand.

rhythmisch Rhythmically.

rim click On a drum, striking the rim with the drumstick.

rim shot (r.s.) On a snare drum, striking both the drum skin and the rim simultaneously with the same drumstick; or laying one drumstick on the drum, with its tip on the skin and its shaft on the rim, and striking it with the other drumstick.

rinforzando (rinf.) Strengthening; used for a rapid crescendo or an accent less strong than a sforzando.

risoluto Resolute.

ritardando (rit., ritard.) Gradually slackening in speed.

ritardierte Slowed-down.

ritenuto (riten.) Holding back.

ritmico Rhythmic.

r.s. Rim shot.

rubato A certain elasticity and flexibility of tempo, speeding up and slowing down the performance of written music.

ruhig Calm.

ruhig schreitend Calm pace, moderate andante tempo.

ruhiger Calmer; more calmly.

rùvido Coarse, rough.

S Soprano.

Saite; pl. Saiten String; e.g., *C-Saite* means C string. *5. Saite nach C zurück*, tune the fifth (lowest) string back to C (from B).

samba cubana In the tempo and style of a Cuban samba, a dance originally from Brazil.

sans Without.

sans nuances Without nuances; do not vary dymanic level.

Schalltrichter hoch Lift the bell of the horn up.

scherzando Playfully; jesting.

schleppend Dragging.

schnell Fast, quickly.

schneller Faster.

Schnellpolka Fast polka tempo.

schon bei geschlossenem Vorhang verhaltend Stop when the curtain closes.

Schwammschlägel Sponge-headed drumstick.

schwerer Heavier.

schwermütig Dejected, sad.

secco, sec Dry.

segno Sign; especially one indicating the beginning of a section to be repeated.

sehr Very.

semplice Simple, in a simple manner.

sempre Always, continually.

senza Without.

senza vibrato (s.vibr.) Without vibrato.

serré Hard, strong.

serrer Push ahead.

seulement Only; alone.

sforzando, sforzato (sfz, sf, sff, sfffz) With sudden emphasis.

sforzando-piano (sfp) Sforzando, then suddenly soft.

siehe See.

simile (sim.) Likewise; continue in a similar manner.

sin al, sino al Until, up to (usually followed by a new tempo or dynamic marking, or by a dotted line indicating a terminal point).

Singstimme Singing voice; vocal line.

smorzando (smorz.) Getting slower, as if dying away.

snares off On a snare drum, disengage snares so they do not sound when the drumhead is struck.

soft stick Use padded or sponge drumstick.

solo, sola (pl. soli) (1) To be played by one performer. (2) Indicates the most prominent part in an ensemble texture.

sombre Dark, somber.

somit Consequently, accordingly.

son fluté, vers la pointe On a string instrument, played near the tip of the bow, producing a flute-like sound.

sonore, sonoro Sonorous, with full tone.

soprano, Sopran (Sop., S, Sopr.), pl. Soprani, Soprane The voice with the highest range.

sordino (sord., pl. sordini) Mute.

sostenuto (sost.) (1) Sustained. (2) In piano music, press the *sostenuto* (middle) pedal, which sustains the notes that are being held when the pedal is first pressed.

souple Flowing, smooth.

sourdement (sourd.) Muffled, muted.

sourdine (sourd.) Mute.

soutenu Sustained.

s.p. Sul ponticello.

Spieler Player or players; *1. Spieler allein*, one player.

spirito Spirit; *con spirito*, spirited, lively.

staccatissimo (staccatiss.) Very staccato.

staccato (stacc.) Detached, separated; held for less than the full notated duration.

Steg Bridge on a string instrument; see *am Steg*.

stem in, stem out On a Harmon mute, indicates whether the stem of the plunger is pushed in, cutting off most of the air flow, or pulled out, allowing more air through.

Stimme Voice.

stopped On a horn, produce a muted, metallic sound by tightly inserting the right hand in the bell and closing off the air column.

straight mute (st. mute, str. mute) Conical mute for brass instruments, placed in the bell and held there by cork strips that allow some air through.

stringendo (string.) Quickening.

subito (sub.) Suddenly, immediately.

suivant les dynamiques, employer baguettes douces ou dures Following the dynamics, employ soft or hard drumsticks.

suivre Follow; *suivre le Ier*, follow the first player.

sul On the; *sul G.*, on the G string.

sul ponticello (sul pont., s.p.) On a string instrument, bow over or very near the bridge; this emphasizes the higher harmonics to produce a thin, metallic sound.

sul tasto (s.t.) On a string instrument, bow near, or over, the fingerboard; this minimizes the harmonics to produce a flute-like, ethereal sound.

sur On; *sur Sol*, on the G string.

sur la touche On a string instrument, bow near, or over, the fingerboard; *sul tasto*.

sur rebord On the rim.

sustaining pedal (damper pedal, Pedale, Ped., P.) On a piano, the pedal farthest to the right, which when pressed lifts the dampers off the strings and lets notes continue to sound after the fingers have left the keys.

s.vibr. Senza vibrato.

T Tenor.

Takt Bar, beat.

tanto So much.

tasto Fingerboard of a string instrument; *sul tasto*.

tempo (1) The speed or relative pace of the music. (2) *A tempo*; used after rit. or calando.

tempo blues In the tempo of a blues.

tempo di marcia March tempo.

tempo giusto Moderate or appropriate tempo.

tempo primo (tempo I, I. Tempo, 1º tempo), tempo initial At the original tempo.

tempo rigoreux Keep rigorously to the tempo.

tempo rubato Play with rubato.

teneramente Tenderly.

tenor, tenore, Tenor (T., ten.), pl. tenori, Tenöre High male voice or part; in choral music, the second voice from the bottom of the texture.

tenuto, tenute (ten.) Held, sustained.

tiefer Lower.

tight mute On a horn, insert a mute tightly into the bell to close off the air stream, producing a sound similar to a stopped tone.

touche Fingerboard or fret (of a string instrument).

tr Trill.

tranquillo Quiet, calm.

tre corde, tre corda Three strings; cancels *una corda* marking.

tremolo (trem.) (1) On string instruments, a quick reiteration of the same tone, produced by a rapid up-and-down movement of the bow. (2) A similar effect on another instrument or voice.

très Very.

trill (*tr*) The rapid alternation of a given note with the note above it. In a drum part it indicates rapid alternating strokes with two drumsticks.

Triller ohne Nachschlag Trills without final auxiliary or grace note.

Trio Second or middle section of a minuet and trio, a scherzo, a march, or a rag.

Triole Triplets.

tristement Sadly.

troppo Too much.

tumultueuse Tumultuous.

tutta forza, tutta la forza Full force.

tutti, tutte Literally, "all"; usually means all the instruments in a given category as distinct from a solo part; cancels the designation *solo*.

übergreifen Reach over; in piano music, indicates that one hand should reach over the other.

übertönend Drowning out.

Übrigen (d. Übrig.) The others, the remaining; used to designate the other players in an orchestral section when one or more players in the section are given separate parts.

un, una, une One; a.

un poco, un peu A little.

una corda One string; tells the player of a grand piano to depress the left pedal, which shifts the hammer mechanism over so that only one string is struck for each note (rather than three or two).

und (u.) And.

unison (unis.) The same notes or melody played by several instruments at the same pitch. Often used to emphasize that a phrase is not to be divided among several players; cancels *divisi*.

unite, uniti Unison.

unmittelbar anschließend Immediately following.

Unterbrechung Interruption, breaking off.

vamp Brief introduction which may be repeated ad libitum until the singer begins.

veramente Truly.

verhallend Fading away.

verklingen lassen Let the sound die away; do not damp.

verlöschen Die out.

verstimmt Out of tune; *ein verstimmtes Pianino*, an out-of-tune upright piano.

Verwandlung Change of scene.

vibrato, vibrez (vib., vibr.) Slight fluctuation of pitch around a sustained tone.

via Away; *via sord.*, remove mute.

Viertel Quarter note.

Viertel schlagen Beat quarter notes.

vif Quick, lively.

vigoroso Vigorous, strong.

vocalizzando con "ah" Vocalizing (singing) on "ah."

voce Voice.

voilé Veiled.

voix Voice.

voll Full; without mutes.

Vorhang auf Curtain up.

Vorhang fällt, Vorhang zu Curtain down.

voriges, vorigen Preceding.

wechselt zum Klav[ier] Move to the piano.

weg Away; *Dämpfer weg*, remove mutes.

wieder Again; still more.

womöglich If possible.

ziemlich Rather, fairly.

zögernd Slowing.

zurück Back.

zurückkehrend zum Tempo I Returning to the first tempo of the movement.

zusammen (zus.) Together; unison.

INDEX OF COMPOSERS

INDEX OF TITLES

INDEX OF FORMS AND GENRES

chorus (*continued*)
    Stravinsky, *Exaudi*, from *Symphony of Psalms*, 219
concerto grosso:
    Schnittke, Concerto Grosso No. 1, 861
contrafact:
    Ellington, *Cotton Tail*, 305
    Parker and Gillespie, *Anthropology*, 555
cumulative form:
    Ives, *General William Booth Enters into Heaven*, 271

duet:
    Gubaidulina, *Rejoice!* Sonata for Violin and Violoncello, 856

electronic music:
    Babbitt, *Philomel*, 691
    Varèse, *Poème électronique*, 687
étude:
    Bartók, *Staccato and Legato*, from *Mikrokosmos*, 236
    Ligeti, Étude No. 9, *Vertige*, 842

fanfare:
    Adams, *Short Ride in a Fast Machine*, 795
film score:
    Prokofiev, *Alexander Nevsky*, 378
fugue:
    Bernstein, fugue from Act I, No. 8, "Cool," from *West Side Story*, 567
    Milhaud, First tableau, from *La création du monde*, 346

jazz composition:
    Ellington, *Cotton Tail*, 305
    Parker and Gillespie, *Anthropology*, 555

lament:
    Saariaho, *Je devrais être l'homme le plus heureux du monde*, from *L'amour de loin*, 912

Lied:
    Mahler, *Nun will die Sonn' so hell aufgeh'n*, from *Kindertotenlieder*, 6
    Schoenberg, *Enthauptung*, from *Pierrot lunaire*, 95
    Schoenberg, *Nacht*, from *Pierrot lunaire*, 92

march form:
    Joplin, *Maple Leaf Rag*, 1
melodrama:
    Schoenberg, *Pierrot lunaire*, 92
minimalist composition:
    Adams, *Short Ride in a Fast Machine*, 795
    Reich, *Tehillim*, 732
minuet:
    Ravel, *Menuet*, from *Le tombeau de Couperin*, 54
    Schoenberg, Minuet and Trio, from Piano Suite, Op. 25, 105
minuet and trio form:
    Ravel, *Menuet*, from *Le tombeau de Couperin*, 54
    Schoenberg, Minuet and Trio, from Piano Suite, Op. 25, 105
    Shostakovich, Allegretto (second movement), from Symphony No. 5, Op. 47, 395
monodrama:
    Babbitt, *Philomel*, 691
musical:
    Bernstein, *West Side Story*, 561
    Gershwin, *Girl Crazy*, 279

operatic excerpts:
    Adams, *Doctor Atomic*, 963
    Berg, *Wozzeck*, 112
    Britten, *Peter Grimes*, 621
    Saariaho, *L'amour de loin*, 901
    Strauss, *Salome*, 23
    Weill, *Die Dreigroschenoper*, 359
orchestral song:
    Mahler, *Nun will die Sonn' so hell aufgeh'n*, from *Kindertotenlieder*, 6